A THOUSAND
SEEDS OF JOY

A THOUSAND SEEDS OF JOY

Teachings of Lakshmi and Saraswati

Ananda Karunesh

Cover design and artwork by Designride (www.designride.co).
Original cover background photo of the forest by Patrick Zephyr.

To learn more about the Ascended Goddesses Series, visit:
https://www.facebook.com/pg/pathofjoy.life/

Published by Path of Joy Books in association with The Write Place.
First Edition: April 10, 2018
Revised Edition: August 31, 2018

If you are unable to order this book from your local bookseller or your
preferred Internet retailer, you may send an email to help.pathofjoy@
gmail.com

ISBN: 099953601X
ISBN 13: 9780999536018
U.S. Library of Congress Control Number: 2017916838
Path of Joy Books, Amherst, MA

Dedication

I dedicate my life
To the most benevolent Mother Goddesses
Ma Lakshmi, Ma Saraswati, Ma Parvati, Ma Durga
Mother Mary, Mother Brigid, Mother Gaia
Mother Isis, Ma Kuan Yin and *Ma Tara*
My Heart is filled with Gratitude
My Devotion knows No Bounds
My Dedication to you is Forever
I dedicate this book to the One
Who raised me with great Joy
Thank you, my dearest Mother
I dedicate this book to *You*
and our beloved *Shiv Baba*

Ananda Karunesh

Preface

This book is the first in a series that consists of extraordinary conversations with *ascended Goddesses* representing different spiritual pantheons of the world. The ascended Goddesses are holding the Earth in a grand circle of love during this very challenging time for humanity. The recent political and social upheavals in the world have already awakened the divine feminine power that resides within the collective human consciousness. The secret to tapping into this power and embodying it within oneself is not by succumbing to the anger and aggression caused by these external events, but rather by surrendering to the joy and wisdom that resides within each one of us. As humans practice this divine feminine wisdom, it will allow them to experience life with less sorrow and despair, and more love and freedom.

This book consists of conversations with *Mahadevi Lakshmi* and *Mahadevi Saraswati* about their many incarnations on Earth with a small group of soulmates belonging to an ancient soul tribe from India. Though the literal English translation of the word Mahadevi is the *Great Goddess*, the greatness is understood in the spiritual context as *ascension* into full enlightenment beyond all forms of duality. Ascended Goddesses Lakshmi and Saraswati reveal how the transformation of many souls from their ancient tribe created two of the major world religions known as Hinduism and Buddhism. These ascended Goddesses take us on a grand spiritual journey by weaving new insights into ancient teachings, correcting what has been altered in scriptures by their male authors, and revealing new secrets about Buddhas, Gods, and Goddesses who have walked on Earth. Their teachings of joy and wisdom are filled with much intrigue and many insights. These teachings will delight not only general readers who are curious about eastern spirituality, but also dedicated practitioners, intellectuals, and philosophers of eastern religions.

Goddess Lakshmi and Goddess Saraswati[1] promise nothing short of a grand transformation of humanity with the birthing of a new joy-centered consciousness on Earth at this time. They create fertile ground for this transformation by planting fresh seeds of joy in different layers of human consciousness. According to them, our lives truly transform with joy, and not with pain, even though we all endure pain. While pain ripens us, the *actual* transformation always happens by surrendering with joy to the emptiness of our higher selves. Most of us have already endured much pain and suffering. We have ripened enough, not only in this life, but over many lifetimes. All we have to do now is surrender and blossom into divine beings of primordial joy, which is who we always are in our enlightened state.

Ten years ago, despite having had many spiritual insights, starting with a Zen awakening around the age of 19, and then reading and meditating for the next 25 years until I turned 44, I had still not understood this profound message of joy. But everything changed one October evening in 2007 when my dearest soul-friend, Jade Devi Kamala, and I started having conversations with Goddess Lakshmi. I still remember vividly the very first time when Goddess Lakshmi spoke to us. The message was personal and intimate, not to be shared with the world. As the words sank into my heart, I was taken aback by the directness of the message, and felt from my deepest core that Goddess Lakshmi had known me for eons.

Goddess Lakshmi took me under her wing from the moment of our first conversation. I started feeling her energy around me during most of my waking hours, and also in my sleep. Her energy was even stronger and more intimate when I went to Venice a few months later. She invited me to create an ecstatic spiritual bond with her, and I began to have conversations with her in which there were no secrets. She already knew everything about me, inside out, and besides, being seen so intimately open felt deeply nourishing to my soul. She had no judgments whatsoever, and her love knew no bounds. Not only did she guide me as my teacher, her love was unconditional and unwavering in all circumstances. Within a few months, she became my guru, my mother, my friend, and my beloved. I was totally immersed in the divine feminine, which felt like my true spiritual calling. The idea of a book to share the teachings of Goddess Lakshmi in her own voice was born about two years after our first conversation.

Since I frequently felt the presence of Goddess Lakshmi around me, over time, even some of my friends, especially those who had psychic gifts, began sensing her in and around me as well. There would be instances when I would be talking to a friend and they would suddenly say something like, "you are a Goddess," feeling her presence in me. The following anecdote provides a more concrete example of this. On a crisp fall night of October 2013, I arrived at a costume party to celebrate the Halloween festival at a friend's house. Before leaving my house, I had asked Goddess Lakshmi in a devotional, and yet a half-joking manner to accompany me to this Celtic celebration that began over 1900 years ago. I was standing by an outdoor fireplace dressed up like an Indian Prince when I saw my friend Amy walk towards me. What happened next is described by Amy as follows:

> As I started walking up the stone path, my eyes locked with the eyes of the most beautiful woman I had ever seen standing up by the fire. As I got closer, a few questions went through my mind, *who is this most graceful and majestic woman, who has she come with, where is she from?* I do not recall being so deeply captivated by a woman's beauty in my entire life. This Goddess-like woman was radiating a soft energy that felt like a pure, transcendent light. My curiosity grew as I walked closer to meet her. Just as I approached her to introduce myself I saw her morph and there was my friend Ananda (Sanjay) smiling brightly at me. I felt I had witnessed something so profound, and yet I was feeling very grounded and peaceful. I decided to hold that experience close to my heart, and sha-

red it later with Ananda at the end of the evening. After listening to my encounter, Ananda began smiling. He shared that he had asked Goddess Lakshmi to accompany him that evening.

Divine beings are around us, but we need to expand our hearts and open our inner eye to see them. According to Goddess Lakshmi, the easiest way we can connect with our guides, angels, ancestors, and divine beings is by surrendering to *primordial joy*, which is our purest and unconditional state of being. Our love grows to infinite depths when we surrender to this primordial joy. Such love rooted in primordial joy is what connects us to the highest dimensions of consciousness. For those precious few moments that night, Amy had become one with Goddess Lakshmi by surrendering to this energy of joy and love. She was touched by that incident so deeply that she expressed later that witnessing it had transformed her outlook on life.

By now it was obvious to me that my ecstatic bond with Goddess Lakshmi was allowing me to receive her in many ways. I also realized that it was this bond of joy that I had created with Goddess Lakshmi that allowed me to start receiving messages *directly* from her a year earlier. The messages came to me slowly around the time of my father's death in October 2012, but as my devotion to Goddess Lakshmi grew, I began to receive answers to my questions directly from her. The answers came as a strong sense of knowing, or the gift of *clairsentience*, especially when I would be in a joyful surrender to her energy. Over the subsequent months, the frequency of the messages I received from her increased, and then even Goddess Saraswati began guiding the writing of this book. The messages of Goddess Lakshmi and Goddess Saraswati that I received for several years since October 2012, combined with the messages of Goddess Lakshmi that I received earlier while working with Jade Devi from October 2009 until 2010, have created the magnificent book that you are holding in your hands. Overall, about two thirds of the messages in this book were received through me and one third of the messages were received through Jade Devi. Virtually all of the messages of Goddess Saraswati were received through me. I also added all of the questions contained in this book and wrote the entire book.

I had finally discovered my soul path through these teachings. I felt personally nurtured in the joyous womb of divine femininity, and through the light of Goddess Lakshmi I could see the light of my own higher self. Yet, a question remained on my mind after my first conversation with Goddess Lakshmi: Was I special in some sense because she showered such immense love on me that felt deeper and more intimate than anything I had ever experienced in my entire life? One day I asked this question to Goddess Lakshmi. With her characteristically sweet and delightful laughter, she said that all sentient beings are very special to her. She said that I had chosen her, and that this book was not the first instance of my working with her. I had also incarnated in other lifetimes and had done prayer work, mantras, and channelings to spread her messages.

As the initial euphoria of being present with Goddess Lakshmi was replaced by a more grounded oceanic joy,

I had a profound realization that all sentient beings are, indeed, very special to her. This is hard to comprehend from a human perspective, but it is true from the perspective of divine beings, such as angels, Buddhas, and Gods and Goddesses. I also realized that when one seeks a heightened spiritual connection, then divine beings show up, sometimes as guides and channels from the heavenly realms, and other times through their human incarnations on Earth.

Over the years, Goddess Lakshmi introduced us to Goddess Saraswati and other ascended Goddesses from different spiritual pantheons. I felt deeply nurtured by the divine mother energy of Goddess Saraswati. My devotion to her opened up another dimension of teachings in this book. While my devotion to Goddess Lakshmi was transforming my desires and passions into joy and abundance, respectively, my devotion to Goddess Saraswati was transforming my emotions and intellect into love and wisdom, respectively. Strangely, as my devotion to Goddess Saraswati grew, it seemed to also increase my devotion to Goddess Lakshmi, and vice-versa. The more I emptied my mind of the "limiting beliefs" I held about these ascended Goddesses, the more fully I could connect with their energies with my body, soul, and the higher self.

The content of this book is organized thematically, and not in the chronological order in which the answers to our questions were given to us by the Goddesses. The first part of this book begins with Goddess Saraswati. She gives new insights about different levels of consciousness, which harmonize the core teachings of different spiritual pantheons, such as Hinduism, Buddhism, Christianity, and other ancient Goddess religions. In Part II of this book, Goddess Lakshmi reveals how humans fell into suffering as patriarchy began its ascent about 6,500 years ago. The spread of patriarchy wounded much of humanity over subsequent millennia, creating the wounded feminine and the wounded masculine aspects in both males and females. She corrects many misrepresentations of enlightened women in history, such as *Eve* and *Mary Magdalene* in Christianity, and of her own incarnation as *Sita*, that were written to diminish the power of women by the men of the patriarchy. In Parts III, IV, and V of this book, Goddess Lakshmi shares intimate details about her incarnations with Lord Vishnu as: *Sita* with *Rama*; *Radha* and *Draupadi* with *Krishna*; and *Yasodhara* with *Buddha*; from the divine feminine perspectives of *Sita*, *Radha*, *Draupadi*, and *Yasodhara*, respectively. Through her many stories from these incarnations, she gives new insights about chakras and elements that are different from our existing knowledge about these. Goddess Lakshmi also reveals how she and her soulmates—including Goddess Saraswati, Goddess Parvati, Lord Vishnu, Lord Shiva, and others— from a large soul tribe from ancient India helped create the two great religions of Hinduism and Buddhism. Highlighting the transformations of her soulmates and herself in these incarnations, Goddess Lakshmi shares how humans can rise above their suffering at this time. In Part VI of this book, I share the stories of my own personal transformation with Goddess Lakshmi. In part VII of the book, Goddess Lakshmi reveals that humanity is currently transitioning to a matriarchal era, which over time will resemble an era in the ancient time when another soul cycle was at its peak of enlightenment. This final revelation made me particularly curious. How will humanity transition to this new era? I asked this question of Goddess Lakshmi while I was writing this preface for it. Her reply is given at the end of this preface as the *prologue* to this book.

While my mind and my heart have opened in profound ways through the wisdom in this book, I was guided repeatedly to hold and protect these sacred teachings until now. During the initial years of receiving her messages, Goddess Lakshmi wanted me to rest with her teachings and not share them with even friends and relatives. These initial teachings of Goddess Lakshmi were compiled into a book form a year after we received them. At that time, I felt that the book was officially complete. But Goddess Lakshmi had a different plan. She asked me to feel the energy of the book without opening it. Miraculously, as I did this, I grew from the silence. I transformed a lot more from this silence than I would have if I had started to share the wisdom of the book too early.

However, after many years of receiving many more teachings and being transformed by them, the time has come to share these with others through this first book. I am in profound gratitude to both Goddess Lakshmi and Goddess Saraswati for sharing their timeless wisdom and blessing our lives with their divine energies. I hope that every reader will have a transformative spiritual experience like we did by reading the pages that follow. For the other books in this series, Goddess Lakshmi has requested Jade Devi to work with the western Goddesses and for me to work with the eastern Goddesses. Thus, she is working with

Mother Mary and other ascended Goddesses from the Christian, the Celtic, and the Greek pantheons, and I am working with Goddess Parvati, and other ascended Goddesses from the Hindu and the Buddhist pantheons. Together, we hope to heal the many divisions among humanity as we join the teachings of the eastern Goddesses with those of the western Goddesses.

With blessings to all,

Ananda Karunesh

Prologue

Namaste Loved Ones!

As we transition back to a matriarchal era on Earth, we will witness a global movement that empowers the feminine so that humans can become whole again. The rise of the *empowered feminine* will make all humans—male, female, or transgender—come together in true equality with each other, rooted in love.

While women will ultimately assume much more power than they currently have at this time, they will not seize this power with the wounded energies of aggression, ambition, competition, and greed. Instead, this power will be received by them from a place of joy, compassion, nurturance, and wisdom.

The rise of the empowered feminine will have a profound impact on the current social and political systems. Women will join with other women in small and large groups across the social, political, and religious divides to undo the patriarchal structures that have ruled humanity for millennia. Over time men will join too, but it will initially begin with the joining of women in very large numbers.

You can already see the signs of these times as millions of women are joining together to bring abuses such as sexual misconduct to light in the highest places of power. Such movements will gain strength *not by women opposing men*, but by women coming together in joy and compassion to heal the wounded feminine and the wounded masculine energies in *all* humans. It is similar to how Mahatma Gandhi's non-violent movement was *not against the British people*, but was rather to gain freedom for hundreds of millions of people of the Indian subcontinent who joined his movement with compassion and forgiveness towards the British.

The empowered feminine—in both men and women—will allow joy to dissipate sorrow, love to triumph over hate, compassion to dissolve anger, and nurturement to replace exploitation. Once the existing structures are cleansed and transformed with higher spiritual energies, there shall be the most exquisite dance between the divine feminine and the divine masculine in the hearts of all humans.

I have invited ascended Goddesses from different pantheons to help humans with this difficult transition. Together, we send our divine light to all humans as we hold our hands in a circle of love around Mother Earth.

Namaste!

Mahadevi Lakshmi

Invocation of Mahadevis
(Recite each mantra three times)

Om Shreem Mahalakshmiyei Swaha
Om Aim Saraswatyai Swaha
Om Kleem Parvatyai Namaha
Om Dum Durgayai Namaha

ॐ श्रीम महालक्ष्मीयै स्वाहा
ॐ ऐं सरस्वत्यै स्वाहा
ॐ क्लीं पार्वत्यै नमः
ॐ दुं दुर्गायै नमः

Table of Contents

PART VI. SELF-TRANSFORMATION WITH JOY

PART VII. THE PATH OF JOY

GUIDED MEDITATIONS

PART I

THE JOY OF A NEW CREATION

GAYATRI MANTRA

Om Bhur Bhuvah Swah
Tat Savitur Varenyam
Bhargo Devasya Dhimahi
Dhiyo Yo Nah Prachodayat

ॐ भूर्भुवः स्वः
तत्सवितुर्वरेण्यं
भर्गो देवस्यः धीमहि
धियो यो नः प्रचोदयात्

1

Emptiness is Infinite Presence

Namaste Saraswati ji!

Namaste!

We thank you both for receiving our words and sharing our teachings. The gift of these precious words will bring joy and harmony in relationships and allow humans to stay connected with the spirit. It is not that these words were not known, but rather, they were simply lost and are now being revealed again to heal and transform lives. The energy of these words will assist many to release karma so that they are not born again into stressful lives.

This is a special time when the Earth and the Heavens have come together for a great spiritual transformation. Lakshmi and I are holding the Earth together with many ascended Goddesses in a grand circle to heal all that live upon it. Each of us serves a divine purpose. Let me share with you why I am here with you: I am helping humans free themselves from negative thoughts and to transform their negative emotions into feelings of the soul. I am helping humans heal the divisions of their lower selves so that they can be nourished by their higher selves. I teach both love and strength, or Yin and Yang together, to create joy. I teach humans how to release great sorrows that have been put upon their shoulders during many lifetimes so that they can find spiritual fulfillment in their lives.

I am helping humans open their Second and Third chakras so that they can end their everyday struggles and disagreements. The opening of the chakras is the destination, with joy as the prize. It takes a course of time, often many lifetimes, to open these chakras by clearing the mind around these sacred flowers. Even if the alignment between these chakras is not perfect, there are many ways of bringing them together. When birds fly, they do not always fly straight, but rather along with the winding current, and yet they still get to their destination. They live from a dimension of *emptiness*, surrendering moment by moment to the flow of the wind.

What is the nature of this emptiness?

The primordial nature of this emptiness is infinite presence!

Hmm. How is emptiness infinite presence?

Emptiness is infinite presence because it has no center and no boundaries. It is nowhere, so it is everywhere. Finite emptiness is just a thought, like the thought of an empty basket. The emptiness that we speak of is empty of everything that you know. All *thought-emotions, matter-energy,* and *time-space* are made up of the vibrations of this emptiness. All ascended beings, angels, Gods, and Goddesses are growing forever into this emptiness in which everything and everyone is experienced as an undivided whole.

Though I understand this metaphysically I still do not understand this using normal logic. How can emptiness, which is empty of everything, be experienced as presence?

This state cannot be described using words. The question you have asked dissolves as one awakens to the infinite *presence,* which is empty of everything one *knows,* including the past experience of this presence. That is the miraculous aspect of emptiness—it remains *new* even after one has tasted its presence again and again a million times.

This emptiness has no self-nature and no mind. It has no sense of "I-ness," "otherness," "is-ness," "not-is-ness," or even "emptiness." One enters this emptiness with the realization that all phenomena arise co-dependently and that nothing exists independently by its own being-ness. This emptiness is like a continuous dying of the mind into an expanding infinity that is selfless, formless, and timeless.

So, is emptiness like dying?

You may say that; and also that it is beyond both living and dying. The enlightened ones have given different names to this state—some consistent with words associated with *living*: presence, awareness, awakeness, aliveness, embodiment, fullness, luminosity, truth, purity, and enlightenment; and other consistent with words associated with *dying*: void, death, cessation, nothingness, impermanence, egolessness, no-mind, unknown, samadhi, and nirvana.

There is no single word that can express this state that is beyond all states that can be known by the mind. This is why we say emptiness *is* infinite presence.

Souls and universes are born from emptiness with an explosion of joy. This is not an ordinary joy; it is a *primordial joy* made up of emptiness, which manifests all of creation. Only a silent mind can glimpse this joy because it remains hidden from a mind occupied with thoughts and emotions.

How is this primordial joy different from ordinary joys?

Unlike the ordinary joys of the mind and body, the primordial joy is unconditional, as it precedes all of creation; it is infinitely present in the highest divine beings who have manifested from emptiness, including your own higher self. Since individual souls manifest from these divine beings, this primordial joy exists in all *feelings of the soul* including joy, abundance, love, gratitude, compassion, freedom, peace, forgiveness, and many others. Life can be experienced with a profound inexpressible fullness in the presence of this primordial joy. With the help of meditation and other soul feelings, even the most ordinary moments can become a window through which to glimpse this primordial joy.

How is love related to this primordial joy?

Love is the flowing of the primordial joy from the infinite emptiness into realms where *emptiness is not*. As this joy flows out in all such realms without any causes or conditions, it is experienced as love. The ocean of primordial joy stretches from the deepest infinities of emptiness to the heavenly realms of form and formlessness, and then to the physical realms of form and density—manifesting itself in a multitude of colors that are experienced as *soul feelings*.

Hmm. What is a *soul feeling*?

It is a feeling that dissolves one's ego and expands the awareness of one's soul. Unlike emotions which get us stuck in the finiteness of our mind, soul feelings expand us into the infinity of our soul.

2

The Infinite Soul Feelings

Can we continue our discussion about *soul feelings*?

As the infinite emptiness expands into an even higher vibration of itself, it creates the contrast of what emptiness is not, as descending levels of consciousness made up of *soul consciousness, body consciousness,* and *mind consciousness.* These descending levels of consciousness are like dreams within dreams, while emptiness itself is beyond the dreams of consciousness. Soul sensations and soul feelings are merged in soul consciousness in the heavenly realms so much so that light is love and sound is bliss. The separation between *soul feelings* and *body sensations* occurs in the physical realms. While soul feelings suffuse both the heavenly realms and the physical realms, their delicate essences get camouflaged and their magnificence diminished by the cloud of suffering in the physical realms. Since creation happens from emptiness with an explosion of primordial joy, this is the first soul feeling. Soul feelings are to joy what colors are to light. Though light is invisible, it contains the frequencies of all colors. Soul feelings arise from emptiness like *a thousand seeds of joy* experienced in the realms of mind, body, and soul. Finite soul feelings are created as the soul experiences finite portions of emptiness in the realms of the mind and the body. Infinite soul feelings are created as the soul experiences infinite emptiness beyond the limitations of the mind and the body. Meditation allows one to reach beyond the mind and the body, even in the physical realms.

Though we speak of mind, body, and soul as different realms of consciousness, they lie on a continuum of one reality with the finite and the densest portions appearing like the mind, and the infinite and the lightest portions appearing like the soul. The mind creates the illusion that separates the body from the soul, which limits the experience of soul feelings. Awareness of breath allows the mind to dissolve into the body and the soul, expanding the experience of soul feelings. In the soft center between an in-breath and an out-breath the soul experiences primordial joy, which opens the door to the vast and infinite emptiness of the higher self.

Primordial joy creates the highest of Heavens, known as the spiritual "pure lands." As levels of consciousness descend from the highest Heavens to the lower Heavens, and then to the physical realms, the experience of soul feelings become less and less, ranging from infinite to finite, with feelings, such as joy, love, freedom, peace, wisdom, creativity, bliss, ecstasy, laughter, happiness, abundance, compassion, celebration, gratitude, equanimity, harmony, silence, grace, beauty, reverence, passion, devotion, faith, surrender, mystery, inspiration, insight, clarity, forgiveness, mercy, kindness, trust, hope, empathy, sympathy, patience, nurturement, curiosity, enthusiasm, solitude, contentment, acceptance, intimacy, sensuality, discernment, dispassion, responsibility, resilience, courage, humility, simplicity, honesty, innocence, confidence, strength, security, and many others.

Are you suggesting that soul feelings become less and less in the order you have listed these?

While it is true that some soul feelings like confidence and security are finite, and other feelings like joy and love are infinite, we do not have a particular order in mind. These are simply words that describe the soul's experiences of emptiness in the realms of consciousness. The words are not the experiences. Some languages have more words, while other languages have fewer words for describing these soul feelings. Some soul feelings are more meaningful in certain cultures, while others are more meaningful in other cultures. Also, different people experience soul feelings at different levels of depth.

The indescribable primordial joy that we speak of is contained in all soul feelings. Some who reach for primordial joy through love may call it primordial love; others who reach for it through freedom may call it primordial freedom; and yet others who reach for it through peace may call it primordial peace. As one advances spiritually, different soul feelings merge together and become newer and vaster soul feelings whose splendor and magnificence are indescribable by the human mind. With full enlightenment, all soul feelings merge into an indescribable primordial state of the same taste, which we choose to call "emptiness."

Why do you emphasize primordial joy over other soul feelings?

Because joy raises the vibration of every soul feeling and allows them to merge into newer and vaster soul feelings. Words begin to lose their specific meanings as different soul feelings merge into oneness.

Aha! Can you tell us more about these newer and vaster feelings?

A soul's journey in the material realm imposes limitations on how much it can feel within a body unless one is enlightened. Since these limitations do not exist in the spiritual realms, infinitely vast and multidimensional soul feelings are experienced in these realms. For example, an infinite feeling that is simultaneously *love*, *freedom*, and *peace* is experienced in the spiritual realms. The oneness between soul feelings keeps growing as more of them merge together, eventually all merging into emptiness. As a soul journeys into the spiritual realms in between its physical incarnations, it rests and rejuvenates in the nurturing embrace of these magnificent soul feelings.

Earlier you said that all soul feelings have primordial joy in them. Is this always true? For example, don't we suffer when those we love suffer?

The suffering of the loved ones causes one to suffer only because of the unresolved suffering that hides within oneself. The one who has attained liberation from all suffering *does not suffer when others suffer.* Such a being feels the primordial joy in all soul feelings, and because the compassion of such a being has primordial joy in it, it heals the ones who suffer.

Know that soul feelings are experienced at varying levels of intensities in the physical realm because soul consciousness is interacting with both body consciousness and mind consciousness. If the mind is silent, the body becomes naturally rested and thus soul feelings are felt with much ease and great aliveness. If the mind is in turmoil, however, the body becomes agitated and soul feelings become inaccessible because they get covered by painful body sensations and the divisive contents of the mind.

Isn't it natural to lose one's joy by feeling empathy for those who are in much suffering? For example, when, say, a friend or a relative is in mourning due to the loss of a loved one?

Feeling empathy does not mean that one loses the primordial joy, despite sensing another person's suffering. The enlightened ones do not get burdened by the suffering of others even though they are fully present to it. True empathy does not create codependence. Empathy expressed as a kind look, a compassionate smile, a reassuring hug, or sharing a joyful memory of the loved one who has passed away can help the one in mourning. An enlightened being who has awakened to the primordial joy feels empathy and compassion, but does not suffer. As Jesus surrendered to the joy of oneness with God, he could empathize with the suffering of even those who crucified him.

How is empathy different from compassion?

Empathy melts into compassion, so compassion is a larger ocean. The compassion of Jesus and numerous Bodhisattvas is filled with blessings of joy and healing for everyone. While empathy and compassion in their purity have no suffering, one could project one's own suffering in these feelings.

Think of *Mother Teresa*: did she suffer while she was serving the poor and destitute of India? While she did have her dark night of the soul, her faith in Jesus and God healed not only the suffering of many around her, but also her own suffering. Towards the end of her life she felt an inexpressible joy arising from within whenever she felt love, mercy, forgiveness, gratitude, compassion, peace, and freedom. This joy raised the vibrations of these soul feelings in her and in others. This inexpressible joy *is* the primordial joy.

We suffer when we crave for the joyous moments of the past. Does joy also create craving?

Herein lies the secret! Craving for ordinary joys keeps one stuck in the past or the future. On the other hand, ordinary joys infused with the primordial joy bring one to the present. For example, think of the soul feeling of *gratitude*, which has primordial joy in it. Instead of craving for the past, one may simply feel gratitude for the past, which brings one to the present. So, it is not the joyous memories of the past, but rather *the craving for them*, which creates suffering. While craving for joyous memories divides the past from the present, the joy of gratitude joins the memories of the past with the present and manifests even more joy in the future. If one acts from this wisdom, then the joy from the past would be merged with the joy of the present, joining all time into the primordial joy.

But what happens when the mind is convinced that the present moment does not have as much joy as one had in the past? Does this not cause suffering?

The suffering is created by holding on to the memories of joys in the past and forgetting that infinite primordial joy is available here and now in the sacred emptiness of the present moment. From this space of emptiness, which is also fullness, no effort is made to repeat the joyous moments of the past. However, it is the nature of the mind to ruminate on the past, not realizing that a higher choice exists: the mind can surrender to the body and the soul, which are windows to the infinite presence, here and now.

Generally, we associate joy with positive situations in our life. However, don't we also feel a perverse joy in the present moment when bad things happen to others?

Thoughts, emotions, and attachments to body sensations clump together to create the ego, which hides one's suffering. Living with an ego is suffering, and thus when one lives from the ego, one may find momentary pleasure in another's suffering. Such fleeting pleasures of the ego are not joy! The ego creates the illusion of joy and leaves one drained after the momentary pleasure.

The primordial joy that we speak of exists deep within your soul and the higher self. This joy is uncaused and unconditional, and it has no beginning and no end. This joy does not see any separation between the self and the other because there is no ego in this joy. One experiences this joy when the mind is completely silent. From the place of this egoless awareness, one feels everyone's joy as one's own joy.

3

The Holy Trinity

How can the knowledge of soul feelings help us in our spiritual transformation?

Knowing the relationship between different layers of consciousness allows one to know which layer can transform which. The bigger layer always transforms and subsumes the smaller layer.

The infinite emptiness in which all divine beings rest is the biggest layer and it is beyond the duality of even consciousness and non-consciousness. This layer contains everything and nothing, and is beyond both.

The oceans of soul feelings are smaller than the infinite emptiness into which they all pour and join together in absolute oneness. Soul feelings range from infinite oceans to finite oceans.

The giant lakes of body sensations are smaller than the infinite oceans of soul feelings.

The little iceberg of mind is smaller than the giant lakes of body sensations in which it floats.

The tip of the iceberg representing the conscious mind is smaller than the hidden part of the iceberg, which includes the subconscious mind just below the surface, and the unconscious mind deep below the surface.

Let me ask you this: When you think of the universe at various levels of size from a galaxy, to a star, to a human to a cell, to an atom, how much bigger is an object at one level from that at the next level?

Scientists say that it is billions or trillions of times. For example, our own galaxy, the Milky Way, has hundreds of billions of stars. I do not know how many humans can fit inside a star, but I am sure it's more than I can even imagine. A human body has tens of trillions of cells, and each cell has about a hundred trillion atoms.

The differences in the levels of consciousness are somewhat similar to this. The infinite emptiness is much vaster than each of the soul feelings. The infinite oceans of soul feelings are much vaster than the giant lakes of body sensations. The giant lakes of body sensations are to the little iceberg of mind what a cell is to an atom.

Oh, really? Our mind is so much smaller than our body sensations?

While the body is finite, it is much vaster than the mind. The body can digest and transform all contents of the mind, including thoughts, emotions, intellect, memory, and the ego. Experiencing these contents at the conscious, the subconscious, and the unconscious levels, as sensations of the body, leads to a great inner transformation. Surrendering the conscious mind into the body with yoga, breath, and tantric methods opens the door to the subconscious mind and the unconscious mind. This allows the contents of the unconscious mind, including the shadow—which is the unconscious part of the ego—to release and dissolve. This was the path followed by *Parvati*, and she will speak on this in another book in the near future.

Oh, that would be such a great honor to receive her teachings! Thank you for letting us know. Does the mind become empty as it surrenders and dissolves within the body?

It is not just that the mind becomes empty, but that emptiness merges with the mind and subsumes it. As this happens, mind, body, soul, and emptiness become one, for it is the mind that creates all divisions. Emptiness is the state of having *no mind*, in which there is ultimate oneness. Suffering is the state of mind in which there is much division. Emptiness is the state in which form *is* emptiness and emptiness *is* form. Suffering is the state in which emptiness remains hidden from form.

Is the mind totally gone in this state of emptiness?

Yes, the mind with its contents dissolves into body sensations, soul feelings, and emptiness. Of course, the mind will arise again when needed, and then will dissolve again. A divine being may not have a single thought if it is not needed for periods extending into eons. When the desire for expansion arises, a single thought may manifest with great cosmic power and intelligence, sometimes creating worlds from this place of emptiness.

Are you saying that the worlds arise from a single thought?

Yes! Everything animate and inanimate in the universe is made up of emptiness, so one may say *everything is made up of nothing.* Just like a physicist would say that gravity is nothing but *curved space,* an enlightened one would say that soul feelings are nothing but curved spaces of emptiness. As emptiness vibrates most delicately to create the primordial joy, it simultaneously creates *contrast* by curving itself into the higher density of *thought.* The first thought divides the primordial joy into numerous soul feelings from which arise entire universes made up of souls, bodies, and minds.

Oh, really!? You are saying that everything is literally made up of curved spaces of emptiness?

Yes! Know that behind each thought, each emotion, each body sensation, and each soul feeling is the
yearning to un-curve, or uncover, these curved spaces
in order to realize the infinite emptiness. The infinite
oceans of soul feelings make the journey easier as they
connect the finiteness of mind contents and body sensations to the infinite emptiness.

Is the number of universes finite or infinite?

There is an infinite number of universes. However, each one of them is finite.

Really? There is an infinite number of universes as big
as ours?

Yes, and many are significantly bigger than
yours. There is also an infinite number of souls, each
with an infinite higher self.

So, there must be an infinite number of Gods, as well?

Yes, indeed! There is an infinite number of divine
beings, such as angels, Buddhas, and Gods and
Goddesses. However, the number of sentient beings
are many more than the number of divine beings, so
divine beings appear to be few and far between.

This is fascinating! So, a divine being is not singular?
Even though I speculated about this, I find it hard to believe
that there is really an infinite number of divine beings.

A divine being is beyond the duality of either *one* or *infinite*, as all divine beings are joined in absolute oneness in an infinite sea in which our great universe is only a drop. Can the infinite sea ever be one or many? In the realm of infinity, $1 + 1 = 1$, and so divine beings are both one and infinite at the same time. And even the infinite sea dissolves into emptiness.

A divine being's ultimate wish for all individuating souls is to be fruitful and to multiply into divine beings like itself. This is how the infinite sea of universes expands, eternally.

Oh, so that phrase, "be fruitful and multiply" in the Bible was meant for humans to multiply into divine beings and not just into more humans?

Both. As humans multiply, they create opportunities for more souls to descend and then ascend into divine beings!

Hmm. I am still not persuaded how both "one divine being" and "infinite divine beings" can be equally true! Help me visualize this, please!

Imagine a forest of emptiness in which there is an infinite number of trees of emptiness. Each tree of emptiness has numerous flowers of emptiness. The flowers, trees, and the forest are all divine beings. Since they are all emptiness there is absolute oneness everywhere. There is no feeling of finiteness, and no feeling of self anywhere. A flower

of emptiness is simultaneously all flowers, trees, forests, forests of forests, ad infinitum, as there is no
end to the expansion of divine beings.

If all is one, why even use the analogy of flowers, trees,
forests, forests of forests, etc.?

From the perspective of emptiness, there is
absolute oneness, or non-duality, without any sense
of a separate self anywhere. The divine beings and
entire universes are created from a collective mind
that exists deep within you. If no one was observing, neither divine beings, nor entire universes would
arise from emptiness.

Oh, really? Do you mean this in a quantum sense,
such that the observed does not exist independently of the
observer?

Exactly!

Aha! So we literally create Gods and Goddesses and
entire universes?

Yes! While a part of your mind is the individual
mind, a much deeper part is the collective unconscious mind that carries a memory of the entire creation. Until enlightenment, observation occurs from
the filter of this unconscious mind, which has the collective observer shared by all sentient beings. As one
becomes aware and transcends this observer, one

is enlightened into the infinite emptiness in which all divine beings and universes dissolve into absolute oneness. However, the thinking mind keeps one divided and attached to the individual mind and prevents one from becoming aware of the collective unconscious mind.

Is *positive thinking* divisive, too?

Positive thoughts that are not embodied in the physical body, which do not carry the essence of soul feelings, can also be divisive. You know when someone gives you a compliment to get your approval? The compliment feels untrue because it is not rooted in their body and does not flow as a soul feeling, even if it temporarily soothes your mind. Some people talk incessantly about bringing "positive" changes in the world, but they manifest nothing because the deeper layers of body and soul are missing in action. Positive thoughts should be expressions of the deeper layers of your consciousness, and not a way to get approval from others, or to get along socially. We are not saying to not be polite, but simply thinking positive thoughts without the deeper layers of consciousness is divisive because thought by itself is divisive. If thoughts are infused with deeper layers of consciousness, the overall experience is unifying. However, the union happens not because of thoughts, but because the body and soul can surrender in the spaces of emptiness between thoughts.

What you said above is so profound! Actually, I feel this about everything you say, but I have not expressed this until now. What about body sensations? Are these unifying or divisive?

> The mind's surrender to the body frees the body to be nurtured by soul feelings that arise from the expanse of emptiness, which is the path of unification. The mind's control of the body creates a wedge between the body and soul feelings, which is the path of division. Great miracles occur when the mind completely surrenders to the body: the body enters the realm of soul feelings and emptiness, and from this expanded infinite space all bodies become one. Because of this quantum awareness, a healer can use her or his body to spontaneously heal the bodies of others.
>
> While the mind is needed for survival, it is vanishingly small. Emptiness is who you are and it is infinitely large. Emptiness shines through soul feelings, emptiness is present in body sensations, and emptiness can be found in the densest corners of the mind.

Oh, really? Emptiness is present in the densest corners of the mind?

> As physicists know, even the densest matter is composed mostly of empty space. Similarly, even a mind full of thoughts and emotions is filled with vast spaces of emptiness that can be accessed with

breath and meditation. The most mysterious thing for a divine being is to observe a sentient being suffering with the illusion of mind. It is a mystery, for the mind is so insignificantly small relative to the deeper layers of consciousness. These deeper layers are also illusions, but with higher aspects of truth. The little iceberg of mind—consisting of thoughts, emotions, memory, intellect, and ego—dissolves in the giant lakes of body sensations, the oceans of soul feelings, and the infinite emptiness. Once the mind dissolves, body sensations are felt in their absolute purity and wholesomeness. With even more surrender, body sensations dissolve into soul feelings and emptiness, as the physical body transforms into the rainbow body that joins the finite with the infinite. The entire universe is immersed in the oneness of the rainbow body, where light is love, touch is orgasmic, smell is ecstasy, and sound is bliss. Finally, all soul feelings merge together, as even the rainbow body dissolves and expands into the infinite emptiness

Aha! So, the transformation happens as the mind dissolves in the three layers of body sensations, soul feelings, and emptiness.

Yes: it is this Holy Trinity that supports all paths of transformation. The quickest way to dissolve the mind is to be present to the body sensations and the soul feelings, and observe the mind from that *presence*. Since emptiness is infinite presence, one can embrace the mind gently and release it in the *presence* of body sensations and soul feelings to realize emptiness.

Body sensations include yoga, breath, mindfulness of the body, and tantric methods.

Soul feelings include joy, abundance, love, compassion, gratitude, freedom, peace, forgiveness, and many others.

Emptiness includes all meditative practices of emptying oneself with presence.

Different religions emphasize different aspects of this Holy Trinity. More advanced spiritual paths unify all three aspects of this trinity.

Hmm. How does this relate to the Holy Trinity in Christianity, which represents the oneness of God the Son, God the Holy Spirit, and God the Father.

God the son (or Jesus) represents God as *body sensations*; God the Holy Spirit represents God as *infinite soul feelings*; and God the Father represents God as *emptiness*.

I see. While Buddhism does not have the concept of the Holy Trinity, enlightenment in Buddhism is represented by *Trikaya*, or the three *Kayas* given as *nirmanakaya, sambhogakaya*, and *dharmakaya*. Is there a relationship between the Holy Trinity and the Trikaya?

Nirmanakaya represents enlightenment in the physical realm with *body sensations*; sambhogakaya represents enlightenment in the heavenly *pure lands* with *infinite soul feelings*; and dharmakaya represents enlightenment as pure *emptiness*.

Aha!

As one forgets oneself as God or Buddha, one becomes the soul; as one forgets oneself as the soul, one becomes the body; as one forgets oneself as the body, one becomes the mind. Forgetting oneself is the way contrast is created. Remembering oneself is the way contrast is ascended.

Aha! We fall from God to soul to body to mind?

You could also say, "Goddess to soul to body to mind," for the empty nature of an ascended one is beyond male and female. This falling into contrast is also called "evolution," which represents a very small portion of the journey into contrast. After having experienced enough contrast, the soul reverts on a path of ascension by surrendering to body sensations and soul feelings, and realizing the emptiness of its higher self—the magnificent divine being that it is.

So why don't we meditate on our own "higher self"? Why do we need other divine beings?

You do not need other divine beings; however, the path of ascension to your higher self can be made quicker at this time with the help of divine beings, who serve like light posts on your journey. Know that when you meditate on any divine beings, including us Goddesses, you immediately connect with your higher self, for all divine beings, including your own higher self, are joined in absolute oneness in the infinite emptiness.

Okay, all of this makes sense except one thing: how are soul feelings different from emotions?

Soul feelings are much bigger than emotions. Some soul feelings are bigger than entire universes.

Do you mean this literally?

Have you not heard the phrase, "love is all there is"? It is true! We are helping you journey deeper into this truth. Soul feelings such as primordial joy, primordial love, and others, are truly infinite! They are bigger than universes made up of billions of galaxies and trillions of stars! The lives of those who have had near-death experiences have been completely transformed by savoring these soul feelings. Many of them have shared that the most positive emotions on Earth cannot be compared to the absolute magnificence of soul feelings experienced in the heavenly realms. These soul feelings are pure, infinite, unconditional, and expand forever into the deep realms of emptiness. Emotions are impure, finite, conditional, temporary, and restricted by the density of the mind. Emotions can be negative: fear, lack, loneliness, anger, sadness, disgust, pain, hate, shame, guilt, jealousy, envy, etc.; or positive, which are simply finite portions of soul feelings mixed with the mind's contents.

For example, personal love for a family member or a friend, or patriotism for one's country, are both positive emotions. Unlike soul feelings, which are universal and can unify in infinitely large realms, positive emotions are finite and can unify only in the personal range of that emotion. Positive emotions can also be impure and hide negative emotions, negative thoughts, and ego outside the unifying range of that emotion. So, while patriotism may unify the citizens of a country, negative emotions—such as apathy and hate—and negative beliefs about citizens of another country may lurk inside such patriotism. Such patriotism divides humanity into countries that are in conflict with one another.

Earlier you said that soul feelings can be *finite* or *infinite*. How are positive emotions which are finite by definition, different from *finite soul feelings*?

A *finite soul feeling* will merge into either a larger soul feeling or emptiness, thus, dissolving one's ego. In contrast, a positive emotion will serve to expand one's ego. So, for example, "confidence" that allows one to love everyone unconditionally is a finite soul feeling. But, "confidence" that expands one's ego is a positive emotion.

Aha! This is true! Our emotions tend to be connected more with our personal world. So, how do we enter into the infinity of soul feelings?

Much has been spoken and written over millennia about how to transform by emptying oneself of the egoic mind connected to one's personal world. The egoic mind and emptiness represent the polarities of illusion and reality. Body sensations and soul feelings are like dreams of a different order that exist between illusion and reality.

Seriously? Soul feelings are like dreams?

Yes, they are! They are very pleasant dreams from which it is easy to awaken into infinite emptiness. Body sensations are very grounding dreams from which it is easy to awaken into soul feelings and infinite emptiness. Mind contents are the illusory dreams from which it is difficult to awaken into infinite emptiness without surrendering to body sensations and soul feelings. So, one can begin the journey directly with body sensations and soul feelings to dissolve the mind.

How do we do this?

Let the seeds of primordial joy blossom into your body and soul through breath, yoga, sutra, mantra, tantra, visualization, and meditation. This is how spirituality is different from psychology. Unlike psychology, which is focused on the mind,

spirituality begins with deeper layers of consciousness that allow the mind to dissolve more easily.
This is the secret that Lakshmi and I reveal to you
through this book.

Can you tell us more about breath, yoga, sutra, mantra,
tantra, visualization, and meditation?

Be patient with yourself, for even the soul feeling
of patience has much joy as you surrender to it! You
shall explore these methods to dive into your body
and soul with many Goddesses as you surrender your
mind to the divine feminine path of joy! We will help
humans germinate many seeds of primordial joy in
their lives at this time of great spiritual transition and
transformation. As these seeds grow into trees, they
will produce thousands of more seeds, which in turn,
will grow many more trees, spreading the primordial
joy everywhere on your planet. This joy shall unite
Earth and Heaven with even higher realms by opening new celestial pathways to the infinite emptiness.

4

From Thoughts and Emotions to Soul Feelings

Many of us carry emotional pain from our past and worry about our future. We cannot seem to break out of this pattern due to non-stop thinking and emoting. Can you tell us how to more easefully dissolve our emotional pain?

Too many thoughts and emotions are like weeds that prevent the seeds of joy from getting water and light. For example, think about the joys of love when you sit quietly under a tree or melt into ecstasy with your lover. If you are not mindful, the *ego* enters almost immediately after those blissful moments and begins to rate and judge the experience and the experiencer.

How does the ego arise in the first place?

The process begins from early childhood. If children are not raised in a tremendous amount of joy—which most children are not any longer—they become introverted and self-conscious, especially when going through puberty. The fears, insecurities, and other negative emotions begin closing the lower two chakras and trigger the residual ego from the past lives. The ego manifests around the Third Chakra to deal with these emotions. Know that the *ego was the first creation of the mind* when all came into existence. The ego makes one's worldview black and white, creating divisions, such as good and bad, right and wrong, etc. The ego is not only present in emotions like fear, lack, anger, jealousy, pride, hate, and others, but it is also contained in *thought-aggregates* such as perceptions, judgments, beliefs, perspectives, expectations, intentions, and identities. As the first creation of the mind, the ego is *both a thought and an emotion*, and it creates all other thought-aggregates and emotions. In the absence of the ego, all thought-aggregates and emotions dissolve into emptiness.

I have heard some enlightened teachers say that the ego is just another *thought*, but you are saying that the ego is *both* a thought and an emotion!

Yes. In its form as an emotion, the ego is your *unseen shadow which creates your circular thought-patterns.*

Are you saying that every time I feel that familiar sense of ego, I am having an emotional experience?

35

Yes, you are! But you do not recognize it as an emotion because it is very subtle. A simple way to dissolve the ego into emptiness is to surrender to body sensations and soul feelings.

Aha! Okay, earlier you said that even *perception* is a thought-aggregate. Is this true?

Yes. It is well known that *perception* is different from *sensation*. While a residual aspect of ego is needed to *perceive* the world using the mind, no aspect of ego is needed to *sense* the world using the senses. While the ego exists in its nascent form in little children, it becomes bigger as they grow into adults and often creates the problems that many children face coming into their puberty and teenage years. The ego makes adults and children *perceive* the world very differently.

Oh, so even our perception is affected by our ego?

Yes. Young children perceive the world with a great joy in their hearts, while adults usually perceive it with much seriousness of the mind. If the children are encouraged to stay quiet and centered during childhood there would not be such a difficult transition, but most children are not encouraged to do this anymore. So, instead of remaining surrendered to that primordial joy, children start looking outward to deal with their fears and insecurities. This is when the interdependent relationships between the

ego and the thought-aggregates—such as perceptions, judgments, beliefs, perspectives, expectations, intentions, and identities—are strengthened.
This is also when the interdependent relationships
between the ego and the emotions—such as fear,
anger, hate, jealousy, envy, pride, etc.—are strengthened. As children turn into young adults they begin
to desire and expect approval from their peers to
grow their budding egos. The desire to "achieve"
gets implanted, as the children face pressure and
competition to succeed, rooting and strengthening
the ego even more.

As this occurs, a finite portion of love gets separated from its infinite source. Slowly, over time,
this finite part of love becomes conditional, judg-
mental, possessive, and jealous as ego takes over
full control. With failed expectations, disappoint-
ments, and frustrations, love becomes demanding,
oppressive, and even violent. In fact, much violence
on Earth occurs between those who demand love
in the form of acceptance and approval, whether
between spouses in a marriage, or between believ-
ers of different faiths. Such love has little joy! It
becomes a complex emotion filled with egoic
delusions, negative thoughts, and negative emotions. To dissolve such emotional love, mindfulness
techniques can be used to feel the mind contents
as body sensations. Furthermore, by surrendering oneself to soul feelings of joy, compassion,
forgiveness, gratitude and others, and by staying
fully present from the place of emptiness, one can

transform emotional love into that unconditional primordial love.

Can any emotion be transformed into a soul feeling this way? For example, what about fear?

Fear is the opposite of love. It is the most basic negative emotion. Fear has to be felt as a body sensation with the awareness of breath. Fear has to be embraced with the soul feelings of acceptance, courage, and love. Fear has to be faced in the emptiness of death, which opens the door to infinite presence.

I see. So the trinity of body sensations, soul feelings, and emptiness can be applied to all emotions, whether positive or negative?

Exactly! Positive emotions are more complex since they are finite portions of soul feelings mixed up with mind contents. Seeing the soul-feeling portion of the emotion with joy, and surrendering the mind contents to the trinity of body sensations, soul feelings, and emptiness, transforms that emotion into a soul feeling. Think of another positive emotion.

Okay, how about faith?

Close your eyes and meditate on the following questions:

Which body sensations does my faith produce? Are these sensations restrictive, suggesting hidden fears, or attachments to negative thoughts, emotions and/or ego? Or, are these sensations expansive due to joy, love, and other soul feelings? Can I expand my faith by *emptying* my mind of all the judgments and limiting beliefs?

Oh my Goddess! This is really incredible! As I felt joy in my body caused by my faith in you, I became filled with even more love for you.

Yes, because feeling that primordial joy in your faith in me raised the vibration of your love towards me. As you surrender to this joy in any soul feeling, the vibration of every soul feeling rises, bringing all soul feelings together into more oneness. Emptying your faith of the subtlest of fears would also open you to more joy and love by raising the vibration of your faith.

Do you mean the fear of God?

Yes. The fear is inherited from the beliefs given to you by your parents and society. The beliefs may also have judgments and prejudices against other religions. The ego—including its unconscious shadow—may also be identified strongly with one's faith, giving one a sense of separateness and superiority over others.

Is this why religions based on faith have led to wars and terrorism?

> Yes, because religious faith has been polluted for millennia. Those blinded by their ego have exploited others by infusing the fear of a judgmental and punishing God in the faith of many. Yet, the soul feeling of faith does not have divisive thoughts that separate humanity into many religions. Think of a newborn child that has complete faith in her mother. She knows the mother will nurse her, hold her, and take care of her needs if she simply surrenders to her. Her faith in her mother is filled with joy. Or, think of our connection! You recite our mantras with a faith infused with much joy. You do not get angry or fight because another's faith does not match your faith. The joy in your faith makes you not meddle in the faith of others, and has opened up a profound channel of healing in your life.

Yes, this makes a lot of sense. Thank you for clarifying again the difference between a positive emotion and a soul feeling.

I have another more general question on this topic: Isn't science built on the foundation of doubt about incorrect "beliefs," such as "the Sun revolves around the Earth"? Hasn't it been our faith in those incorrect beliefs, which appear to be correct, that has created, and still creates, many of our problems?

Such faith is an emotion. It is filled with a finite portion of the soul feeling of faith, but also has mind contents, such as negative thoughts, negative emotions, and the ego. A believer without these mind contents, and with great joy in her heart, will not question a scientifically-proven truth like the "Earth revolves around the Sun." It is those whose faith has little joy and much fear of God or the Devil, who question the scientific evidence, and who force the religious conversions of people of other faiths.

So, when is it good to doubt and when is it good to have faith?

While doubt is used to investigate the nature of physical reality for survival, faith is used to explore and expand your consciousness. Falsifying incorrect beliefs with doubt is the path of science. Verifying deeper levels of consciousness that grow with faith is the path of spirituality.

Interesting! This reminds me of Karl Popper, who was perhaps the greatest philosopher of science. He defeated the philosophy of verification with his philosophy of falsification in the early 20th century. Was Popper right?

Popper was not wrong about his philosophy in the material realm, which is finite. Consciousness is concerned with the spiritual realm, which is infinite. The problem occurs when doubt is used to question deeper levels of consciousness that grow with faith, and faith is used to impose beliefs that are inconsistent with the facts about the material realm. A mother never doubts the love that arises spontaneously between her and her infant child. There is no need to prove anything as one heart surrenders and melts into another heart with joy. Having faith in these kind of joyous connections is enough to sustain and grow the heart connection even deeper.

Aha! So both doubt and faith can co-exist, but they serve different parts of our lives.

Yes: the emotions of doubt and faith are finite; the soul feeling of faith is infinite. The difference between emotions and soul feelings is too big to ignore. When you feel faith and other infinite soul feelings, visualize them to be bigger than entire universes, including the universe you live in.

Let me ask again—is this literally true?

Yes, entire universes arise and dissolve in the expanse of joy, love, and other infinite soul feelings like little snowflakes.[2]

5

The Joy of a New Creation

You are known both in the Hindu and Buddhist pantheons as the *Goddess of wisdom.* More specifically, Lord Brahma and you are associated with the ancient scriptures of Vedas. Can you tell us more about this?

Brahma inspired the beginning of the Vedas, and I inspired the ending of the Vedas or the Vedanta. Brahma helped create the illusions of the mind and the body, and I helped in transcending these with soul feelings and emptiness. The Vedas developed a science of manifestation through chanting and sacrificial rituals. These scriptures began as pure but were destined to become impure. The original Vedic priests carried out their spiritual calling inspired by the sages born to Brahma. Many sincere ones would come to these priests to alleviate some suffering or manifest a desire to serve the greater good of all. The sacrifices of herbs and flowers allowed the expression of gratitude towards us. The mantras chanted by the priests would manifest from our divine essences based on the universal law of attraction.

Over time, however, the Vedic priests fell into the trappings of material wealth, which corrupted the use of the law of attraction and its power to manifest. Some priests continued to be authentic, but others compensated for their lack of spiritual attainment by creating elaborate rituals that resonated with the minds of the greedy and the unwise. All of this was meant to be, for the souls desired to know the contrast of everything: good versus bad, light versus dark, and spiritual versus material.

The fall from grace happened in many places on Earth during this time. As the Vedas were corrupted in India, the ancient Goddess temples were destroyed in the rest of the world. Fear and sorrow spread as billions of brave souls incarnated into the Kali Yuga to willingly fall into the illusion of suffering in order to know all. The patriarchal religions defined themselves in opposition to a path that existed earlier which empowered both the feminine and the masculine. Many wars were fought in the name of these new religions.

The Goddesses hid themselves from the world and Gods like dear Vishnu incarnated in order to usher in the Kali Yuga. As this Yuga descended with full force, some Goddesses, including myself, incarnated again to balance the ebb with the flow, and to begin new paths for freeing humanity from its suffering. Now, as Kali Yuga is in its final chapter, many Goddesses are moving forward to bring the joy of soul feelings back on Earth.

Can you tell us more about your path in Vedanta?

I wish to speak about an incarnation in which I came in with many of my soulmates. We had journeyed together for some lifetimes, and in this particular lifetime everything was in place for the next stage of the expansion of the universe. A new soul cycle was about to begin, and many from our soul tribe incarnated in that lifetime to help with the spiritual unfolding of this cycle. A part of my soul divided from my larger soul and incarnated as Gayatri in that incarnation. So, I was both Gayatri and Saraswati in that incarnation.

Brahma received the first vision of the new soul cycle. He chose to perform a Vedic ritual with Gayatri, who took my place as his partner. While this angered the larger part of myself for a moment, the emotion of anger dissolved fully in my body and transformed into the soul feeling of passion. From the place of this passion I co-created the futures of my soulmates with the agreement of their higher selves. I uttered the words describing the many incarnations of my soulmates in which they would fall into contrast and rise into enlightenment. Unfortunately, my words were interpreted as curses on my soulmates.

Were they not curses on your soulmates?

When I spoke, it was to allow myself to say
what needed to be said. It was not with anger, but
a boundless passion that arose from the dissolution of my anger. My words also taught the masses, especially women, to speak from their heart.
For had I not spoken, what manner of Goddess
would I have been to not say anything? There were
many there, and my saying nothing would not
teach women to speak as they needed to speak.

Could Lord Brahma have chosen differently?
Perhaps! Either way, the expansion of emptiness
would continue. I was thankful for the choice made
by Lord Brahma, for my path was to bring the
timeless wisdom of Vedanta into the world. I simply observed the events that would unfold, which
were conditional on the choice made by Lord
Brahma. Though my prophetic words were interpreted as curses, they came from a place of deep
knowing. After my ascension, the foretold events
came to pass, and I watched over and guided
my soulmates to ascend to their higher selves in
their human incarnations. Know that many spiritual
paths have begun with the dissolution and transformation of anger into passion. Even Jesus spoke
with a great passion in the Temple of Jerusalem.
His words set a chain of events that eventually created the great religion of Christianity. Such passion is creative, like the sexual passion that creates

life. It is what birthed Goddesses like Durga and Kali when the anger of Gods dissolved and transformed into passion.

There are many layers of teachings in this story and one of the great lessons is about trust—trusting to say what is in the heart. For if one does not speak from the heart, does that not curse oneself and lay Karma upon oneself? The words I spoke allowed me to receive what I desired from my heart. It was not so much about a man and woman relationship between Lord Brahma and myself as it was about the Ying and the Yang energy, and the forgiveness, allowing, and not sacrificing myself, which would have been of a lower energy. If you are in a river and you attempt to row against the current, you use a yang energy to fight a greater yang energy, which in turn creates nothing. But if you flow with the river and keep rowing, you remain balanced because you use your yang energy with the greater yin energy of the river.

Were you enlightened when your anger transformed into passion?

I was enlightened as I already had six chakras open when this occurred. I could see all of the past, present, and future, but the tiniest tail of my ego was still there since the Seventh Chakra had not opened. After I ascended fully with the opening of the Seventh Chakra, the portion of my soul

in Gayatri also ascended in the same moment, and
merged completely with myself.

So, did the two of you become one in that moment
after your ascension? Or were you still two?

Both! Our inner oneness was not affected by
our external forms. So we were completely one,
manifested as two at that point.

Aha! Your story reminds me of different manifestations
of Goddess Tara. The Buddhist scriptures say that both
Green Tara and White Tara manifested from the tears of
Avalokitesvara, the great Bodhisattva of compassion.

It brings a smile to my face that you would
bring this up. If one is fully present to the emotion
of sadness without any resistance, then the sadness dissolves and transforms into the soul feeling
of compassion. Compassion is creative and it heals
many. Think of how Jesus healed so many with his
great compassion. Compassion blesses both the
giver and the receiver as the suffering melts into
joy.

Compassion cannot be realized if the ego
either represses the emotion of sadness or attaches itself to it. When the ego represses sadness, it
becomes blind to the suffering of oneself and others. When the ego attaches too much to sadness,
it creates sorrow and depression.

Many Bodhisattvas vow to heal the suffering of others before becoming fully enlightened. A very tiny residual of the ego attached to their sadness about the suffering of the world remains, which prevents them from being fully enlightened. However, as sentient beings are healed into joy, it allows bodhisattvas to release that residual ego and grow into Buddhas. Know that the whole universe expands into a greater primordial joy when we melt our sadness into compassion.

Does compassion always have some sadness in it because it is created by the dissolution of sadness? Similarly, does passion always have some anger in it, because it is created by the dissolution of anger?

If you throw the tiniest particle of sand into an ocean of pure water, does the water become impure? It is similar to this. Divine beings know anger and sadness, for they have experienced physical realms before their ascension into the spiritual realms. They dissolved these emotions and transformed them into the oceanic soul feelings of passion and compassion, respectively. Think about it: if divine beings did not know soul feelings such as passion and compassion, and were only immersed in their emptiness, then how would they recognize suffering and respond to it? Soul feelings are what join sentient beings to the heavenly realms and beyond. Using the guidance system of soul feelings, divine beings can manifest from their abode of emptiness into those worlds that are out of balance.

The words of passion that I spoke to Lord Brahma and my other soulmates were filled with the joy of a new creation. The words came from a great knowingness and were completely aligned with the mission of our soul tribe. Spoken with strong intention, these words helped manifest the incarnations of Lakshmi and Vishnu in the Hindu epics of Ramayana and Mahabharata, and in the great religion the world knows as Buddhism. The words were aligned with the soul paths of Lakshmi and Vishnu, who out of their infinite compassion incarnated again and again on Earth to create new paths of spiritual wisdom.

As Lakshmi surrendered to the events of her life in Ramayana, she was taken from the abundance of the palace into the wild forest to realize the soul feeling of true abundance through her First Chakra, which represents the earth element. Thus, she is a Goddess of abundance—the joy of true abundance that Mother Earth provides. As she surrendered to the events that occurred in the lives of her different incarnations in Mahabharata, she realized love in many different forms—the love of a maiden, the love of a matron, and the love of a crone. Thus, she is a Goddess of love, and more specifically, the Goddess of passion that unites the First Chakra with the Heart Chakra. As she surrendered to the events of her life with Gautama Buddha, she realized the emptiness in which all soul feelings merge into oneness. Thus, she is also the Goddess of enlightenment, representing the opening of the Seventh Chakra. As Lakshmi and Vishnu experienced the contrast of these incarnations, the emptiness of their higher selves expanded even more.

We are so elated to talk to you directly about these incarnations of you and your soulmates.

We are delighted to speak to you. Together we will create this book so the rest the world can also benefit from these teachings. It is not only divine beings like Lakshmi and Vishnu who experienced contrast in their incarnations— but also all humans have experienced contrast over many lifetimes to expand the emptiness of their higher selves.

Can you tell us more about contrast?

The first duality that created contrast was the division of all creation into the polarity of the feminine and the masculine. This polarity exists in all things, including even the four elements. While religions, cultures, and nations have also divided humanity, the biggest division underlying all divisions was created by the identification of the two sexes with the wounded archetypes of feminine and masculine under the reign of patriarchy. The alignment of the two sexes with the wounded feminine and wounded masculine has created the most basic conditioning that underlies all other conditioning of humans at this time. The ascended Goddesses and other divine beings are pouring much light on Earth at this time to heal the split between the wounded feminine and the wounded masculine. Now, in the next part of this book, dear Lakshmi will speak about how to step outside the box of this wounded feminine-masculine polarity and step into the dance of the empowered feminine and empowered masculine to heal the Earth and all sentient beings that live upon it. The recent events in the world have already awakened the empowered feminine in both men and women. Our wisdom shall join with the wisdom of other Goddesses, who shall also speak in future books, and together we shall create a new path of spiritual awakening for all of humanity.

Namaste!

Namaste Saraswati ji!

PART II
THE TRUTH ABOUT
EVE, MARY AND SITA

SELF-LOVE MANTRA

Aham Prema

अहं प्रेम

6

Eve and Mary

Namaste Lakshmi ji!

Namaste!

Can you tell us why have you chosen this particular
moment to speak to humans?

I am here for a moment of opening to bring
joy and teachings as I have done in the past. The
timing that is spoken of and that you have questioned has to do with the aligning of the stars and
the signs of past eons, so it is only an unbuckling
of a record. The energies of the Earth are calling for its emotional stability. This was the task
I was assigned several generations ago. There
have not been many teachings that I have been
able to bring forward, as my teachings have been
buried. I wish to manifest aspects of myself that
were hidden in the past. I desire to assist many
in overcoming the hardships of their lives as well

as their endeavors for companionship. Not only shall I speak, but also, as Saraswati mentioned, other Goddesses from other belief systems will as well. You may see Goddesses in other cultures come forward and correct the beliefs and transferences that have been made toward more of a masculine energy so that we may become balanced once again.

We humans seem to have completely lost our way. Is this part of some karmic cycle? The intensity of suffering is too much.

Think of a harsh winter storm. If one stands calmly at the center, in the eye of the storm, one experiences the beauty of the storm with its ultimate peace and quiet. Most humans, however, stand outside the eye of the storm, living in much fear and chaos; they cannot simply rest in that tender place of surrender. All of nature finds joy and silence in the whiteness of winter, bringing forth fruit in the spring again. So, your question about the karmic cycle is a small part of a great spiritual unfolding.

Do we have to suffer so much?

Suffering is a learned thing. A child is born with suffering because the mother has no peace with the child in her womb. In past generations, women would take time away from everyday work and rest for the length of pregnancy and birth. The children would have an opportunity to be born in peace. The human race has turned its back to the teachings of the original ancestors as it pertains to caring for their children. There has also been violence of some sort or other in recent generations; because of this, children have experienced only fragmented joys in life. Furthermore, there has not been true nurturing for many generations in these lands ruled by men. Because many patriarchal structures are built with rigidity, the mind has not opened and expanded in ways that bring Heaven and Earth together. This has manifested diseases of body, mind, and spirit that have been the cause of the tears of this Earth mother that you live upon. This was not always so, and even now there are those who desire to become connected to the ancient spirits of the Earth. In order to assist in their awakening, one of the tasks I have been given is to bring new knowledge and to help this land bear a fruit of a different kind.

Some believe that Eve's eating of the forbidden fruit from the tree of knowledge caused men's distrust of women. This distrust then led to men's control over women, and the creation of patriarchy.[3]

This is a metaphor, and Eve did not eat any "forbidden" fruit. The original story was changed over generations, creating an incorrect belief that women have caused men's separation from their higher spiritual aspects. It brings us a sigh to think that, when presented with a forbidden fruit, an enlightened one, such as Eve, would have been tempted, knowing in her heart that this would cause a great separation.

Oh really? Eve was an enlightened being?

Yes. Eve enjoyed the garden greatly. The garden was spontaneous and alive. There was hearth and home there. Many teachings were given to her. Her gifts were to speak to the angels who came and went as the Sun moved up and down. She also was a care-taker of many angels. Eve spoke to these winged ones and also to animals, as did Adam. Everything was in complete harmony at this time, and only joy resided there. The belief that she somehow did not know what her action would cause is unseemly. She was given the most divine choice to create more from the inner tree of knowledge *within her*. In contemplation with higher divine beings, Eve and Adam made a decision to remove themselves from a place of joy and harmony because they were evolved to a point where they needed to move forward into even greater spiritual realms. The idea that they did not decide this together is incorrect. The "forbidden fruit" was a metaphor created by men after many generations to make women feel guilty about following their joyous feminine path of spiritual awakening. They changed Eve's moment of awakening into the "original sin."

What about the story of the snake who persuaded Eve?

The serpent is a sign of the Egyptian God, *Thoth*. He is the messenger of the Gods. He lived in the garden that would manifest its fullness in divine timing. This unfortunate reptile has been branded as a "lower form"; however, this is not consistent with its gentle and non-aggressive nature. The association of a woman with a serpent was created to portray the woman as a being of lower nature.[4] It was done to disempower women: the image of a snake that bites and attacks became a symbol of women's inherent evil nature. However, all beings exhibit higher and lower energies, so while a snake's venom is poisonous, it is also used for healing. More often animals are used as examples of truth and wisdom, as we see in many indigenous cultures. In eastern cultures particularly, this is so.

Think of Ganesha: why did they put an elephant head on him? They could have put a human head on him. But they used an elephant head because the elephant is a representation of the higher nature of longevity, posterity, wisdom, and gentleness. The truth about Eve will come to light, and will be rectified by the future generations.

The story of Eve's original sin reminds me of another story in Christianity about Jesus and Mary Magdalene. Mary Magdalene has been portrayed as a repentant sinner in Christianity since Pope Gregory I (also known as Saint *Gregory the Great*) identified her as a prostitute in 591 CE.[5] However, some writers have suggested that Mary Magdalene was Jesus's closest friend, beloved, and spiritual partner. Can you speak about Mary's life and her role with Jesus Christ?

Mary was one of several sisters in her family. She had high intuition and could manifest many things in her life. She was known for her beauty and amazingly attractive eyes. She had comely limbs and dressed simply. Her hair was also her crowning glory. She was chosen by Jesus, the beloved ascended being from high above, and was pre-ordained to be his spiritual partner, for they had already spent lifetimes together. She recognized him and asked the Goddesses to bring them together. They met during a family ceremony. She had never been one that would bring herself to the attention of a man. She sequestered herself spending much time alone before Jesus came to her, a fact that has not been written in scriptures. She was also very musically inclined and talented. She had no fear of the tasks that would lie before the man whom she loved. She also saw him for the man that he was and did not just worship him as a God. This endeared him towards her. He pursued her through the ceremonial and traditional dating rituals of those times. She was wooed by this beloved ascended being and their love was blessed by Mother Mary and Joseph, and by her own family.

Jesus was able to listen to the advice she provided. He shared some of Mary's teachings, which she received in the edifices that were built and dedicated to those pure in heart and brought them to him. So, the teaching that Jesus received his wisdom from his father only is not correct. This will also be brought to light as more records are revealed in future times. Jesus and Mary also had children together since it was the law of the time to consummate a marriage and have children. She kept herself away from the masses. This is why so many in the past had incorrect information. Jesus protected her from the burden that would become his. Thus, Mary traveled faraway and spent much time alone, yet again. She took her children with her to raise them. She also taught them many lessons, devotionals, contemplations, poetry, and songs. Those will also come to light later.

So much of what we think about Eve and Mary is untrue.

Yes. As some do know, there were other enlightened women that were like Eve. She had a place as an angel in the garden, and this was her hiding abode. She was given the task of speaking with the winged ones—we have spoken of that before—and these were the messengers of love.

She was tasked with the raising of children, and many women followed that path. Women found joy in the raising of children and their roles at that time were mainly to be guides for their children. The women were guided by angels in order to help the children on their individual paths.

We would also like you to know that there were large groups of women who lived in female tribes with many enlightened priestesses. There were many women who had tasks of taking care of these priestesses as do bees in a beehive. Like the bees who pollinate to sustain much life on Mother Earth, the priestesses in these Goddess temples would send healing energies to sustain other living planets and star systems in our universe and other universes. There were also warrior women who protected these female tribes living in Goddess temples. These temples were almost always high up in the mountains where the energy could remain pure and the vibration would be high so that the women could serve as portals to sentient beings everywhere. There was direct communion from Goddesses to priestesses in these heart-centered places of the universe.

For procreation, the women of these temples allowed the men of high spiritual aspirations to seek them out. The women came down to the flatlands every so many years with other warrior women who protected them in order to find mates to procreate with. There was a specific group of women who would procreate, and their children were looked upon as warrior angels. There was no sorrow among these women and they were close to God like Mary was.

7

From Matriarchy to Patriarchy

The great ancestors had many teachings. There was so much celebration in these Goddess temples of the ancient times. Women nurtured their children deeply and taught them many sacred gifts. It used to be a blessing for even a male child to go into a meditative state and rejoice in the feminine aspects of himself. There was more balance at that time, and the protective masculine energy was whole and creative and not fragmented and wounded. The early commandments brought man and woman together to procreate, and men and women enjoyed their lives without the burdens and sorrows that afflict humans today. All of this changed with the rise of patriarchy created by the contentious energies of the wounded feminine and the wounded masculine.

How and why?

The soul cycles go in phases of expansion and contraction, like the inhalation and exhalation of the breath. This current phase of contraction began with the transition of humanity from a matriarchal system to a patriarchal system close to 6,500 years ago. It accelerated significantly around 2,000 years ago when some things were changed. The protective masculine energy became egotistical in nature, and it no longer desired to honor the feminine energy. The men came together and created power structures that did not need women, except for in procreation. As this creative protective energy devolved into a lower wounded form, it became more patriarchal. Men became aggressive and wanted to control women and even other men. They did so through fighting wars, dominating lands, and imposing beliefs on others. Families and clans were divided as children were taken away from their mothers. All of this caused much grief to women and children as well as the men related to them. This grief perpetuated and multiplied over many lifetimes. The separation of children from mothers was similar to the annihilation of entire tribes of indigenous peoples and languages in more recent times, and the sorrow caused by this separation continued over generations. The guilt and sorrow was perpetuated further in women who could not bear male children. Little-by-little women became slaves to their own minds conditioned by the patriarchal order.

As time went on, fear-driven men usurped the natural order of the universe, so much so that they felt that they would rather be in contention than in peace. Since the turning of humanity to a patriarchal order, it has not been the wish of men for generations that women fill the sacred spaces. Women also succumbed to men's wishes by carrying a deep river of guilt about nurturing everything for many generations. The guilt turned into sorrow as men of coarse nature held women accountable for more than was possible under the patriarchal order, and this created the imbalance that we see today. If you look around, there are many individuals nowadays who do not have a feeling of being nurtured. This is so because so many people have disconnected from their innate nurturing selves. Even babies of many mothers feel an absence of nurturance early on in the womb.

In many cultures women are literally carrying the heavy burdens of the daily chores on their heads and shoulders. Some women have such great sorrow that their pain rises even to their heart. It feels like a deep mourning of the wounded feminine. They carry sorrows of many past generations. There are those who desire to bring forth their gifts but cannot sit in the place of their power due to the patriarchal order. This keeps them from their true path and makes it difficult for them to see the cause of their suffering. It is as if they cannot seem to find the notes of music that can be played in harmony. In their unknowingness, they forget to even look up and see that our light shines upon them.

Women have been demonized as sinners for centuries in many cultures and nations. Is there a deep-rooted fear in some men about women everywhere on Earth?

Yes: the fear is both political and personal. Politically, the fear dates back to thousands of years ago when the patriarchal religions first labeled the high priestesses of temples as prostitutes. These priestesses were deeply connected with Earth and enjoyed the respect and honor of managing the affairs of the lands. As men invaded lands of others and wrested control from women, they spread incorrect beliefs about the matriarchal system that had existed during those times. In matriarchy, women celebrated their bodies and fertility in their personal lives, and were also empowered with leadership roles in their public lives. Many were seen as manifestations of the great goddesses. Men introduced shame about the human body to counter the power of women. The innocence of living with bare minimum clothing was taken from humans in many cultures around the world.

As patriarchy became firmly established, the male priests declared enjoyment of the sensual as sinful and the naked body as shameful. In doing so, they alienated humans from their sacred sensual nature, which in turn created incorrect beliefs about human sexuality. Having classified human joys into "good" and "bad," organized religions weakened the human free will and increased men's control over women and other men. Controlled and repressed masses could be persuaded to fight wars to further the ambitions of men looking for the approval of other men. As a result, men became more exploitative and prone to anger and violence. In this struggle, many women lost harmony with their feminine essence and became more aggressive themselves. This separation continues even now because women are not being true to their own nature.

At a personal level, the fear is quite simple. The fear results from the belief that once a woman has the seed, she does not need the man. She can nourish the roots and allow the sun to shine upon them from above. Some men have a need to be, for lack of a better word, very primate-like, driven by animalistic impulses. These men want to hunt and protect with the warrior energy. They are afraid that if women interrupt this warrior energy that they may not have anything left that is intrinsic to their nature. So look at your own day; look at where we have been since these last fifty years. During this time when women were struggling and pushing against male domination, some men felt the need to conform to a more effeminate nature, thereby feeling demasculated and stripped of their masculine energy. But look at those that have been Zen or Japanese warriors —they have a balance of the masculine and the feminine energies.

Are both men and women acting out of their fears instead of accepting their true nature?

The man has a fear that once the woman has a child, she may not need him much. The woman has a fear that if she does not fight for herself, she may be used and discarded. What is needed is temperance and patience between the masculine and feminine energies and the ability to respond differently, both as a male and a female. The main course is love. Love that comes in service to one another brings balance, and you can see this clearly in nature.

Let us go back to when I shared with you about standing in the center of the storm. The eye of the storm is a warm, nurturing place of great harmony between the divine feminine and the divine masculine. When one speaks of standing at the edge of the storm, one is not standing quietly at the edge of the storm. Instead, one is in the storm struggling to reach the center. The struggle itself is the war between the wounded feminine and the wounded masculine. The war plays out at many levels, both within and without. If one could simply observe the war within and completely surrender, one would already be at the center without reaching for the center. Or, one can continue to battle. When one does the latter, one freezes and creates karma upon oneself. The men of lower nature created this karma by using organized religions and other patriarchal structures to disempower women.

Oh, so if these men of lower nature had surrendered completely, they would have moved to the center without creating so much karma for themselves and suffering for others.

Yes. Is the storm not an illusion created by the mind after all? Let us speak briefly about why it has been hard for those who keep fighting to surrender without ever reaching the center. We talked earlier about women who have had their hearts wrenched apart. The children who are born to these women have a hard time returning to their feminine essence, as they have already been in the storm during conception. It is more difficult for these children to surrender. As the woman has stayed in the storm and even stoked the storm, the child knows nothing but those tumultuous times which cause a breakdown of DNA patterns, thus affecting generations.

I will make it simple for you. Think of those holiday lights on a string. Is it not true that as one light goes out, the whole strand goes out? This is the same for the DNA strand. One stroke can affect the whole strand of generations.

Oh, then much suffering of humanity right now can be traced to some points in history when women suffered much, which would have affected the DNA during conception?

That is right.

So the breakdown in DNA patterns explains why we see a continuation of abuse patterns in families?

Yes.

So, would you say that it is extremely important that women feel loved and cared for during pregnancy?

Mother nature assists in this process as the hormonal changes during pregnancy make the mother feel happy and joyous.

Oh yes—the pregnancy glow! Earlier you spoke about children being taken away from their mothers during Biblical times. Can you tell us more about this? Why did this have to happen? Who benefitted from separating children from their mothers?

Those who gained had much greed for power

and money, for they or their ancestors had themselves been victimized by the patriarchal system.
They pursued their greed with much aggression
by acquiring lands and heritage. They would take
the children from the mothers and use them just as
one would kidnap a person these days for wealth
expropriation purposes. Using these children,
they would ask for ransom that would increase the
power of one family over another. They were very
particular about the children that they took.

Why do humans have such greed for power and money?

Obviously, the greed comes from the human
ego. The ego thinks that it can fill the lack not realizing that in doing so it perpetuates the illusion of
lack. Ego wants approval from others more than it
wants true love or inner peace. Ego likes to please
others with the hope that others would see it in a
positive light. The need for approval is the reason
behind most human conflicts and behind much of
human sorrow. As human societies evolved from
matriarchal to patriarchal structures, the need for
approval became primary, and love became secondary. Children were taken from their mothers and
were enslaved because there were those who were
looking for more power in order to get approval
from others who were even more powerful. If you
think of the many stories from scriptures, you will

see the same pattern. Even Demons were looking for the approval of someone or the other in many of these stories.

What is wrong with wanting the approval of our loved ones?

The need for approval leads to a breakdown of communication even when there is a desire to do good by the loved ones. This is because every person sees the world from one's own perspective. Even children born to the same mother and father have very different experiences of growing up. For example, think of two sisters sitting together for a conversation. Each sister may truly believe that she is right without understanding the other. At the same time, each sister may attempt to please the other in order to get her approval instead of being true to herself. This breaks down the harmony and love that existed before each thought that she was right and desired to get the other's approval. Through this simple breakdown, fissure cracks arise in their relationship. Even if one sister reaches out to resolve the miscommunication, the other sister may refuse to engage. The sister who reached out would take that as a personal insult due to her own insecurity. Thus, even if both desired to love one another, they may end up with a breakdown in their communication.

I share this simple example of two sisters to explain the disharmony between humans on a larger scale. The fissure cracks between the sexes caused by the need for approval have snowballed gradually into much greater conflicts between them, which have led to men taking control and creating patriarchal structures over many generations.

8

Sita

I have struggled to understand the contentious issue of "approval" in my own life. It seems like we are conditioned so deeply to obey social rules and respect cultural norms that I have found myself feeling guilty sometimes for not "behaving" properly and not living a "normal" life like everyone else. Yet, many of these rules and norms serve patriarchal institutions and systems, which do not resonate with my own inner knowing. The conditioning seems to happen at the deepest levels, beginning from early childhood with popular stories from scriptures like the *Bible* or the *Ramayana*. For example, in the great epic of *Ramayana*, the epic's hero *Rama* gives much weight to social norms and opinions when making decisions about his marriage to you in your incarnation as *Sita*. So, is it true that even someone as enlightened as Rama struggled with the issue of "approval?"

> Rama incarnated with a divine mission to which he surrendered with the best of his human abilities. He was not the most romantic person; he was more

task-oriented and dedicated to his spiritual mission. He desired the approval of his parents and his step-mother in the beginning of his spiritual journey until he was enlightened to his true nature. He considered serving and protecting his wife and children his *duty*, which he fulfilled in a good manner. While the conversation between us was sometimes lacking, it is not correct that he put social norms above our marriage. Certain references about our relationship were changed and false stories about us were added to the *Ramayana* over time. Rama listened to his guides, angels, and holy teachers, quite often. His was the *Avatar path* followed by Christ and other enlightened beings, as well.

Hmm...according to the scriptures, Rama was sent into exile for 14 years at the request of his step-mother, who desired to make her own son the King of Ayodhya. After many years in exile, you, as Sita, were kidnapped and taken hostage by Ravana, the King of Lanka, and were hidden in a place called Ashoka Vatika for many months before Rama rescued you by defeating and killing Ravana in an epic spiritual war. Yet, before returning to Ayodhya, Rama made you go through an *Agni Pariksha*—a fire test—to prove your fidelity. Was this done *to prove to everyone else that you were pure*, even though Rama believed in his heart that you were pure?

Isn't it interesting that so much of human history has been written from a patriarchal perspective? There are so many incorrect stories about enlightened women like Eve, Mary, and others. Some have been lost in translation. Others were created to suit male-oriented cultures throughout human history.

Are you saying that you did not go through the fire test?

I *chose* all of the major events of my life in my incarnation as Sita. It was my decision to go with Rama into exile. My soul desired to know the depths of loneliness, so I *chose* to be sequestered with the help of Ravana. The three of us had a soul contract in this. Once Rama and I totally surrendered to our lower chakras, we found our nothingness and blossomed into bliss. We realized who we were, and that is when Rama gathered the strength to defeat Ravana, who was no ordinary mortal. We met as enlightened beings *after* Rama's victory over Ravana. We were open in all our chakras, and so nothing was hidden from us at this point. We could communicate directly using our thoughts without using any words or language. I could have walked on water or disappeared at will if I wanted, for I had full control over the elements at this point.

So, you could have even gone through the fire without being burned. Did you go through the fire test?

No, there was no fire *test!* The fire was a metaphor for my enlightenment. Think of the sun as it melts down over the clouds into the place where you cannot see it anymore. This is what that means. This is to help you understand that the ego must be released into the ultimate nothingness, just as the sun is released into the void of the night. Then, the snake energy, or the Kundalini, rises and one has pure enlightenment. So there is a double metaphor related to my being in the fire—one is the releasing of the ego, and the other is the claiming of enlightenment. It is like the phoenix: a rebirth from the ashes.

I find this hard to believe. Are you saying that the fire is just a metaphor for your enlightenment in the original story and that it has been taken out of context?

Yes. Rama and I were totally united at this point, and he required nothing of this sort from me. We thought as one mind and felt as one heart, so there was nothing that he desired for me, which was also not my wish.

Well, we think of Rama as a benevolent King who is very concerned about setting an example of good conduct for his subjects. Sage Valmiki, the author of the *Ramayana*, clearly states that Rama brought up the issue of your chastity in public, and at that point you asked Rama's brother, Lakshmana, to light the pyre so that you could either prove your chastity or be consumed by the fire.

Valmiki was a great sage!

So, were his writings correct?

His had profound insights in everything he wrote. And he wrote much.

Then why would he write a story about you entering fire, which was meant as a metaphor, but could be easily misunderstood?

He did not write this.

Huh?

The *Ramayana* was altered over centuries to suit the beliefs of its new authors who valued the patriarchy. Some parts were expanded, and whole new sections were added in other parts, that Valmiki never wrote. When you research this, you will find clear evidence that entirely new sections were added to the *Ramayana* hundreds of years after Valmiki initially composed it.

Really?! Very interesting! When and how did this occur?

This occurred around the time when they crucified the beloved of Mary. Many original writings were changed to suit the patriarchal beliefs spreading all over the Earth during a few centuries around this time. These beliefs presented the female as submissive with a very subdued fire element. That is when the male priests removed my statues in my glory as Lakshmi that showed me in a way that did not please their eyes filled with shame. In the new writings, the male authors tested my virtue as Sita and "purified" me by putting me through the fire.

Valmiki reincarnated on Earth to correct this soon after the end of the medieval period, when the temples were being destroyed in India. He wrote a translation of Valmiki's *Ramayana* that was closer to the truth, but even he did not recollect everything from his earlier incarnation as Valmiki.

Oh, you mean as Tulsidas, who wrote the *Ramcharitmanas?*

Yes.

So is *Ramcharitmanas* the correct version of what happened?

It is closer to the truth, though not entirely true, as Tulsidas was also human. Tulsidas prayed often and was inspired by angels and gods. In his meditations, he realized that his own words from his earlier incarnation as Valmiki had been changed, and whole new chapters and sections had been added to make me appear weak and submissive.

Can you give us examples of which chapters and sections were added?

Not only were verses about my fire test added, a whole new section was added about my separation from my beloved after we returned to Ayodhya. I have no memory of being separated from my beloved after we returned to Ayodhya.

Oh, really? Are you saying that Rama did *not* ask his younger brother, Lakshmana, to take you to the forest and abandon you there because of a "rumor" about your infidelity that Rama had heard from a washerman?

This story must be put to rest once and for all. Rama turned away from all rumors of this kind and did not listen to those who were speaking ill of me. Rama knew that I was the chosen one; not just the chosen one for him, but also *the chosen one*. The washerman story was a metaphor for those who liked to gossip, but Rama would have none of it.

The timing of the original story was also changed. This gossip that you are asking about occurred much earlier during the time when Rama was searching for me. It might surprise you that Ravana was not seen in a negative light until he was defeated by Rama—he was actually seen as a great King and I was seen as the unchaste one because I had been put away for whatever reason. A woman was sequestered in those days for various reasons and not always of her own volition. Rama's task was a difficult one, for he was considered to be of a holy nature, but he was searching for me—a person who was rumored to be "unchaste." Such is the nature of human gossip! This gossip was manipulated into the fictional washerman story by the male authors of the *Ramayana* who added new verses and new chapters to this epic many hundreds of years after Valmiki wrote it. These authors reasoned that if a Goddess like me could be thrown out of my own home, it would set a great example for ordinary women to not commit adultery and thus make them "behave and be dutiful" towards their husbands, always. Similar changes were made in the scriptures of other religions around that time as well.

So, what occurred after you returned to Ayodhya?

We were both fully enlightened when we met after Rama's victory over Ravana, and we lived happily until the time came to lay ourselves down. I chose to be connected to the forest and would often take our children to be with nature away from the palace. Our sons, Lava and Kusha, grew up feeling the sacred connection with Mother Earth and were also taught by the learned sages who lived in the forest. Rama was close to our sons, but I spent much time with them in the forest. There was no leaving. There was only love.

Why in the forest?

Let me repeat, Rama and I were united in all our chakras and nothing was hidden from us at this point. The forest was the true paradise that we both wanted our sons to experience, but Rama

was more engaged with his brothers and his subjects in the running of the kingdom. I enjoyed the
raising of Lava and Kusha and my meditations with
them in the forest. There was a coming and going
from the palace to the forest, and Lava and Kusha
grew up with a deep connection to nature and to
the wisdom of sages. Since we spent much time
away from each other physically, this was misunderstood to mean we were not together as a
couple.

So is it not true that "you took shelter in Valmiki's hut
after being expelled by Rama"?

I have already stated that Valmiki did not write
any of this and reincarnated to correct much of
what others had added fictitiously over time.

I am finding this extremely hard to believe! Based
upon the scriptures, most Hindus have thought for centuries that for the sake of society's "approval," you went
through the fire test. They also believed that Rama sub-
sequently expelled you from the royal palace because the
people of Ayodhya had serious concerns about your fidelity
given that you had remained in close proximity to Ravana
for so many months.

Not only was the *Ramayana* changed drasti-
cally, but also other scriptures were, like the Holy
Bible. The official versions of the Bible reveal only
a small portion of the mystical truths about the

vast ascended being whom you know as Jesus Christ. Eve did not commit the first sin; she and Adam were few of the last remaining enlightened beings on Earth from a previous soul cycle. Mary Magdalene was not a prostitute but Jesus's most beloved wife and one of the twelve apostles. Rama loved me immensely without concerning himself about "approval" by the people of his kingdom .

The feminine side of humanity has been wounded by the alteration of scriptures and by the creation of fictional stories that marginalized many Goddess-like women all over the world. These stories have deeply wounded the collective consciousness of humanity. The wounded side of the feminine has forgotten the immense depths of love and joy—the absence of which has created the wounded side of masculine.

However, in order to counter the misrepresentations of patriarchy, and to heal the *wounded feminine* and the *wounded masculine*, new writings have also been inspired all over the world in many spiritual traditions. In some places like Tibet, Saraswati and others hid numerous scriptures to be revealed later at appropriate times so that the feminine spiritual wisdom of Buddhism could be protected from the patriarchal human mind. A few centuries before incarnating as Tulsidas, Valmiki's soul inspired another great book, the messages of which survived in their originality.

Hmm…

The knowledge of this book was given to Rama by his teacher, and it manifested Rama's path of enlightenment.

Oh, the *Yoga Vasistha?*

Yes.

Two of my favorite books are *Yoga Vasistha* and *Ashtavakra Gita.* One is a conversation between your husband, Rama, and Sage Vasistha, and the other is a conversation between your father, Janaka, and the enlightened Sage, Ashtavakra.

I was blessed with a wise father and a loving husband.   Laughter!

9

The Wounded Feminine and
the Wounded Masculine

Can you tell us more about the wounded feminine and
the wounded masculine?

Before understanding the wounded feminine and the wounded masculine, let us understand the duality of the feminine and the masculine, which is present in all things and all life. The
heart nurtures and unifies, and so is feminine.
The mind individuates and creates, and so is
masculine. The heart represents the sun energy,
which is introspective and shines from within.
The mind represents the moon energy, which is
reflective and shines from without.

Hmm! So, would you say the sun is feminine and the
moon is masculine?

The sun gives off itself to sustain life. Think of
the warmth a child feels when embraced by her or

his mother. The sun provides the same warmth to the Earth, representing that feminine energy. The moon is more distant but not too far from the sun. It is just far enough to be reflective, but not nearly as warm. However, it is close enough for one to see. Such as the child that looks to the father but is not suckled by the father.

Your answer seems to agree with many ancient matriarchal cultures in which the sun was seen as feminine and the moon was seen as masculine. It seems as if humans changed the answer at some point so that the masculine would be seen as more powerful.

That is true!

Are elements either masculine or feminine?

Yes. The masculine *individuates* and the feminine *unifies*. Metaphysically, air represents thought; earth represents physicality; water represents emotions; and fire represents sensuality, sexuality, insight, and enlightenment. Air and earth are masculine energies that individuate, and fire and water are feminine energies that unify. The masculine energies are physical, intellectual, analytical, logical, and left-brained. The feminine energies are mystical, emotional, synthetical, intuitive, and right-brained.

Reality is like a hologram that reflects the polarity of feminine and masculine at all levels and in all things. It is a constant ebb and flow of more individuation and more union in everything. For example, the individuation of the physical universe from the feminine wholeness is masculine.

Why do earth and air individuate and why do fire and water unify?

Water represents emotions. Fire represents joy. Purified by the fire of joy, emotions become love. Since joy and love unify all back into oneness, fire and water are feminine elements. As Vishnu and I were joined in the bliss of our *fire-water*, we interacted with a higher being who was in even a deeper state of bliss and that led to the *first thought* of curiosity after eons. This led to a joyous explosion that divided the oneness of our fire-water to create the *earth* element. I am not talking about the creation of your universe, but rather of a universe that interacts with your universe in those invisible dimensions. But, this is also how your universe came into being from the union of higher beings. Since the first thought—which is represented by the air element—individuated all into uniqueness, it is masculine. Since the earth element represents the physical universe that individuated from the feminine wholeness, it is also masculine.

Aha! So there are many universes that interact with our own universe?

Yes, in the invisible dimensions that you do not see.

Okay! Are male and female associated with the masculine and the feminine, respectively?

The duality of male and female is based on who sheds the seed and who nurtures it, but the association of the male with masculinity and the female with femininity is rooted only in thought, in your mind. It is not always true that the male has more masculine energy and the female has more feminine energy. We are speaking of the four cardinal energies and how they interplay so that people may understand that there are two feminine and two masculine energies that complement one another in every human, whether male, female, or androgynous. So the answer to your question is that masculine and feminine *do not always* correspond to male and female.

Many humans choose to stay with the sex roles assigned to them by parents and society. Most people want to see a person as a male or a female or a transgender identity, and then based on their cultural beliefs about masculine and feminine, they evaluate how each person fits in one of them.

When they do this, however, they are no longer fully present to the relationship. In the extreme case, the relationship becomes sexist depending on what is considered "correct" or "incorrect" at a given time in a given culture. One can look deep inside to move beyond these gender roles. The infinite depths of the soul lie beyond the division of male and female and embrace both the masculine and the feminine. Judging people through the lens of the masculine and feminine causes much misunderstanding between humans.

Aha!

Many people become confused because of the attachments to such beliefs about the apparent duality of masculine and feminine. Similar to the example of the two sisters I spoke of earlier, the confusion begins with the desire to please others to get their approval based on the beliefs passed down by parents and by society. But the fissure cracks resulting from these limiting beliefs snowball into great internal conflicts, creating either a wounded feminine, a wounded masculine, or both. The *wounded feminine* feels emotionally stuck, non-nurturing, joyless, loveless, insecure, nagging, exploited, manipulative, ugly, and complaining; the *wounded masculine* feels absent-minded, disembodied, unstable, uncreative, argumentative, aggressive, greedy, egotistical, violent, and impotent. The wounded feminine triggers the wounded masculine, and vice-versa, creating a feminine-masculine dance of great suffering within oneself and between two partners. For example, the more absent-minded one partner becomes, the more emotionally-stuck the other partner feels. The more complaining one partner does, the more impotent the other partner feels, and so on. The suffering continues unless one is willing to look at the wounded parts within oneself and break free from the beliefs imposed by others.

Such narrow beliefs have divided humans very deeply. Due to the strong influence of civilization, this division has spread to the tribal and indigenous people. In the ancient times before patriarchy took hold, the male child and female child were not loved differently, and there was not a thought of: "is this a boy or is this a girl?" As time went on and societies shifted to the patriarchal norm, men demanded male children of their wives or their concubines. So the separation was projected from the moment the woman conceived. Within a few generations, even the woman wished for a male child and put that divided energy into her body. Her only thought became that this must be so, causing again that breakdown that we spoke of in our first conversation. The patriarchal religions and institutions also spread the belief that the female child is of no value and that everything of valuable essence is male.

Could we talk a little more about balancing the masculine and feminine? Some women become too masculine

to compete with men, while others subdue their masculine
warrior energy to mold themselves according to the patriarchal norms. Likewise, many men cannot hold the balance of the masculine and the feminine within themselves.

There is a great fear in many women to position themselves in a domestic place of home in
these last generations, in a place where they
could raise their arms in joy and surrender to the
raising of children. Other women feel inhibited
about fully embracing their masculine warrior
energy. These fears have resulted from patriarchal beliefs that wrapped a woman in "clothing" that was not suitable for her and led to the
shutting down of her fire energy. These beliefs
made a woman close her heart off and become
just dutiful to that which she had been given. The
bearing of children and raising them became her
mantle of responsibility regardless of whether
it came from a place of joy or not. That is like
shutting down a volcano, which in turn creates an
implosion of energy. There are places on Earth
where the hot fiery energy builds up and the subsequent implosion causes a non-relaxed state in
that part of the Earth.

There are other parts of Earth where buildings
have risen causing the Earth to expand herself in
unnatural ways. This is similar to a woman who is
required not to express herself sexually. She may
either become overwrought and hysterical or she
may expand her body due to an uncreative state in

which she has been asked to refrain from her being. You see more of an emotional unbalance in women than you see in men because men are expected to go forward with their energy and manifest. Men can engage in the creative act with their mates and go forward into the world to express that creation. In contrast, women are expected to stay home in many cultures and many of those who go to work cannot express their creativity in the same way as men. This imbalance gives little freedom to women, and their desires and wishes remain unexpressed.

Didn't the feminist revolution correct some of this, at least in the western nations?

Yes, some of this was corrected! However, many women have succumbed to their wounded masculine side with the feminist revolutions. Like many wounded men, they have also become aggressive, greedy, and egotistical in order to not feel exploited and insecure. Women need to embrace their *divine feminine* and *divine masculine* sides instead of succumbing to their wounded masculine side in order to hide their wounded feminine side. Reigniting the fire and water elements will allow women to express themselves with more joy and love. Many women feel they cannot express themselves like the whirling dervish in its ecstatic femininity. See the women around you. When they express themselves in a balanced manner, they do well and are recognized, even by men. Look at those who express themselves in a wounded masculine way; they are shunned by both men and women. Their energy shifts from the fiery nurturing feminine to a dominating patriarchal energy. It causes an imbalance in the world. The unexpressed fire energy becomes a burden.

Think of the woman in the menopausal season of her life. If she has not expressed herself during her early years, there is an emotional imbalance in her mind and her body at this time. For those who have expressed themselves, there is more harmony and more balance in the body at this time. If those who suffer from the imbalance would seek a quiet practice through yoga or other meditative practices, they could lessen this energy, and so not experience an over-abundance of it.

Would such holistic practices be better than, say, hormonal replacement therapy?

Yes: it would lessen the need for medicines such as estrogen. They ask for these medicines to balance themselves. Think of the indigenous tribes where women were allowed to express themselves at an early age, and there was no shame. Few of these women ever experienced post-menopausal symptoms the way modern women do. These women were always allowed to choose. It is not that they had many partners, but they were allowed to choose from an early age. As men came into power, this was looked upon as a grievous error.

As the male energy subdued these women, they hid from themselves. As that male energy was lodged in their hearts, they closed their hearts off. When these women would come of the age when there was no more bearing of children, there would be an imbalance. In the extreme, this imbalance would drive some of them insane.

Was the fire energy subdued in other ways too, say, in relation to career, creativity, sexuality, etc.?

Everything. Fire energy exists in all Chakras. As women express themselves with the joy of fire, they will not have so many internal health issues, and they will not express themselves as the volcano expresses. It is time for men to open their arms and receive the ideas and expressions of women. With men, it is the opposite, and there is too much expression of the creative energy. It is an overabundance, such as the overabundance of the unexpressed fire in older women. With women *expressing more* and men *receiving more*, the divine feminine and the divine masculine energies shall balance and empower the natures of men and women.

10

The Empowered Feminine and The Empowered Masculine

Can you tell us what you mean by the *divine feminine* and the *divine masculine?*

The divine feminine is unifying, embodied, flowing, nurturing, joyous, loving, melodious, beautiful, devoted, and that which is of a full heart. The divine masculine is free, present, stable, creative, protective, confident, silent, strong, dedicated, and that which is of the no-mind. The divine feminine and the divine masculine energies flow from higher levels of consciousness represented by your soul and your higher self. As these energies are expressed through your body and your mind, they manifest into the world as the *empowered feminine* and the *empowered masculine.*

In most of the animal kingdom, the male is more colorful, the more ornamented, the more *beautiful* one. In most of the invertebrates, in many types of fish, amphibians, reptiles, birds, and in some mammals, the female is the *stronger* one. You can learn from the animals by watching them. That will truly open your heart to the empowered feminine and empowered masculine energies in all beings, male or female.

Aha! Very often what humans think of as "masculine" exists in females, and what humans think of as "feminine" exists in males in the animal kingdom.

Yes. While there is physical duality between sexes, this duality does not have to correspond with the feminine and masculine energies. Let me repeat, both the feminine and the masculine energies are in *all* beings: male, female, or transgender.

So the "male" and "female" distinction is *different from* the energies of "masculine" and "feminine."

Exactly! There are times when you walk through the supermarket and you look at a child and you say to yourself, "is that a boy or a girl?" It is your thoughts and beliefs about the child's clothing and appearance that make that child surrender to a specific energy. In ancient times, the child was raised in the balance of feminine and masculine energies. The sexual distinction did not matter. Think of the ones who were enlightened, and there have been some who were enlightened as young children. These enlightened ones carried no attachments or beliefs regarding male and female except in their biological distinctions.

Those who went beyond such beliefs—that feminine and masculine energies must correspond to biology—have had greatness. For example, think of some great musicians of the past. Take Beethoven, for instance. Though he felt the burden of family responsibilities on his shoulders, and he suffered from physical illnesses, there was a joyful balance of feminine and masculine in his music. Finding himself in male clothing, there was a concern about how to play out his lifetime. However, as he surrendered to the oneness of himself, there was the *joy of nothingness*, and all males and all females could relate to that. Because the music came from nothingness, it was all and for everyone. It is the way of music.

So, it came from some depth of oneness, which was...?

It came from the *ether*, the fifth element, which is emptiness and fullness. It is the spirit, which is beyond feminine and masculine. It is formless. When it enters form, it enters as a combination of fire and air. As the fire element it can be felt as energy, and as the air element it can be felt as a thought.

That is why when we channel you, we feel you as bursts of energy with thought?

Yes. Though I am beyond elements, I express myself through elements. Like all ascended beings, I am emptiness, and so I am fullness.

So, if feminine and masculine elements do not define female and male, respectively, then why do humans carry these beliefs?

The attachment to beliefs comes from the air element, because metaphysically speaking the *air element equals thought. Thought* separates the masculine from feminine, as individuation is the nature of thought. This is the burden of human conditioning that comes not only from cultures and parents, but also from being born as a human. So, look to the lovely dancing peacock and meditate with nature to free yourself of the human conditioning.

Is there male and female duality even in the angelic realms?

Yes, but the human understanding of this duality has been distorted by patriarchy. Humans have imposed beliefs even on angels. Laughter! Patriarchy conditions human beings to align masculine energy with being male and feminine energy with being female; however, this is not so. Like all sentient beings, angels have both the feminine and the masculine aspects, and they choose to express themselves as male or female and sometimes as androgynous. As the world turned more patriarchal, female angels were made into male angels. For example, Gabriel was known as female and is now seen as male. Additionally, Uriel was known as female and is now seen as male. I tell you that these two are females.

What about Archangel Michael?

Michael is male and Rafael is male. Also, Jovial is male.

Does the male and female duality continue in all realms? For example, do we have this duality even at the level of divine beings, such as angels and Gods and Goddesses?

When the soul reaches perfection, or rather, when it discovers what it was before it individuated, it sees its own nature as neither male nor female, but that in which both exist in perfect balance. Before remembering what it once was, there is a breakdown of balance and the uniqueness of the soul, and that may lead to different outcomes. It puts the soul into a non-androgynous state, reaching for what it feels it does not have.

So, you may ask of me, "am I androgynous?" The answer is both Yes and No. I am androgynous because my *nature* has the balance of both male and female. I can sow a new universe and also nurture it, but I choose to *express* myself as a female. It is the same for all divine beings. They have a balanced, androgynous, *nature* about them, but they choose to *express* themselves in one way or another.

So, when Lord Vishnu sees you, does he see you without any concepts of gender in his mind?

He sees me *fully*. Laughter! Even as he surrenders completely to my beauty and my sensuality, he sees a perfect balance of feminine and masculine in my *nature*. Our union heals worlds within worlds as his masculine expression yields to my feminine wholeness. Humans can also create such a bond with each other, and with divine beings as well.

How do we do this?

You can see divinity in every person you meet. For example, if you were to simply practice what I have asked you—to see *me* in every woman and in every man you meet, you will experience all humans in their fullness without the shadow of "beliefs" about their gender.

I actually visualized seeing *you* in my father who passed away in 2012. As I did this I felt an endearing feminine energy in him which I had not felt so much when he was alive. After this experience, I visualized seeing *you* in other men and women, especially those who seemed too masculine to me. Something shifted deeply in my relationship with each one of them after this visualization.

> Your awareness of the divine feminine in all humans shall bring a profound healing to you and transform your world into a softer, kinder place. Know that everything in its unmanifested *wholeness* is feminine, just like everything in its manifested *individuation* is masculine. So, by seeing myself in all humans, you are awakening to the wholeness that joins us all.

Oh, really? Everything in its wholeness is *feminine?*

> Yes. So, "what about the masculine?" you might ask. As existence evolves into more complex levels, masculine energy individuates from the feminine at every step with the help of the *mind*. Yet, most of nature lives in the no-mind and continues to be feminine. For example, animals live mostly from their body and soul. So, they continue to be mostly feminine: they create *round* nests and they dig themselves into *round* holes. Almost everything in nature is either curved or round. There are no square trees or square oceans. The Earth and the Sun are mostly round, as are virtually all big objects created in the universe. Even in your body there are no organs that are square, yet

the masculine mind creates many square things. Do not judge this, for the masculine individuation is needed for feminine wholeness to know itself. Since humans have created much masculinity and squareness in recent times, they can now surrender to femininity and roundness in order to bring back balance. Seeing *me* and other Goddesses in everyone will allow humans to awaken to this *roundness*—the unmanifested wholeness present in all humans and all things.

Like myself, even Mother Earth has an androgynous *nature*, but she expresses herself mostly in a feminine way. Sometimes when her hot, fiery energy builds too much and expresses itself wildly, she becomes masculine in that expression. So, when we say that Mother Nature destroys, it is not the "mother in balance" who destroys, but the overabundance of feminine energies that lead to a masculine expression. As you know when humans act out of balance, Mother Earth brings back the balance.

For example, like global warming leading to flooding on Earth?

Yes. We are getting in "deep" territory here. Laughter!

11

Three Joys of the Divine Feminine

Can you tell us more about the aspects of the divine feminine, especially as it relates to women?

In the ancient times, the Goddess energy represented three aspects of love based on three vibrations of the primordial joy. The first aspect is the more innocent, flirtatious, and sensual. It is the pure, uncomplicated love of a virgin. The second aspect is more matured with the fullness of a grown woman. This aspect has the sexual love for her partner and a nurturing love for her child. The third aspect is like a grandmother who has seen all, who is wise and non-judgmental beyond her childbearing years and is childlike once again. So the first aspect is like the sunrise, the second aspect is like the brightness of the day, and the third aspect is like the sunset in which rests the fullness of the entire day. These are the three aspects of the Goddess energy, and there is a joy in each one of these.

Women can experience all three aspects of Goddess energy if they surrender to and celebrate each stage of their life. Overplay of the first aspect would cause a young female to change her energy from sensual to sexual to attract a male. This aspect can be more volatile and cause addictions if no restrictions and boundaries are taught. I said, "restrictions and boundaries," not judgments, for judgments can shut down the sensual fire and create an emotional imbalance. These boundaries can be taught from one woman to another, and the balance will allow the young woman to grow into the fullness of the second aspect. The third aspect comes full circle, and it is so overflowing that it not only fills oneself, but also pours down on all that is upon the Earth.

Oh, so the third type of love can be more impersonal if it is not directed to a specific being.

Yes. So let us say that if I stayed high up in the mountains for all of my days, then I would be in the third aspect. For I would be there just to maintain a holy place. The Earth itself does that. There are places on Earth that overflow with a healing energy and people go to these places and say, "this is a holy place." This is the third aspect. A woman would go through all three phases. By the third phase, if a woman has not grown herself to the fullness, she could revert to the first aspect. The

first aspect of Goddess is the Maiden, the second
is the Matron, and the third the Crone. This is com-
monly known when you study these phases.

In some religions, the maiden, the matron, and the
crone were associated with the waxing moon, the full
moon, and the waning moon. However, you said that these
three stages are associated with the sunrise, the bright sun,
and the sunset. Can you explain why there is a difference
in the use of metaphor to represent these stages?

As humanity transitioned to a patriarchal system, some men desired to make fire into a masculine energy. So the three aspects of the Goddess
were changed to the waxing moon, the full moon,
and the waning moon. Patriarchal religions also
associated passion with the darkness of the night
since it had to be hidden. The matron in her fullness, however, is like the bright sun as she embod-
ies her passion without shame.

I have all three aspects, which is true for all
ascended Goddesses. I choose to express myself
as a maiden and also a matron. You would visualize me as a maiden and a matron if you desire to
connect with me. As a maiden, there is a genuine
openness in my femininity. There is sensuousness
in that aspect, and there is no shame. If you see
little children, they have a sensuous nature. They
have not yet learned that humans have a sexual
nature. Unless they are taught shame, they accept

themselves as they are. In her positive aspect, a maiden is like a young girl whose life is simple and joyful. There is no energy in her surrounding the belief about death. She also feels completely free and from her joy and freedom she manifests from the Earth. She manifests easily because she does not have negative thoughts attached to whatever she desires to manifest. There is no karma upon the maiden in her positive aspect, for she is not attached to thoughts and beliefs. She has a deep intuition and closeness to the Heavens. There is also a connection between her and the angelic realm.

Scriptures say that you were with others before you married Lord Vishnu. Was this as a maiden or as a matron?

I was in many relationships, but I did not participate in them sexually. So I was in these relationships more as a maiden. There were men with me who were great thinkers, men who were soldiers, men who were great men among men, and men who were caretakers of others. I made myself partners with every aspect of male energy rooted in all elements—water, fire, earth, and air—so that I would know all aspects of a male, and the male would know all aspects of myself. This is the true pregnancy of a female, receiving all aspects of a male and being able to manifest what is the highest for all concerned. This is also a part of Saraswati's path.

Did all of this take place before you married Lord Vishnu?

Yes.

What were these relationships like?

We shared what I had to offer without an attachment of sexuality. I was not overly flirtatious. It was of emotional value, sweet and joyful. I simply trusted myself. There was always a natural intuition guiding me, and there was not a judgment about this as there is now in many human cultures. With every man there was sensuousness, but it was not sexual until I found my beloved, Lord Vishnu. All things in the Earth are sensuous. They have a feel to them. Even when you touch the leaf or the petals of a rose, there is sensuousness about them.

Sensuality was celebrated in the ancient times. This is also what will happen in the future. Preparations are underway in the next few years for humanity to transition to a more matriarchal system. The new system will have true equality and will resemble the matriarchal systems of the past. The transformation may seem gradual at first, but it will happen fast as belief systems begin to shift rapidly.

So, will women assert more control of human societies?

It is not so much about women taking more control, but both men and women surrendering their minds to their hearts, and thus restoring the *harmony* between the masculine and the feminine. The Earth and all things on Earth are already in that state of transition. It is the minds of humans that are not in that place. This is the cause of many taking vows of walking an angelic path. Though human societies were surrendered to the feminine in the ancient past, it did not mean that we had an empress or a queen who was above everyone else.[6]

In the rest of this book, I wish to share the stories of my different incarnations on Earth.

In the third and the fourth part of this book, I will share stories of my incarnations as *Sita* with *Rama*; and as *Radha* and *Draupadi* with *Krishna*, respectively. My stories have been changed through the ages with the spread of patriarchy. As I will share my stories of love with my beloved, I will correct all that is incorrect and reveal all that has been hidden so that these stories may become whole and heal many. I will share new insights about chakras and elements focusing specifically on the first three chakras and their role in manifesting your world using the law of attraction.

In the fifth part of this book, I shall reveal secrets about our soul tribe that created many spiritual paths, which are now seen by humans as the "religions" of Hinduism and Buddhism. I will share new insights about the life of *Gautama Buddha* from the perspective of my incarnation as his wife *Yasodhara*. I will also reveal new secrets about Saraswati's path with Vishnu, including his transformation into the primordial *Adi Buddha* through her. We shall discover different stages of enlightenment as we unravel the mysteries and the mission of our soul tribe. My revelations will join the feminine sides of Hinduism and Buddhism into oneness.

In the sixth part of this book, you may ask me questions about your own life journey and spiritual transformation. You are in the process of moving from your Third Chakra into your Heart Chakra, and so you may ask me questions about these two chakras in more detail. In the final part of this book, I will provide guidance for the transformation of the whole of humanity through the empowered feminine path of joy.

As more Goddesses speak in the near future from different pantheons, you shall see a joining of different spiritual paths into oneness through the divine feminine wisdom. This shall be the next turning of the wheel of dharma that will empower the feminine while honoring the masculine. These Goddesses shall speak on how the Heart and the higher chakras can nurture the lower chakras, and will tell many stories of enlightenment from different spiritual paths. You may ask us any questions that arise in your mind, and we shall answer everything to your heart's content. We may begin with my incarnation as *Sita*.

Namaste!

Namaste Lakshmi ji!

PART III
CHAKRAS AND THE LAW OF ATTRACTION IN RAMAYANA

UNIVERSAL HAPPINESS MANTRA

Lokah Samastah Sukhino Bhavantu

लोकाः समस्ताः सुखिनो भवन्तु

12

My Soulmates, Rama and Ravana

Namaste Lakshmi ji!

Namaste!

We are so delighted to hear directly from you about your incarnation as *Sita* in the *Ramayana.* According to the *Ramayana*, Ravana was the evil king who kidnapped you and wanted to marry you. Your husband, Rama, had to fight a long war to defeat Ravana and bring you home. You had to endure even more suffering and humiliation after coming home. Is this correct?

> The time that you speak of was an epochal period for humanity's transition from one Yuga to another. Like most stories, there is truth and there is also a romantic version to this epic. Laughter!
>
> This was a long and arduous incarnation for me. I was very lonely because I was sequestered. I did not have much to eat and had many restless nights. I suffered much, and there were times

when I felt I was close to death. There were also times when I lost faith. But I allowed myself to have that place of suffering. I knew it was my soul path, for there is purpose for the human to go to the depths of sorrow. As low as I would get in that lifetime, as sorrowful and desperate as I would feel, I would turn inward at the last moment and be told by my guides and ancestors that I had a bigger path than what I was allowing myself to embrace. This saved me many times.

What is the purpose of so much sorrow?

As we have already spoken, the soul desires to know *all*. That is the purpose of incarnating as a human. Without knowing the contrast, there cannot be growth and flowering. It was my path in that lifetime to experience what I did. It was a humble path for me. Many on Earth are choosing this path at this time. It is part of the natural cycle. Even those in the heavenly realms may incarnate as humans, for there is not as much contrast and growth in these realms.

Is that why Rama took so long to come and rescue you?

Rama kept looking outward and building his external strength for a long time. This is why it took him so long. He was not completely surrendered to himself and he was not looking inward, initially. He was willing to play out this war for as long as it took.

When he did surrender to the great healer that he was, the illusion went away immediately and he was able to come to me. His war was within himself, which created an outer war of his greatness over evil. Even I had to surrender to the same lesson.

What created the war within?

The internal war was created by the thoughts that were given to him while he was growing up. In order to survive, he needed to fight for what he truly desired. His stepmother had a projection of what she desired for him. That created the internal conflict that resulted in the external war for him.

But didn't the war between Rama and Ravana happen because Ravana kidnapped you?

Ravana wanted to unite with me for my spiritual powers. Obviously, he invited the war upon himself by kidnapping me. Rama also attracted the war to himself. That is how all wars happen. Those in a war attract one another at a deeper level.

Most Hindus think of Rama as "good" and Ravana as "evil."

This distinction is true from the mind perspective of duality, but there are higher truths of the heart and the soul that are beyond simply good and evil.

What are these higher truths?

Rama and Ravana were *soulmates*. They were also my two soulmates, one in the positive aspect, and the other in the negative aspect. The three of us served each other's life purpose in that incarnation. Rama desired to please his stepmother and his father as he wanted their approval. Remember we said earlier that pleasing others for approval creates fissure cracks in any relationship. It is because the desire to please others for approval comes from the place of ego. Rama found his inner guidance eventually, and that is when he found me. But he was meant to learn important lessons through the suffering on his ego path during his exile.

So how did he awaken from his ego path?

Rama's soul path deviated from his ego path as he realized that the only voice he needed to listen to was that of his higher self. As he surrendered to the higher voice during the final days of the war, it allowed him to receive guidance from his guides and ensured his victory over Ravana.

In the ancient times, everything was more surrendered to the feminine, and much guidance of one's soul path came from the higher self and its heart connection with one's angels, ancestors, and divine beings. This changed as humanity shifted to a more patriarchal order. The purpose of being with nature in silence and meditation is to become attuned to oneself, such that one does not desire to please others for the sake of their approval.

Was your kidnapping by Ravana meant to be?

Yes. I was sequestered with the help of my own family.

Huh?

Yes.

So, Ravana was your own family?

Yes.

Are you saying Ravana and these people were relatives of your family? I did not know this.

Yes.

This is interesting.

If you look at the history of wars, they have often happened between people who are related, even between brothers at times. There was not so much distance between our families, and I was the *prize*. The *thought* was that if the two of us came together there would be greatness! So, a division was made by this thought. It is always thought that separates the union of fire and water to produce the earth. This is how elements are separated. Sometimes this produces an Earth full of desolation and lack. Ravana's task was to separate us so that we could experience what our souls had come to experience before coming back together in even greater harmony. I made the choice to experience all of this during my incarnation.

Really?

The level of suffering was not revealed to me before I incarnated. It is not possible to know suffering from the spiritual realm. The only way to know it is to experience it in the material realm. However, my angels and goddesses were with me, and Saraswati was watching over me. I created many songs during this time. Saraswati gave me hope and helped me have the fortitude to stay strong. She was like a very kind mother.

These were the years when Ravana attempted to take the knowledge that I had. It was part of my suffering to not give him that.

So, Ravana was more interested in your knowledge. Was he not in love with you?

He was not in love with me. This is more about what I had to offer as a Goddess. Why would he want romance?

...because you might have been the most beautiful princess for him.

Beauty, as we hear these days, is in the eye of the beholder. He was more interested in the knowledge and the siddhis that I had.[7]

So, Ravana was a deep person? Was his soul more evolved than we assume?

Well, if you think about it again, all things mani-fest with the law of attraction. I would not have chosen that life with his role in it if he were only a romantic person at heart. He saw the Goddess I was, and he understood what he wanted from me. It was his soul path to separate Rama from me, which helped in bringing us together spiritually. He has no Karma for doing this.

...he has no Karma even though he fought Rama and was killed by him?

That is okay. But he has no Karma.

You said earlier that even you had to surrender. What did you have to surrender to?

I was born in complete harmony with the Earth, so my First Chakra was open and rooted in the Earth. Since I was surrendered to the Earth, I had little difficulty in finding food and taking care of my body. I had much loneliness and sorrow, and would often think thoughts of suffering. Eventually, the switch happened as I surrendered even to that. My thoughts turned to manifesting joy and love. As I meditated truly upon that and treasured even the simple pleasures of life I had, I raised my vibrational field, which, in turn, brought Rama and I together.

So, your thoughts about your life changed even though you were sequestered?

Yes: my thoughts went from deep despair to great joy. As this occurred I would sing to Rama. I created many songs during that time of my life. This is what transformed me. Soon after this transformation, I was "enlightened" to the nature of who I was and made the connection: the joy *within* us not only manifests everything we truly desire, but it also opens the door to one's enlightenment. This is the way of every enlightened being. That is when Rama found me.

Aha! So, we have it backward! We think that we will be happy when our desires are fulfilled, but what you are saying is that *we manifest what we truly desire when we have the joy within us or when we are happy from the inside.*

Yes, and until you taste this joy from within, you do not even know what you *truly* desire. As Rama surrendered also, I was able to attract him to

myself because we both came to the same place
of emptiness which is filled with joy.

Earlier you said Ravana was not evil. What was he like?

No, he was not evil. He was a bridge that
separated us and then brought us back together even closer. He was a devotee of Lord Shiva
and a descendant of the holy ones. He pos-
sessed knowledge, and he was a skilled warrior.
He did penances and engaged in ascetic practices that gave him powers to manifest his body
in the way he chose. But these practices were
also his downfall for they did not enlighten him
to his true nature, but instead increased his arro-
gance and ego. This is the danger of opening
the higher chakras before the lower chakras are
fully open. It was his path to show this danger
of seeking after siddhis by taking the suffering
upon himself.

So, Ravana was not "evil" in the ultimate sense, even
though from a limited human perspective he is seen as evil?

Yes, much as those who are deemed "evil"
such as Judas or Lucifer. They all played a part in
the separation of the feminine and masculine energies, so that contrast could be created. Evil does
not exist in an absolute sense, as everything is
nothing.

Why did Ravana choose to incarnate as what we think is "evil?"

His soul was a part of Lord Vishnu's higher self. Lord Vishnu and he decided together how he was going to fall and come back as his enemy in his different incarnations so that contrast could be created.

Aha! Ravana was part of Lord Vishnu!

Yes, just like Lucifer is a part of God.

So, what happened to Ravana after Rama killed him?

Both were enlightened! Ravana realized the great illusion created by his ego as Rama's divine arrow pierced through his Third chakra, a little above his navel. The fatal blow aligned and opened his lower three chakras instantly. Thus, liberated from his suffering and his Karma, he entered his Heart Chakra as he lay dying. Though his suffering ended with the opening of his lower three chakras, he did not experience enlightenments of higher chakras in that life because he had already left his body at that point.

While death was Ravana's soul path to enlightenment, Rama's soul path called for a more gradual blossoming into enlightenment. As his battle with Ravana continued for days, he realized the invincibility of Ravana. Though his arrows struck

Ravana's repeatedly, they did not kill him. Rama was transformed by watching this happen. It made him surrender fully to his higher self for strength and inspiration. As he did this, he realized that Ravana was a part of his own shadow self. Then, in a flash of insight, Rama realized that the *ego is never destroyed if one seeks to destroy it.*

Aha!

That is when Rama reached deep in his heart and embraced Ravana's soul with compassion. As he did this his ego melted, and he felt Ravana's suffering as his own suffering. At this point, he received guidance to use the Brahmastra to liberate Ravana. As he shot this divine arrow with prayer and compassion, it hit Ravana in his solar plexus area just above the navel, and both were enlightened in that instant. There was an explosion of light in which both realized that they were soulmates who had great love and devotion for one another. Both found themselves in the emptiness of no-mind as their lower three chakras aligned and opened. Unlike Ravana who died instantly, Rama was still alive to embrace the enlightenments of the higher chakras. These higher chakras opened on their own accord over a short period of time as Rama surrendered himself fully.

This is an amazing story of the enlightenment of two soulmates.

Yes. Ravana had come very close to enlightenment through long penances and ascetic practices even before he found himself on Rama's path. But these practices opened his higher chakras before the karmic attachments in his lower chakras were fully resolved. This was his downfall; the siddhis he attained from his higher chakras expanded his ego, which *increased the imbalance* of *elements in his lower chakras.* This is why focusing on opening the higher chakras, such as the Third Eye, before opening the lower chakras can be dangerous.

13

Chakras and Elements

Can you tell us more about chakras and elements?

Chakras are energy centers where the soul interacts with the body at high frequencies. The vibrations of these energy centers can be felt when the mind becomes silent. There are numerous chakras, which are like energy vortices where the body and the soul interact at higher frequencies. Some chakras are also below and above the physical body. Unlike the physical and the mental bodies, which are finite, the soul is infinite, and extends into the Earth and the Heavens, and even beyond. Even within the finite body there are many minor chakras in addition to the seven major chakras. For example, between the Heart Chakra and the Throat Chakra is the *Higher Heart Chakra* that opens with the feelings of devotion and prayer. These soul feelings are of a much lighter vibration than the emotions of the mind.

Much of the work human beings do on Earth are about opening and aligning the lower three chakras, the culmination of which then naturally opens the Heart Chakra. As a new soul falls into contrast, numerous incarnations are spent on the opening of the First Chakra, fewer incarnations are spent on the opening of the Second Chakra, and even fewer incarnations are spent on the opening of the Third Chakra. Once the Heart Chakra opens together with the lower three chakras, the rest of the chakras open rather quickly, either on Earth or in the Heavens.

Chakras are interconnected in numerous ways so their opening is often simultaneous and non-linear, and not sequential. Overall, it is safer to first open the lower three chakras instead of attempting to open the higher chakras. The higher chakras are already open but are inaccessible due to the closing of the lower three chakras. Surrendering to the nurturing energies of the higher chakras with body-centered yogic and mindfulness practices, and through the awakening soul feelings can accelerate the opening of the lower chakras.

The lower chakras are also associated with specific *elements*. The earth element is associated with the First Chakra, the water element is associated with the Second Chakra, and the air element is associated with the Third Chakra. *The fire element is associated with all chakras.* All elements come together in oneness with the *ether* element in the Heart Chakra.

Hmm...According to the conventional wisdom on chakras, the earth element is associated with the First Chakra, the water element is associated with the Second Chakra, the fire element is associated with the Third Chakra, and the air element is associated with the Heart Chakra.

> The conventional wisdom is incorrect. Ravana's imbalance was in his Third Chakra, which had circular and egotistical thought patterns, representing the air element. And let me repeat that all elements unite in the Heart, so it is not true that the Heart has only the air element.

Oh, I see! The books on this subject do not have correct information.

> Most are written with information borrowed from just a few original books, and the original books have incomplete information. Also, some of the information was misinterpreted.

Is there a reason for the way the elements are organized in the lower three chakras?

> The lower three chakras are organized in the human body, just like they are organized in Mother Earth's body starting from its center. Earth's core represents her First Chakra, which has the "earth" element; her oceans represent her Second Chakra, which has the water element; her atmosphere represents her Third Chakra, which has the

air element. *And fire is everywhere*—in her hot core, in her great waters, and in her atmosphere. Without the fire, her waters would turn into ice, and even the air would freeze.

Aha! So fire is in all chakras?

Yes—take the Second Chakra, for example. This Chakra is the seat of *both sexuality and emotions*, which represent the fire and the water elements, respectively. Sexual expression is most joyful when not separated from the emotional connection in the Second Chakra.

That is true! Does the fire have a different function in each chakra?

Yes. Fire creates, preserves, and destroys as you move up in the chakras. Fire changes its character in a continuum, so there is not a sudden jump from one chakra to another. There is no limit to the complete expression of the fire energy. A complete surrender can make the fire energy move higher and higher, destroying the subtlest beliefs of the mind.

That makes sense. It reminds me of Kundalini Yoga.

The practice of Kundalini Yoga requires much guidance and surrender. In the ancient times, high priestesses of great honor and virtue practiced this path. Raising the Kundalini too early or too fast can be dangerous if the lower chakras are not in a state of complete surrender. One must be careful and patient.

In my incarnation as Sita I was fully enlightened with the raising of my Kundalini energy, but this required much humility and surrender for many years. My First Chakra was already open from my previous incarnation, so I began my work in the Second Chakra.

Is this where Lord Rama began too?

My beloved was in the Third Chakra when we left Ayodhya. He was already peeling layers of his ego in his Third Chakra when his stepmother requested his exile from the kingdom. He had received many wise teachings in his childhood that prepared him for the grand spiritual quest we would embark on together.

Why would you both start in the lower chakras if you were already incarnations of Vishnu and Lakshmi?

Because we desired to experience the physicality of incarnating as human beings. We chose the humble path. How would we inspire and guide if we did not know the experience directly?

Can you tell us which chakra most humans are stuck in at this time on Earth?

About 80% are in the First Chakra.

Can you tell us more about the First Chakra?

This chakra is the closest to the Earth and the most connected to it. This chakra allows perception by your senses. It is connected to your basic needs for food, survival, and shelter. This chakra is mostly concerned with security related to home, health, and even relationships. This chakra is one that helps release old patterns. Eating green, leafy vegetable helps balance this chakra. The basic human response made in this chakra is "fight, flight, or freeze." When unbalanced, this chakra creates patterns of fear and aggression. Physical conditions such as addictions, exploitation, poverty, diseases, and violence are all results of humanity's imbalance in this chakra. Many at present are attempting to balance this chakra.

You said earlier that all chakras have the fire element. So, what is the role of fire in this chakra?

Fire creates the experiences of our senses and sensuality in this chakra. The purely physical expression of sexuality comes from this first chakra. Most humans have difficulty in moving the fire upward for spiritual growth. Many humans cannot even connect emotionally with their partners, as their sexual energy is experienced only from the First Chakra. There is nothing wrong with this, but it remains a partial expression of joy when it doesn't integrate with the higher chakras.

The unbalanced fire element in the First Chakra can lead to either inertia or violence, making humans feel either weak and afraid with too little fire, or aggressive and violent with too much fire. The fear may either keep them stuck in circular thought patterns, creating the inertia of stagnation, or lead to aggression and violence, even in a sexual way. A balanced and healthy fire in the First Chakra allows one to stay physically healthy and active, and connected with nature.

Did Ravana have some imbalance in the First Chakra that would have made him aggressive towards you when you incarnated as Sita?

No! But he had a huge imbalance in his Third Chakra. As I said earlier, he wanted my spirituality, and not my body. He wanted me only if I chose him of my free will, which I did not. But there were others around me who would attempt to take the energy of my Second Chakra. As far as my First Chakra was concerned, that was not something that was taken from me because I knew how to remain rooted to the Earth.

So, you figured out ways to eat and survive on your own?

Well, I could manifest things myself as I needed them.

We do not know much about your childhood in your incarnation as Sita. Can you tell us a little about that?

I had great joy as a child in many lifetimes. In the lifetime that you are speaking of I did not know that I was chosen, but I incarnated with an open First Chakra. I had access to understanding nature, so there would be things that nature would offer me that I would receive. Let us say that as a bird taught me its habits, I could eat as a bird. The suffering was not like in these days. As I said to you earlier, I knew how to live off the land. As a child, I knew only that life was play. I was open to making others happy, and being quite considerate of others. I would have people come to me and ask me to make them certain things to help them heal.

...like certain healing substances?

Yes. As they would take these things within themselves, it would help open their minds. I did not receive any money or trades for doing these things. I knew how to manifest things that I needed through my thoughts. I knew about these things even as a young child. This was a transformation that came to me around the age of nine. I had these things born inside of me and I was able to manifest my path in that lifetime as I stayed clear. There were those that came to my family to ask for my guidance.

I know that some other enlightened beings, such as Buddha, went through much physical hardship in the forests in search of enlightenment. I know he came to the "middle way" in the end, but initially how did he deal with all this hardship? Did he also have an open First Chakra, like you?

Sometimes one gives away all as one begins one's quest for spiritual attainment. It takes a great amount of faith for one to surrender and to have the patience to accept what one knows inside. With our beloved Buddha, the enlightened one, his First Chakra was not only connected to his surroundings, but also to his name and the family name. Walking away from that caused dissension in his family, for he was required to attend to duties that would maintain the security of the family. He felt that it would tear the family apart by giving up all of these things. It was this, and not the physical hardships that he would face on his path, that made his decision difficult. But he chose to leave knowing in the end that it was not his responsibility to carry on the family, and that the family itself was bigger than his immediate family.

Was he thinking of the world family?

Yes. When he came to that realization, it became easier for him to let go because he understood that his path would also affect his immediate family in a spiritual way. His suffering was not so much from being in the forest as it was due to his separation from his family. There were those who were angry with him leaving, but through meditations he saw the bigger picture. As he left the palace, the First Chakra responded to him as he was deeply connected to his mother for security.

The connection to our mothers maintains openness in this chakra. When we close ourselves off from our mothers, this chakra also closes and becomes a different color than the bright red it naturally is.

Buddha did not have the fear that he would be taken down by the forest. Like Sita, he learned from the flora and fauna, and from the animals, how to survive. Trial and error and knowledge of plants allowed him to see what was good for him.

It sounds like Sita and Buddha could be on any of our "survivor shows" on reality TV. Laughter!

Laughter! Yes.

Why does the First Chakra respond if one is deeply connected to one's mother?

The mother represents food, security, and home for the child, all things related to the First Chakra. The first impressions of the child about food and security begin in the mother's womb, and the first thing the newborn wants instinctively is the mother's breast. The mother's love for the child is also the foundation of its emotional well-being. The mother is deeply connected with the child with both the First Chakra and the Second Chakra, and if she has grown spiritually, then also the higher chakras. The one who has a connection of pain and sorrow with one's own mother walks with too much weight on Earth. Both Sita and Buddha had very loving and nurturing mothers.

How did you protect yourself from others around you who were interested in stealing your virtue?

I was protected through sacred symbols and energies, so my virtue could not be stolen. At times, it would seem to others that I was barren, and at other times, others would see me more like a child than a young woman. Angels attended me and helped me to not to be seen at times.

Aha! So the ones interested in stealing your virtue would not see you at all with the help of angels?

Right. It would seem as if I was not there.

You must know that I love these conversations.

I know.

I feel more fullness in my life these days. I feel very fortunate not to be struggling with issues related to health, finances, etc. I feel gratitude for being able to have these conversations with you.

Yes, because your First Chakra feels balanced and open. It was not always so in the past.

I remember! There were intense periods of struggle in my life related to health, career, etc., throughout my 20s and 30s.

And relationships. Laughter!

Yes. And relationships.

As you surrendered, things came into balance by themselves. Like two magnets that find the opposite poles of each other on their own if they are close enough. This is the way of all chakras. From your surrendered space came the creative spark of your actions, which had the balance of the feminine and the masculine. But sometimes, the Karma simply takes its time to play out, as your choices are more limited in the First Chakra.

Why is that?

If you are born under physically challenging conditions, there may not be much you can do to change that. Only a complete surrendering can open this First Chakra more quickly.

What happens with complete surrendering?

> *Your choices increase,* because when you are
> in surrender, the fire energy can shift the earth
> element into balance without any striving on your
> part, opening more possibilities and deepening
> your connection with the higher chakras.

Why can't we move the earth element into balance by
striving or pushing hard, instead of surrendering?

> You can, and if you push in the right place, it
> might work temporarily. But without surrendering
> you do not know where to push, where the earth is
> too dense and unmovable, and where your push-
> ing can create the great balance. That is why you
> need to surrender.

Earlier you said that Sita had no issues in her First
Chakra and that she began her journey in the Second
Chakra. Can you tell us more about the Second Chakra?

> The Second Chakra is connected to both
> emotions and sexuality. This chakra is bright, and
> though they say it is orange, it is bright like the
> orange Sun. The energy is very electric in this
> chakra, like a summer storm. It connects easily
> with the Crown Chakra, which helps one to stay in
> an inner bliss and make choices from that fullness.
> If you touch a plant and feel the softness of its

leaves, or if you feel the soft fur of an animal, that feeling of softness comes from the Second Chakra. While the First Chakra allows one to *sense* using the body senses, the Second Chakra allows one to *feel* what one senses. Two people may taste something sweet using their First Chakra; however, one may *like* the sweet taste while the other may *dislike* it. Such likes and dislikes and the emotions tied to them come from the Second Chakra. Though emotions are felt in multiple chakras, almost all of them—except the primal fears—*originate* in the Second Chakra. The energy of the Second Chakra helps in maintaining good skin tone and good hair. When not functioning properly, it can either unleash raw fiery energy, causing one to become angry or violent, or excessive water energy, causing one to become too emotional. There is more choice in this chakra than in the First Chakra.

Why?

The First Chakra is related to your physical being, which is the earth element, and the Second Chakra is related to your emotional being, which is the water element. What you have physically is not as easy to change as changing how you feel about it with your emotions. But if you can transform how you *feel* about what you have, you may even transform your physical reality using the law of attraction.

Can I choose to feel good even when bad things happen?

There is always something good happening in your life even when it does not feel so. Besides, you create what is good and what is bad because these do not exist independently of you. It is an illusion that you create in your Third Chakra, so you might as well create a happy illusion. The secret to feeling good is that you *choose to feel good*.

14

The Law of Attraction

Is this "secret" what the law of attraction is all about?

When a farmer plants his crops, he does so from the First Chakra, but when he has the insight from his Third Chakra to send positive emotions from the Second Chakra, he helps harness the energy of the First Chakra to manifest a good harvest. Similarly, when you cook food, you do it from the First Chakra, but when you have the insight to feel positively about what you are cooking, the food will feel that energy, and it will be more nourishing for you.

The law of attraction is based on the reciprocal relationship between the First Chakra and the Second Chakra, which is allowed by the transformation of your worldview in the Third Chakra. It is a universal law about how your feelings manifest your physical world, and how your worldview manifests your feelings. When you change your worldview and *choose* to feel differently about what you already have, you can begin to consciously use the law of attraction.

I see. So *choosing* one's worldview in the Third Chakra is guiding the law of attraction to work in one's favor?

Exactly! The law of attraction is directly working through the lower two chakras, either consciously or unconsciously. The transformation of your worldview in the Third Chakra makes you aware that this law is manifesting both positive and negative outcomes in your life. A deep awakening to this wisdom in the Third Chakra makes you surrender your negative emotions by being completely present to them without any judgment and fear. The higher chakras, including the heart, help to transform the worldview in the Third Chakra. This is why a change of heart changes everything! By aligning your thoughts with positive feelings about what you have in your life, the law can work in your favor. The question is not whether the law of attraction is working or not, because it is always working. The question is whether the law is working for you in a way that allows you to manifest what you truly desire.

Most of us desire something else to replace what exists in our lives.

And that is the problem. If you *want* something else because you are not happy with what you have in your life, then you will remain wanting *because the feeling of wanting-ness arises from your Second Chakra.* The best way to manifest using the law of attraction is to feel the joy of what exists in your life together with the joy for what you would like to be created. If you wish to use the law of attraction to *escape from that which you do not want in your life,* it will only create more of that.

Many spiritual paths emphasize surrender to the present moment, or the "law of acceptance," and others emphasize the "law of attraction" as the way to manifest something different in the future. So, what is the right approach?

Both; but unfortunately, both approaches are misunderstood very often. Surrendering to the present can be misunderstood to mean that it does not include the past or the future. The truth is that *the present moment contains all*: the immediate present, which you perceive through your senses, and all of your past, which exists in the present moment through your mind. And the future is simply the past projecting forward, so it is also in the present moment, again through your mind.

Aha! So the present moment includes all, either through your *senses* or through your *mind*?

How can there be anything else but the eternal present moment? Laughter!

True!

So, it is not the present versus the past or the future that transforms the inner self. What transforms the inner self is when one's present moment is seen in total harmony with the entire timeline. Then you do not desire to manifest your future in order to escape from your past. Instead, your present holds your past with immense gratitude for the journey already undertaken and a deep surrender to the unknown future. The positive feelings are felt in the entire timeline. Then and only then does your life have true happiness, because even if you did not manifest what you desired, you are already in the fullness of your being. And from such fullness, whatever you think and desire manifests a lot more easily. That is how the law of attraction works.

Very interesting! How can the past be seen with positive feelings, if in reality the past was full of negativity?

By you seeing your past differently in the present moment and by you sending love to your inner child that still lives in you. By embracing that child, and by gently smiling at yourself as often as you can, you give that child what she or he did not receive as a child. Isn't this what psychotherapy is all about? To release your past by surrendering to it through the eyes of the present?

Oh, yes! So are you saying that psychotherapy works? I feel some therapists are a little on the edge of losing their minds themselves.

You have to get out of the mind to understand the workings of your mind. Good psycho-
therapists understand that it is not about psycho-
analyzing anything *using the mind*. It is simply a
direct seeing without the burden or conditioning
of the past. Therapy can be very effective if aided
with meditation, breath work, yoga, mantras, etc.
because these tools get you out of the mind and
back in the present moment.

That makes sense. So therapy would work better if combined with meditation, prayer, etc.?

Yes. And meditation can benefit from therapy
by making peace with one's past in addition to
being fully present to the here and now.

Earlier you said that many people misunderstand the
law of attraction. How so?

The law of attraction does not manifest anything if the *intention* to manifest—which is often,
unconscious—springs from lack and not from
fullness. Most people who intend to use this law
come from the feeling of lack, and so they create
even more lack.

So, trying to feel happy thoughts of becoming a millionaire will not make one a millionaire?

Not until you keep trying to feel happy thoughts because "trying" implies you are unhappy not being a millionaire. So, you have to go deeper and question why you want to be a millionaire in the first place. If the whole idea of becoming a millionaire originated in lack, then how can you become a happy millionaire? Lack only generates more lack, so most likely you will not become a millionaire this way, and even if by some luck you did, you will become an unhappy millionaire. Laughter! You should look at the lives of people who have won big lotteries and see what happened to them. Many of them lost their last shred of happiness. At least they could live on hope before winning the jackpot. Now even that was gone, and their misery multiplied with their money.

So, it is more important to change oneself from the inside, to send positive feelings to all parts of oneself, instead of trying to manifest externally. The external world will shift as the internal world shifts because *the law of attraction is always at work!* You have to be happy to attract more happiness, a fact, which due to its utter simplicity, seems like a secret. When Sita surrendered to the little joys of being in the forest, her thoughts of loneliness transformed into thoughts of love, and that is when Rama found her. When Parvati tried to tempt Lord Shiva with the help of Kama, she created only more loneliness for herself; but when she reached out to him after attaining her inner fullness, Lord Shiva felt her ecstasy and responded to her. When the Second Chakra is open and working in harmony with the First Chakra, the sky is the limit of what someone can create and manifest.

Okay, this makes a lot of sense. So, what happens when the Second Chakra is not open and thus not aligned?

One does not feel connected to others and distrusts others when this chakra is not open. The shutting down of this chakra feels emotionally draining as if one has no joy in relationships. The energy can also feel overly emotional, let's say like a volcano with too much energy. It also leads to the desire to express oneself in a more seductive way. And this causes a lack of responsibility in that individual. The emotional energy expresses itself in a lower form of "wanting," from which the person never feels fulfilled. This can also lead to addictive and unbalanced behaviors as fire energy moves downward in the First Chakra and remains stuck. Sitting near a tree can help, as the energy of a tree is golden within. It is slow, patient, and joyful. The essence of the tree can soften the one with an overactive energy.

So, is that the reason you asked me to sit near the trees recently? Laughter!

Maybe! Laughter! Sitting near the tree would help you create a deeper and more balanced connection with your sexual energy. If the Second

Chakra is in harmony, there is a dance between the inner male and the inner female that is exquisite. Also, if one has chosen a lifetime to meditate, then harmony between the Second Chakra and the higher chakras can bring a faster enlightenment. This is the path of many who choose to be alone in their last few lives to create harmony within the self by opening and connecting all of their chakras. Others choose to enlighten together by using the law of attraction to incarnate with each other as soulmates. In my next incarnation with Lord Vishnu, we used the law of attraction to connect with each other at *three different levels*.

Namaste!

Namaste Lakshmi ji!

PART IV
THE FEMININE WISDOM
OF MAHABHARATA

GOD-REALITY-TRUTH MANTRA

Hari Om Tat Sat

हरि ॐ तत्सत्

15

Radha, Krishna, and the Gopis

Namaste Lakshmi ji!

Namaste!

Earlier you said that in your next incarnation you used the law of attraction to connect with Lord Vishnu at three different levels. What were these levels?

> In his next incarnation, Lord Vishnu incarnated as Krishna to assist in the change of the Yugas. This was an important time for humanity's transition, and so I incarnated myself into three different women who were connected to Lord Krishna. I came as his devotee, as his wife, and as his spiritual friend, and I expressed all three aspects of the Goddess energy through all of my human selves.

Did you incarnate as three women *simultaneously*?

Yes: as the maiden I was his devotee, as the
matron I was his wife, and as the crone I was his
spiritual friend.

So, the soul can divide itself and incarnate in multiple
people?

Yes, if the soul is called to do so. Usually, only
ascended beings would incarnate in this way.

I am guessing that as *Radha*, you were his spiritual
friend, and as *Rukmini*, you were his wife. Who were you as
his devotee?

I was the devotee who had five husbands.
Laughter!

Oh, so you were also *Draupadi* from *Mahabharata*, the
wife of the five Pandava[8] brothers?

Yes. I assisted the Pandavas in their surrender
to Lord Krishna's energy during their many trials
and tribulations.

Aha! I would like to hear more about these incarnations from you, especially those of Radha and Draupadi.
The scriptures say that as Radha were you Krishna's lover
and partner,[9] even though you did not marry him? Is this
true?

Laughter! Krishna was born a *realized Self*. So there was no need to complicate him. Laughter! You do not teach a tree to be whole; you simply appreciate the tree for its wholeness. The tree just is. So as he was himself, both male and female, I was there only to support him. He was much like the enlightened one whose path you were on before you came to me.

...Sri Sri Ravi Shankar, the founder of the *Art of Living*?

Yes. Sri Sri. He is pure joy. There are many women around him who assist him.

Yes, he is a bundle of joy. I used to love his Satsangs.

The world only knows my relationship with Krishna from a distance. While the scriptures have some truth, these are also projections of the minds of their authors. So let me share with you my relationship with Krishna from up close. Laughter! I did not desire to marry Krishna, for he was like a father figure to me. If I had been married to him I would have been tied down with him. I was very independent and I desired to come and go as I pleased.

My path in this lifetime was the same as the path of angels: to assist one such as your mother; to make her understand that she could have been herself in her marriage. This is a good story for women who desire to be whole and free from within, who wish to let go of the patterns that make them feel attached to the dramas of past lifetimes.

I chose to have Krishna with me in a relationship of healing, for he was already whole. The relationship we had was more of camaraderie and adoration and not romantic love. As we would be together when he did his work, I would be like a battery for him. Do not judge this as this sometimes happens even with enlightened beings. They may have relationships of high nature with the women on their path, should they choose to be together. They are careful in such relationships not to entangle themselves in a complicated manner, or as a concubine dancing to an emperor, for that is not the nature of such relationships. In this relationship, it was more a path of truth and honor. It was also a path to learn how to be of an angelic nature.

So if you think of the worm, though it does not need a partner to reproduce, it may choose to intertwine with another worm. Similarly, there are some plants that self-pollinate. Our relationship was of a similar nature. It was very harmonious and of a high vibration. You may even think of the nuns and priests. While they do not get together in the present time, many did so in the ancient past to raise each other's vibration.

So, it would have been okay if you and Lord Krishna were together.

Yes. Think of how the Virgin Mary conceived Jesus. While at one level, the conception can be thought of in the ordinary human way, at a deeper level, Jesus was the *Son of God*, and so the relationship between Virgin Mary and Joseph was of a very high vibration to allow the divine conception to occur.

Earlier, you said that you would be like a battery to Lord Krishna. Can you explain this more?

I was simply stating that our relationship would raise both of our vibrations. So, when you see your beloved teacher Sri Sri and women around him, as he surrenders to the energy between them, his vibration rises. The relationship is of a healing nature, so there is no crossing of certain boundaries. There was an understanding between us. There was an honor between us.

What you said has made me curious. If he was whole, why would you be like a battery for him?

I would be the catalyst for him to come to his joyful state of connectedness from his restfulness. I am not saying that I was the only catalyst, as taking care of the Earth or helping those in need would also expand his fullness.

So, what was Lord Krishna like?

Lord Krishna! He was of a deep mystical nature. He took care of many that were around him, especially assisting those who had sorrow in their hearts. He was also very devoted to his family. He spoke very quickly. So, let's say as a personality trait, that he would answer questions efficiently and to the point, but his speech was rather quick. He was always in a hurry. Laughter! Because he felt he had much to do, he rarely slept. He would spend time with few people when he was in his meditative states. He would take breaks from people about twice a year.

In our relationship, we talked about many things, and we did not always agree on everything. This was because of my independent nature. This made for good conversations in which I could be simply myself. He would sing to me. At times, I would travel away from him, but when we would rejoin, we always rejoiced in one another. Again, remember it was my choice not to marry him because society was not so patriarchal in those days.

Was this incarnation after you incarnated as Sita?

Yes, approximately twenty-one human lifetimes after that incarnation.

Could you share a story of love between you and Krishna?

There was a time when he was on his spiritual journey and traveling for many months at a time.

The knowledge that he brought was not in books. He would manifest simple things. For example, he knew how to go to a tree and the tree would bring forth fruit of whatever nature he desired. His energy field, especially his Heart Chakra, would be completely open during these times when he would manifest. The strongest times were at sunrise and sunset, when he would manifest these things. He would speak to me across the stars, or rather, he would speak to the stars, and that energy would flow to me like through a compass. After receiving communication from him I would then speak back to him through the stars as well.

I stayed in places that were high up in the mountains, not along the seas. So one would have to go through mist to climb up to where I lived. Such places would allow me to connect with his energy and be near him. There was a place where I stayed that had trees at the very top, but the path was quite steep, so it would be difficult to get to this place on any animal, even a horse. The angels spoke to me often, and I would do ritual-like dances to create patterns of weather through my joy. That was the gift I shared, and as prayers would float up to me in a feminine way, the lands would be plentiful. As I would envision what I desired for Lord Krishna to manifest, he would receive the guidance and would manifest that.

He had both the masculine and the feminine energies, and I had developed these energies, as well. So there was always oneness between us.

This may not be like a love story, but it was like the caretaking of the Earth. We shared some of the tasks together, and notice I do not say "duties and obligations," for these were tasks that we enjoyed doing together. This was a time when I was quite free, or not guarded.

You could change the weather patterns to take care of the Earth? How did you do this?

Yes. I understood the patterns of the seasons, the movements of the stars, and various other things about nature as well. There was great harmony in our lives, and I felt very secure. There was a lot of change within me during this period. There were others, very few, who also lived with me in this high place that was like a sanctuary for us. I could also speak in a language that was close to an Egyptian dialect. There still may be books and relics that exist from this time with my teachings.

I realize that we know so little about you as Radha.

It was Lord Krishna's path to share what he had learned and discovered, and not my path to reveal too much about me. So, there is not a lot that is known about my emotional nature, what I enjoyed, and how I lived. The world knows more about the teachings of Lord Krishna.

Can you tell us more about the nature of your relationship?

We could move our energy back and forth, which allowed us to be together. At times, I took care of the Earth more, and at other times he did; and then there were times that we danced together to heal the Earth. So this was not a relationship of a romantic nature; it was a healing relationship, and it healed the Earth. It was like two people coming together to create balance in a family, or two people coming together to create wholeness.

Did you love him emotionally, spiritually, or both?

True love is always of the heart, as this is the place where different elements come together in oneness. Though my love for Lord Krishna was physical, emotional, and spiritual, it was always purely of the heart. It did not have any wantingness, and it was unconditional. It was what some eastern religions refer to as Vajra love. So, if you think about some of the stories that we spoke about, we can wrap them up by saying that our love was Vajra love; it was physical, emotional, and spiritual, and yet beyond all of these.

Vajra love?

Yes: when the lower chakras surrender and align with your higher chakras, the body unites with the soul, and love is experienced as Vajra love. The word Vajra means pure and clear like a diamond. While diamond has the essence of coal, it is not coal. Similarly, while Vajra love has the essence of the intimacy of all types of love, the experience is more blissful and devotional.[10] As we danced in our union with our higher selves, we were in the same energy whether we danced together or we danced separately. There was physical contact but not consummation.

Why not?

Vajra love is an embodiment of one's higher self in the physical body, which allows a transformation of different loves to a much higher vibration of the spirit. Unlike sexual love, Vajra love is not focused on an outward exchange of energy from the lower chakras. Instead the energy movement is inward, and the alchemy happens within, as the inner masculine surrenders to the inner feminine. The joining with a partner may happen, but it is not necessary on this path of awakening. It is how a Crone expresses herself. As we loved one another and became one with our surroundings, it healed the Earth. Though sometimes we shared this love together, at other times, we expressed it individually in our intimate connection with the Earth.

Talking about love, there is much celebration of the love of the Gopis for Lord Krishna. There is also a story in the scriptures according to which these Gopis were sages in a previous lifetime who were surrendered to Krishna. Is this how they met their Krishna in this life?

> Well, about half and half. In other words, half were sages and half were followers of the sages. So, as Gopis, the first half were like matrons and the other half were like maidens. They were all following Lord Krishna, but Lord Krishna did not require it. Their hearts were full of love for Lord Krishna. Their love was similar to the love between Radha and Krishna. Lord Krishna taught about the completeness of love, the ecstasy of love. Laughter! Imagine two people who are dancing, drunk with the nectar of the divine. Whether they dance holding each other or dance separately, they remain in the same energy. Even if there is physical contact, it does not mean that every part of the body makes contact.

So, there is physical closeness and possibly some intimacy, but it does not mean that it is sexual?

> Physical contact can allow sacred transmission of life energy that is not always based on just romantic attraction. There is wholeness in such energy, such that it is not divided as physical, emotional, or spiritual.

16

The Soul Cycle

Earlier you said that you also incarnated as Draupadi, who was Krishna's devotee and married to the five Pandava brothers. Can you tell us about the nature of your relationship with the five Pandava brothers?

In that incarnation, my energy was more of a maiden, though I went through all stages of womanhood. I grew up very innocent, rebellious, and fiery, and I accepted Lord Krishna as my spiritual master. I had opened my first three chakras, and I was growing into my heart when I got married. Finding out that I had married five husbands was surprising and shocking, but it did not create any sorrow, as I was already in the no-mind. I was moved by the boundless love Pandavas seemed to have for each other. I was bestowed with great beauty and a joyous nature that attracted the brothers to me like bees to honey. They loved me in different ways and my coming into their lives bonded them even more instead of making them jealous. This was their true greatness. I supported the brothers in the difficult journey they had chosen together as new souls. Occasionally, I would bring them messages from Lord Krishna, which I would receive in my prayers and meditations. I was open to the path that lay in front of me.

You said the brothers were *new souls*. What do you mean by that?

Their souls had just individuated from Gods before they began their journey, so they arrived on Earth as new souls. Since they had come from a place of great magnificence, their hearts remained open in the most trying circumstances. They did not see and understand evil like others; for example, they understood evil differently than their hundred cousins who had begun their human journey many lifetimes earlier. The eldest Pandava brother was always willing to forgive and forget for the sake of what he understood was his dharma, his spiritual path.

So, their cousins, the Kauravas,[11] were older souls?

They were already on their Karmic paths from previous lifetimes. Human incarnations go in cycles. Pandavas were just beginning their descent in human incarnations, while Kauravas had descended much more. So Kauravas were the older souls.

When a new soul arrives on Earth, it lives more from its heart and the higher chakras, as Karma does not accumulate so much in their lower chakras. As the soul takes more births, it gets entangled in Karmic journeys based on the choices it makes as a human using the gift of free will. This gets the soul trapped in the lower three chakras, and that begins a great forgetting of its sacred connection to its higher self. Fear, anger, hate, sorrow, and other negative impressions are carried into the future lifetimes in the lower three chakras, attracting more situations that remind the soul of what remains unresolved. Then, instead of resolving, it often adds to the existing Karma, getting buried into the quicksand of Karma.

After the soul has experienced enough contrast, which it came to experience through the human incarnations, it opens itself to a spiritual path and begins the reverse journey of releasing and rising above its Karma. During the current transition period, many humans are in the last stages of releasing their Karma. At this time, many older souls are embracing wisdom to release their Karma. During the beginning of the soul cycle, the younger souls are innocent, as they have not accumulated much Karma. Wisdom is received only after innocence is lost and regained.

So, are you saying that the Pandava brothers were innocent but not necessarily wise?

Exactly, and they were going to lose their innocence with their descent in human incarnations.

Can you tell us a little more about the soul cycle of human incarnations?

Everything in the universe unfolds in a rhythm, so the soul's cycle is divided into a rhythm of Yugas. The journey has similar Karmic paths and lessons for most humans during a given Yuga. The transition periods between Yugas are very special, and Gods may incarnate, new souls may individuate, or old souls may get enlightened, during these epochal periods in order to help with the transition of the rest of the humanity. However, the majority of souls choose to be enlightened in the Satya Yuga, the Golden age of joy, love, and peace.

How many incarnations do we have before we finish the entire soul cycle and get enlightened?

It varies with each soul because there is free will. All souls experience the contrast—some may experience a little less, and others may experience a little more. Occasionally, a soul may individuate for only one life, as I have done in some lifetimes.

Some religions say that it takes millions of lives before one is enlightened, and some say like 84 lives, with 21 lives in each Yuga, etc. So, is it hundreds, or thousands, or millions?

It is all of them for there are cycles within cycles within cycles as a divine being expands into even more divinity by dividing itself into many souls and then rejoining. Most human souls who have incarnated in the current soul cycle have evolved in many universes across multiple dimensions before coming to Earth. Most of you have lived anywhere between sixty and one hundred human lives on Earth. Because of free will some of you will take less time, and others will take more time until all of you are fully enlightened.

Why would souls desire to experience the contrast?

A new soul is made in the image of a divine being, such as a God/Goddess source that it individuated from. It is full of joy, love, purity, light, truth, and magnificence, but it wishes to know that which it is not. Unlike an enlightened being, who is always expanding in oneness with its opposite, the new soul does not know its opposite. The new soul is born without any past, and so it has no reference point to know that which it is not. So while the new soul experiences its divine splendor, it does not know itself in its full glory, as it once was a part of the divine being. It does not know anything about darkness and pain, and a great curiosity arises in it to know *all*. Through its incarnations in human lives and by going through the Karmic cycle, it experiences that which it is not. At first, resistance to that which it is not causes it to experience suffering. After having experienced the contrast of suffering, it learns to embrace that which it is not, which is the beginning of the end of its suffering. Growing into oneness with that which it is not, it realizes its blissful nature, which is beyond all opposites of the mind. It is on the path of realizing itself as a divine being, like a Buddha or a God/Goddess.

Can every soul become a divine being?

That is the final destiny of all souls.

Going back to the Pandava brothers, you said that they were new souls who had just individuated from Gods. What were their experiences like as new souls on Earth?

New souls live from the heart and have difficulty in seeing evil intention in human actions. So, at first, the Pandavas could not see their Kaurava cousins in a negative light. They would get very confused by the actions of their eldest Kaurava cousin.

Do you mean Duryodana?[12]

Yes. Initially, they saw Duryodana with the same love they shared between themselves, but over time their lower chakras got clouded with the accumulated hurts, and that soured their emotions. Even after being hurt so many times, their hearts remained open to love, so much so that they were willing to forgive and forget at any point until the war began.

If the Pandava brothers were willing to forgive and forget, then why did they have to fight the war?

The point of their lives was not to ascend to where they came from. Most of humanity was at the end of third Yuga when the Pandava brothers incarnated on Earth. The brothers came to help humanity transition to the Kali Yuga, which is the most intense period of experiencing the contrast. At that point, most of the souls journeying in the soul cycle desired to experience more contrast.

So, the Pandavas came as new souls even though many human souls had already lived through three Yugas by then. Am I understanding what you are saying correctly?

Yes. The great war of *Mahabharata* marked the transition from Dvarpara Yuga to Kali Yuga. Because the Pandava brothers had incarnated as new souls, they were very familiar with the divine energy of Lord Krishna and could assist him in this spiritually challenging task of changing Yugas. It was a mission they agreed upon with much excitement and enthusiasm before incarnating on Earth.

They saw Lord Krishna as their savior and were born with superhuman strengths that they inherited from the Gods from whom they individuated. While they wanted to forgive and forget, Lord Krishna knew of the deeper soul journeys they had come to experience. Like the rest of the humanity, the Pandava brothers had to descend into the darkness of Kali Yuga. That was the wish of many souls who, at that time, wished to experience more contrast. Being new souls on Earth, the Pandavas had a more difficult task, as they were so connected to the spiritual realm that they could not see what good would come out of killing. Duryodana's soul had descended enough on its Karmic path to stay true to the soul contract.

Duryodana was true to the soul contract?

Souls are joined in immense love before they incarnate on Earth. All of us—including Lord Krishna, the Pandavas, the Kauravas, and everyone who was connected to us—co-created the drama that we would act out in that lifetime. Duryodana's soul path was to help in the creation of contrast through his ignorance. All of us stayed true to the soul contract, more or less, but the Pandavas' task was harder because they were new souls on Earth, and the contrast between the spiritual realm and the material realm was too much for them to bear at first. Lord Krishna and I (as Draupadi), would help them stay on their soul path, which they chose *using their free will.* When Lord Krishna could not be with them, I would receive messages from him, which I would convey to them.

From what you said, it seems everyone is always on his or her soul path. For example, Duryodana was on his soul path as he stayed in his ignorance, and the Pandavas were also on their soul paths with your help and the help of Lord Krishna. Is there ever a time when someone is not on their soul path?

Ultimately, one of the greatest truths of life is that you are mostly doing what you are supposed to be doing except for the judgments of your ego. The ego resists wanting a better way. Sometimes, this makes you deviate from your soul path but most of the time it does not.

Can you explain this more?

The ego does not always deviate from the soul path. If the soul wishes to learn about contrast, and the ego supports that by creating contrast, then the ego is being true to the soul path. So Duryodana was on his soul path. The ego does deviate from the soul path, and it deviates more both when the soul is beginning its journey and when it is close to ending its journey in the cycle of human incarnations. When the soul is beginning its journey, the ego is too attached to the spiritual realm, and it does not wish to experience the contrast of suffering by falling into the material realm. This is the *spiritual* ego, which resists the soul's path of falling. When the soul is close to ending its journey, the ego is too attached to the material realm, and it does not wish to let go of the suffering in order for one to rise into the spiritual realm. This is the material ego, which resists the soul's path of rising. The Pandava brothers were at the beginning of their soul journey and were thus in their spiritual egos. They would have deviated from their soul path if I had not encouraged them to fight the war.

So you, as Draupadi, kept the Pandavas on their soul paths by encouraging them to fight their cousins?

Yes. Because I was enlightened, I received messages from my higher self, and one message was always consistent: the Pandavas were supposed to fight their cousins, the Kauravas, without any emotional attachments if they wished to be true to their soul paths. They could also choose not to fight by their free will. Since I was married to them, I felt a deep calling to serve my husbands by reminding them of their soul paths.

Were you fully enlightened with all seven chakras open?

No, I was not fully enlightened. Unlike Lord Krishna, who had opened all seven chakras and realized his God nature, I had aligned and opened my first three chakras and was in the process of opening my Heart Chakra. Sometimes I would feel an immense outpouring of love for everything including the Earth, the trees, and all humans including the Kauravas, which is hard to express in words; at other times, however, I remained unmoved by the suffering of Duryodana and the other Kauravas while I was in my joy with my husbands. I surrendered to Lord Krishna often, which kept me growing on my soul path.

17

Draupadi and Karna

It seems no one deviated from his or her soul path in this epic war, which I find hard to believe.

I did not say that the Pandavas did not deviate ever from their soul paths. They did sometimes as most humans do, but in virtually all of the big decisions, including the decision to fight the war, they listened to my advice, and were also guided in this war by Lord Krishna once they decided to fight the war.

So, are you saying that all characters in this epic war more or less followed their soul paths *in making the big decisions*?

Yes, except the one who was destined to be the real *Hero* of the war, however. Laughter! The older three of the Pandava brothers also had another elder brother who was abandoned by their mother. She was unmarried when she conceived him.

Oh, Karna?[13]

Yes. Unlike the five Pandava brothers who had individuated from their source Gods as *new souls*, Karna had individuated from his source God many lives ago, and he was in his last human incarnation. He was ready to ascend to his higher self in that lifetime.

He was the one whom I longed for the most before I married Arjuna. At one point, when we were in exile in the forest, I confessed to my husbands about this, and they understood, so this is not a secret. But Karna chose to react out of his ego instead of surrendering to his soul path *on that day when he could have been enlightened.*

When was that?

It was the day when Duryodana's brother dragged me to the royal court of the Kauravas and tried to strip me naked in front of hundreds of men. I knew Lord Krishna would save me, but I did not ask for his help until I gave every man, except Karna, a chance to speak for me against this injustice.

Some have speculated that you did not ask Karna because of your *ego,* as you had already rejected him once before by not allowing him to compete in your *Swayamvara.*[14]

As I have said before, the scriptures have been changed, and new additions were made over time. Not all that was added over time is inspired and true. I was in constant communion with Lord Krishna. When I looked at Karna, my higher self was guided by Lord Krishna to *not ask for his help*. Karna was supposed to awaken to his soul path on his own by watching my humiliation, and not because I would plead for his help. Karna's ego was triggered *as I ignored him*, and in a rare moment of revengeful weakness in his otherwise exemplary life, he forgot how much he had desired me once, and supported my humiliation. Because Karna chose to be on his ego path instead of his soul path, he did not get enlightened in that most auspicious moment of his life, and Arjuna became the hero in *Mahabharata* instead of him.

So, Karna could have really been *enlightened* in that moment?

Yes, if he had surrendered to his soul path instead of his ego path. There are special moments in every human's life that have the "potential" to enlighten that human. However, very few of us recognize these moments as they occur. I awoke that day with a foreboding of what was going to unfold. I knew it was a day when the Pandavas would lose all and that some people would try to steal my virtue, but that I would be protected. I had no fear, as my lower chakras were open. Instead, there was much anticipation in my heart as I received guidance from Lord Krishna that someone whom I loved might transform and get enlightened in those moments. As I was dragged to the court and faced all of our cousins and relatives, I knew in an instant that it was Karna, the one whom I had desired to marry on the day of my Swayamvara.

Really? But you barred him from even competing in the contest at your Swayamvara.[15]

Yes. It was my soul path to do so. In that fateful moment of my Swayamvara, I surrendered to the guidance I received from my higher self. My barring him from the Swayamvara was for a higher purpose to awaken him to his soul path. My humiliation on that day when the Kauravas tried to strip me naked was supposed to melt his heart and break his bond with Duryodana.[16] In that moment pregnant with the possibility of his enlightenment, *he could have forgiven me for rejecting him at my Swayamvara*. His learning about forgiveness was the most important part of our soul contract, and it required much surrender on his part. As I said earlier, the soul path is more likely to deviate from the ego path, both when the soul begins its journey and when the soul is ending its journey. Karna was close to the end of his journey, and my humiliation was supposed to stir his soul into action by encouraging him to surrender his ego and protect me.

Oh, so you did not have any *negative* thoughts and feelings for Karna?

> Remember, my lower three chakras were open and aligned, so I had already tasted the emptiness that had dissolved my fears, insecurities, and emotional imbalances. I never felt any negativity towards Karna, as I was in the process of fully opening my Heart Chakra in that life. Even my higher chakras would have opened quickly, except that the relationships with my husbands, the long conflict between my husbands and their cousins, and the raising of my children kept me busy, which did not provide me with extended periods of solitude to meditate. I had chosen to be a devotee of Lord Krishna in that lifetime, and I was connected to him in making all such decisions.

Would the events have unfolded differently if Karna had surrendered his ego?

> He felt a bit of unease as I was dragged into the court, but instead of listening to his higher self, his ego got caught up with the rest of them after I ignored him. If he had only opened to his higher self, his guides and Lord Krishna were ready to show him the way, and he could have attained in those precious moments what he had been searching for in many lifetimes. He would have experienced those moments as I was experiencing them, and he would have asked Duryodana to stop my

humiliation immediately. This would have enraged Duryodana who would have then insulted Karna by speaking harsh words. A falling out would have occurred immediately between them. Because Karna had much self-esteem, in a moment of great courage, he would have returned all the earthly gifts Duryodana had showered upon him. As he did this, the deep insecurity in his First Chakra of being deprived of everything in his childhood, the rage in his Second Chakra of being insulted by me at my Swayamvara, and the deep ego wound in his Third Chakra would have all be exposed fully. In the next moment, his lower three chakras would have opened and aligned with his heart, as he would have let himself drop into the emptiness of the no-mind and be *enlightened*. Karna would have realized in that instant that the Pandavas were his own brothers.

Would the *Mahabharata* have unfolded differently then?

Most of the events would have played out more or less the same, except that Karna would have been on the side of the Pandavas. The war of *Mahabharata* would have ended in 11 days instead of 18, and Karna would have fought on the side of the Pandavas and struck only when his brothers needed his help. Almost all who crossed over in this war would have still crossed over and descended into the Kali Yuga in their future human incarnations, as that was their chosen soul path. [17]

What about you and Karna?

> At some point after Karna's enlightenment, the Pandava brothers would sense my spiritual longing for him, and I would confess to them about this. Soon, I would marry Karna, and while I would continue to love all of the Pandavas, my sexual relations would only be with Karna from that point onward. With Karna's enlightenment and my marriage to him, the Pandavas would see us both with much honor and admiration, and would agree to what I proposed.
>
> Karna was a noble and resplendent soul whose path was to be in the *Mahabharata*, what Rama was in *Ramayana*. If Karna had lived up to his soul path, children would have grown up with stories about *Draupadi and Karna* similar to those of Sita and Rama, or Radha and Krishna. Though Karna failed to realize his soul path with me, he had everything that I desired in a soulmate. He had more generosity, loyalty, truth, physical prowess, skill, and courage than was in all of the Pandava brothers. The only hurts he was carrying in his lower chakras were his abandonment by his mother and my refusal to allow him to participate in my Swayamvara. These abandonments made him feel deprived and because of this feeling he got attached to Duryodana as his loyal friend.[18]

Very interesting! What would Karna represent in terms of spiritual wisdom on his soul path?

He would symbolize *listening* to the higher self because he would have listened to the voice of his higher self on the day of my humiliation.

Aha! The name Karna means *"ear"* in Sanskrit.

His name and the big celestial earrings that he wore were to remind him of his soul path: *to listen with Karuna and with his inner ear.*

Interestingly, the word *Karuna* meant *"sadness"* in Sanskrit in the ancient times, but later it came to mean *"compassion."*

Karna's soul path was to have Karuna, to feel the sadness and listen with compassion to the one who was being shamed and violated, but who was ultimately his highest soulmate. On his soul path, Karna could have transformed his sadness into compassion.

Aha! The word *Karuna* is also the root of my spiritual name, *Karunesh*. Can you tell us how sadness can be transformed into compassion?

By emptying your mind through the soul feeling of *forgiveness*. The meaning of the word *Karuna* evolved from sadness to compassion through *forgiveness*, which is the missing link in the evolution of this beautiful word over millennia.

What happens if we do not forgive?

If you do not forgive then your sadness may devolve into anger and hate against those who you think are responsible for your sadness. The others may hurt you temporarily, but whether you transform your sadness into compassion, or let it devolve into anger and hate is a *choice*.

You have transitioned from your ego path to your soul path because you have surrendered to forgiveness in some key moments in this lifetime. In some of your previous incarnations, you were more on your ego path. In one lifetime in Egypt, you were so blinded by your ego that it caused great suffering for many women in your life.

I am truly sorry!

You are forgiven! Let the untold story of Karna's soul path inspire everyone to grow in Karuna by truly listening with their inner ear. Karuna is the great gift we give to ourselves by apologizing sincerely and forgiving generously. Know that forgiveness is one of the fastest ways to help grow compassion in your life. Let your new name guide your work for healing the wounded feminine, not only in women, but also in men. Let the untold story of Karna's soul path awaken the empowered feminine in all of humanity, as the aggressive masculine apologizes and the violated feminine forgives, while maintaining the boundaries when needed.

18

Great Lessons of Mahabharata

I am feeling inspired by what could have been the soul path of Karna even though he did not live up to it. Can you tell us what is the main lesson in the *Mahabharata*, as I have been often confused about this epic more than any other?

There is not one but many lessons in *Mahabharata*, and the first one is *to surrender to one's soul path*. The soul path and ego path merge in the middle of the soul cycle of human incarnations, but diverge both at the beginning and the ending of the soul cycle. At the beginning of the soul cycle, the soul is full of light and the birth of ego allows it to descend into darkness, but with great difficulty; in the middle of the soul cycle, the soul does not have as much light, and the growth of the ego keeps the soul in darkness; and finally, at the end of the soul cycle, light starts pouring in again but the ego resists its own ending, which makes it difficult for the soul to return into light.

The Pandavas came into the first human incarnation of their soul cycle, so that their egos resisted descending into darkness. Lord Krishna and I helped them on their soul paths. Duryodana was in the middle of his soul cycle, and his ego kept him in the darkness. Karna was at the end of his soul cycle, but his ego did not surrender totally, delaying his return into light until the moment of his physical death.

Isn't the main lesson of the *Mahabharata to be fully present to your action without any attachment to the fruit of your action?*

This is the second lesson of *Mahabharata*, which the divine helps you remember both at the beginning of the soul cycle and the end of the soul cycle. This lesson allows you to live in the present moment. The lesson is almost always forgotten in the middle of the soul cycle when the soul descends into darkness. This is how it is supposed to be, for the soul wishes to experience the contrast of suffering. *Bhagavad Gita* could have been preached either to Arjuna or Karna, but, not to Duryodana, who was in the middle of his soul cycle.

Really? Lord Krishna could have preached the *Bhagavad Gita* to Karna?

Yes, indeed! Lord Krishna would have been Karna's charioteer, and not Arjuna's, if Karna had lived up to his soul path.

But wouldn't Karna have already been enlightened on his soul path? If yes, why would he have needed spiritual guidance from Lord Krishna?

Standing up for me on the day of my humiliation would have enlightened Karna by the opening and aligning of his lower three chakras. But there are higher enlightenments which Karna would receive as he would ask questions to Lord Krishna on the battlefield. The answers would be similar, but unlike Arjuna, who remained unenlightened and mostly unconvinced by Lord Krishna until the very end, Karna would have had flashes of enlightenments that would have successively opened all of his higher chakras. *Bhagavad Gita* would be a story of Karna's ascension into full enlightenment, as the conversation with Lord Krishna would have culminated. Lord Krishna's main task would be to unveil spiritual wisdom to Karna, and not so much to help the Pandavas in the execution of the war. But in reality, Lord Krishna had to interfere in the war quite often because Karna remained on his ego path. The divine has infinite degrees of freedom in manifesting that which is the highest good of all.

So, in reality, what happened to Karna after his death on his ego path?

As he was dying, he surrendered himself fully to Lord Krishna. The door opened instantly, and he was fully enlightened in those precious moments.

I am confused now. On the one hand, Karna did not live up to his soul path, and on the other hand, he was enlightened as he was dying. Did it matter in the end, what Karna did or did not do?

It did not! *Divine never interferes with free will and yet nothing matters in the end for divine always prevails.* This is the third lesson of *Mahabharata.* It allows you to appreciate your ego path in the larger context of the whole universe. Ultimately, Karna's path was that of a compassionate Bodhisattva but without him knowing this. If Karna had saved me from my humiliation that day, then he would have been enlightened, but a great opportunity would have been lost, which was to show that *divine always prevails,* even against the most difficult odds. He delayed his enlightenment but opened the path of surrender to the divine for billions of humans. His ego path was joined with a higher universal soul path for the rest of humanity.

Aha! That is insightful. We should not cast judgments on those who we think are living from their egos because they too may be serving a higher purpose. Is there a lesson for all humans based on the story of Karna's life?

Acting out of your ego at the key crossroads of your life does not condemn you to stay on the ego path, forever. Instead, think of your ego path as crisscrossing your soul path at many key moments—such as moments of humiliation, failure, success, disease, divorce, reunion, death, survival, etc. How you act in these moments, brings you either to the soul path or the ego path, both at the beginning and the end of your soul cycle, when these two paths diverge. Karna received many opportunities to return to his soul path, as Lord Krishna reached out to him in different ways, and he surrendered eventually as he was dying.

The final lesson of *Mahabharata* is that *it is never too late to surrender to the divine.* Like Karna, you can find your soul path even in your dying moments. Remember, it was the plan that we all agreed upon when you individuated as new souls and co-created the drama that we are living today. The *Mahabharata* war was a turning point for humanity that amplified the intensity of *contrast* that many humans are now experiencing in this Yuga.

Namaste!

Namaste Lakshmi ji!

PART V

THE SECRETS OF
A SOUL TRIBE

UNIVERSAL COMPASSION MANTRA

Om Mani Padme Hum

ॐ मणिपद्मे हुम्

19

Buddha and Yasodhara

Namaste Lakshmi ji!

Namaste!

The scriptures say that after your incarnations as Sita with Rama, and Radha with Krishna, you incarnated as *Yasodhara* with *Buddha*. Were you able to keep your heart open when Buddha suddenly left the palace?

> This was a marriage of tremendous love, born out of choice and not out of a lower karmic nature. We came to know *love* as we realized our *freedom*. We began our journey in the palace, but our relationship truly blossomed outside the palace. It was his path in this lifetime to search without for that which is neither within nor without.

But were you not disappointed that he abandoned you?

I had my wholeness whether we were together or separate. My experience of the relationship even when he left was not one that was not pleasurable. I simply blossomed as I did my everyday work. When my time came, I laid myself down.

Did you blossom even while he was away?

Yes, I am speaking of the time when we realized ourselves in those years after he had left but before he returned. After he returned I travelled often and took the teachings that I had learned to others across waterways, but not tremendously big waterways. The things that I have written are not hidden.

Did you learn these teachings from Buddha?

Remember, I had already learned of myself in other lifetimes.

But the story goes that after Buddha was enlightened, he came back for you, and later you joined his Sangha.

Yes, but I was already in that place of enlightenment before he returned, so again the story that you know is of a man enlightening a woman.

Oh, I see! You were already enlightened?

Yes. As Buddha and I came together, we both got enlightened in ways similar to those in our previous lifetimes. There were lifetimes when we already were who we were, and this one was similar as well; our separation created the space for us to grow spiritually. For example, I frequently sequestered myself in prayers for lengths of time. As I hid myself, I blessed the Earth and things grew unexpectedly; I did this to help feed those around me. Great healings and cleansings took place that helped many at that time; various herbs and their properties were also discovered.

Very interesting! We know so little about you as Yasodhara.

Yes. There are written words about me that are not in the books that you know. It is not hidden but protected by those that have been charged to do so even to this day. Again, divine timing...

Will these teachings be revealed at a later date when the time is right?

Well, yes: for the writings to come forth, these teachings shall be made known in the next few years.

Can you tell us more about your life as Yasodhara after he left the palace?

Before Buddha was enlightened I knew him as my husband, Siddhartha. There were letters written between Siddhartha and I, and our child kept me happy and busy. I did not live a life bound by tradition and convention, even though it appeared to be so. I was quite happy in that lifetime.

My life as Yasodhara is intended to show women that they may be enlightened in their small lives and have great joy in that, for my husband supported me in what I truly desired, which was to share my joy and wisdom with others. But many couples are unable to support one another in this way.

I agree. I separated from my first wife because of my need to meditate, and she got tired of my need to be alone.

Well, you did not meditate as much as you spoke about it to her. Laughter! And the more you spoke about this, the more insecure she became about your need to be alone. Had you been like Siddhartha, you would have simply gone and done your prayers and meditations. Then your wife would have been happy and joyous and found her own spiritual path and things may have been different.

So, I needed to meditate more instead of talking about it so much. Laughter!

Your wife was a bit impatient, and you took a little longer to blossom. Laughter! But neither of you lost anything as you grew from that experience, and you still have love for one another.

According to historical accounts, you were married to Siddhartha when you turned 16 and remained with him until he left to find enlightenment at the age of 29. Can you tell us more about the nature of your relationship with Siddhartha during these years when you were with him?

Let me first share with you about my path and the nature of what I did during the period when he was gone. I worked with younger children. I worked with them until they came of age to marry or to go on their own way. I kept in contact with Siddhartha both psychically and through the written word. We were able to communicate with each other from the other side through higher realms. This kept our marriage very strong. But there were times when months would go by without any written word or any sort of communication. However, our meditative and telepathic nature was developed strongly during this period of our separation. One would think that in our meditative state we would commune with each other only spiritually. But there was a communion also in joy and passion.

That is sweet!

This way of being with Siddhartha was similar to the dance I did with Vishnu. It was both within and without. This allowed us to have joy and fullness within ourselves.

So, you and Siddhartha did not suffer after your separation, as one would imagine.

That is my point. Our separation brought air and fire together. These things can be taught to couples so that they will not feel lack when they are separated, such as during wars or during times when one partner has to maintain the home while the other is away. The feminine joy of waiting is not taught any longer. More often it is women who wait, and they wait in great suffering. This does not have to be so because couples can remain connected through higher realms. You also asked earlier about the period before we separated.

Yes. I'm curious about the period during which you were together before he left the palace. What was that like?

Our marital bliss was conditioned by the societal norms and not the true bliss we received *after he left*. Though I was of a strong-natured mind, I began to question my actions—whether what I was doing was "right" according to the cultural beliefs of the time. We did not have many conversations because it was not my place to speak much. It seemed we did not speak in harmony with each other when we did have conversations about right and wrong. All of this changed with his leaving, which helped me to come back to my own nature.

So, it was not your place to speak much because he was the prince and because society was patriarchal then?

Yes.

It is very interesting that you found joy in your relationship after he left, and not before.

Yes. We became more harmonious in our minds during the period we were separated. *Our separation created our fullness*, because we grew from it spiritually. So, when we came together in later years, we reunited as innocent children. There was a portion of our lives that was not in sync with universal love.

So, is the lesson here that we should not judge when couples separate?

It is impossible to separate, as we are all joined in oneness in our higher selves. We experience the *illusion* of separation in order to grow spiritually. If couples can separate with love, the illusion disappears, and there is no Karma created in such separation. When couples choose to stay together, sometimes one partner may feel that the other partner is not paying attention to their emotional needs. Instead of worrying about why their partner is not paying attention to their needs, one could come into their own knowing and fullness.

Our marriage was not one of great suffering because I had my individual fullness and so could support him when he needed me in his journey, even after he left. I stayed true to myself and we both blossomed into enlightenment.

It seems that couples find it hard to create the right balance of freedom and union in a relationship. Personally, it has been a challenge for me to be in the no-mind state as well as be in a relationship.

The *mind* is there even when one is alone and not in a relationship. So simply enjoy those moments when there is no mind, for there is no desire and no wanting when you are not in the mind. There is simply joy of being present to all that there is.

Our conversation about "wanting-ness" is going to be an important one, as this is where so many get caught up. They become addicted to going to this seminar or that place to get better, or spend years in therapy, attempting to let go of the "wanting-ness." They are looking outside for the treasure that is inside of them.

What should one do to let go of the mind in a relationship?

Relax with yourself and relax with one another. Sometimes one mind is constantly challenging the other mind to get out of the mind, when no one is going to get out of the mind. Laughter!

Think of the time when you and I have been together, when we have been alone, and there has been only a small amount of mind. There is mind, but you have not minded the mind. You have allowed it!

So this is a meditation for you. Relax and focus on each one of the chakras, and do this with a completely open heart. As you do this with love and joy, these wheels, or lotuses, will begin to open. Remember that lotuses are beautiful even though they live in muddy murky ponds.

So, that is what it is like—our bodies are like the muddy murky ponds, and the chakras are like the beautiful lotuses?

Our thoughts and our mind....

Aha! So, our thoughts and our minds are like the muddy murky ponds, and the chakras are like the beautiful lotuses.

Yes. And the lotuses still grow.

Oh, what a beautiful analogy.

That is how it is, and this is how we see it.

20

Yes, He Knew

Can you tell us a little about Buddha after he came back? What was that like?

I saw him often through my inner vision, and he was as I had expected him to be. Even though we were separated physically, we had journeyed together for most of the time that he was away. I was already in the knowingness of his journey, so I stayed with him through the ups and the downs until he finally attained enlightenment.

It was more important for him to see his father and our son when he came back since he and I were already in a spiritual union. I was actually in divine rapture—in total surrender to the immensity of what had occurred and the path that lay in front of us.

Buddha's father still had hopes for the kingdom to be ruled by his kin, and for his grandson to become the next king.

The scriptures say that you wanted your son, Rahula, to receive the inheritance from Buddha.

My wish for Rahula was to receive what he truly desired from his heart. If I had persuaded him to be ordained as a monk in the Sangha he may not have progressed and attained enlightenment as quickly as he did. He may have questioned his journey, as it would have not felt like his own calling. So, I encouraged him to receive his "inheritance" from his father, knowing already that he would choose the spiritual kingdom over the earthly kingdom.

What was it like for Buddha's father, King Suddhodana, to see his own son come back as an enlightened being?

Let us first talk about Buddha's relationship with his father when he left the palace as Siddhartha, and not when he came back as Buddha. Siddhartha did not think that he could be a good father to his newborn son, as he had a dysfunctional relationship with his own father. While he left the palace seeking an end to suffering, the father's expectations of him had made his suffering all the more unbearable.

It was not so much that he desired to leave me, as I was a source of comfort for him, but he felt that he must leave because of his complicated relationship with his father.

What caused the dysfunctional relationship with his father?

The more King Suddhodana sheltered Siddhartha from seeing "suffering," the more unnatural Siddhartha's life became. Siddhartha could sense his father's fear and also felt the heavy burden of expectation placed on his little shoulders. Siddhartha felt that his father wanted to live his own dream through him. It felt like conditional love; it had no joy in it for him. So, as Siddhartha became an adolescent, he became moody and introspective, which bothered the King even more, and that began his dysfunctional relationship with his father.

Should the King not have sheltered Siddhartha from seeing many forms of suffering on Earth?

King Suddhodana's constant sheltering of Siddhartha from "suffering" created the suffering in Siddhartha's mind because Siddhartha began seeing suffering in all things and thought much about it. Suffering is a mental state, and it could not be eliminated by the physical luxuries King Suddhodana provided for his son. The fearful and anxious mind of the father activated the son's lower chakras at a young age, making him a sensitive child. Little Siddhartha may not have understood what he felt, but he was deeply aware of his father's pain. Siddhartha's escape from the palace was to rediscover the primordial joy that he knew as a very young child, but forgot as he grew older.

Do young children suffer when they see suffering in the world?

Children do not suffer because they do not have preconceived ideas about sickness or aging; they do not stop loving their grandma because of her wrinkled face or her aging body. While children do not want to be sick or die, they do not suffer in sickness and death like adults do, unless conditioned by their parents and society. Because children live in the present moment, they do not fear death as adults do; for example, when they go on a risky adventure they are not so concerned with the ever-present danger to their lives.

Furthermore, in many ancient societies of the past, even children participated in the celebration of death, which was seen simply as a sacred transition into the spiritual realm. Such celebration comes very naturally to children because they are joyful by nature and can connect with divine beings easily.

You seem to be saying that Siddhartha knew of suffering long before he went outside the palace where he saw the sick and the dying...?

Yes, he knew. While it was possible to hide the physical manifestations of suffering for a short while, it was not possible to hide the mental suffering of those around Siddhartha, including his own father. The father's sheltering not only failed in preventing Siddhartha from suffering, but it also made him suffer even more as an adult when he saw the contrast of life that existed inside and outside the palace.

However, it was all meant to be, as this was Siddhartha's soul path.

Many parents seem to suffer just like King Suddhodana did. They suffer more themselves because their dreams for their children remain unfulfilled.

Yes, and their children know this. This is the cause of the disillusionment that children feel with their parents. King Suddhodana thought a lot about what may have occurred if Siddhartha had not renounced the world. This is the reason Buddha did not return immediately to see his father after his enlightenment—his father was not yet ready to receive the teachings from him.

The scriptures say that King Suddhodana made many efforts to invite Buddha back to the palace, but all the messengers he would send to invite Buddha *would join the Sangha instead.*

Yes. This is because the King was not ready to transform during these times when he sent messengers to bring Buddha back. Buddha went to Angulimala immediately after hearing about him because this man was ripe for transformation.[19] But he waited to see his own father because the father was not ready yet.

King Suddhodana's messengers kept joining the Sangha until he sent a messenger to Buddha with the condition that the messenger may join Buddha's Sangha *only if* he could persuade Buddha to come back to visit the King first.

Yes, this messenger came to Buddha when the King was ready to transform. The teacher shows up when one is ready to receive the teachings.

2 1

Stages of Enlightenment

The Buddhist scriptures say that King Suddhodana attained what Buddhists called "Sotapanna" soon after meeting Buddha. Is that the first stage of enlightenment in the sense you have described? For example, is this the state when the lower three chakras align and open?

No! A Sotapanna is someone who has opened the lower two chakras and has moved into the Third Chakra. When this happens, a profound shift occurs in one's identity and one's worldview. One may not fully taste the primordial joy of emptiness at this stage, but one is strongly on a path to liberate oneself from suffering. Let's say a Sotapanna glimpses light at the end of the tunnel of mental suffering. This is where Rama began his journey when he left Ayodhya, and this is where Siddhartha began his journey when he left the palace.

According to Theravada Buddhism there are three more stages of enlightenment after one becomes a

Sotapanna: Sakadagami, Anagami, and Arahant. Those who have attained Sakadagami have to return only once more as human being in order to get fully enlightened. Those who have attained Anagami do not have to return as human at all and may get fully enlightened by birthing into the spiritual realms instead. Finally, Arahants do not need to take births even in the spiritual realms in order to get fully enlightened.

> This is mostly true, but let us clarify. A Sakadagami would have to return at least one more time, but he or she may *choose* to return more than once. An Anagami, or an Arahant, does not have to come back in human incarnations, but again, he or she may also *choose* to come back more times, like my beloved and I did after being fully enlightened. The choices increase at higher levels of enlightenment.
>
> Buddha, the fully enlightened one, was talking about the *least number* of human incarnations required at these stages. A Bodhisattva is someone who may choose to come back more times than necessary out of his or her compassion for all beings.

What is the level of enlightenment of a Sakadagami?

> A Sakadagami has opened the lower three chakras and moved into the Heart Chakra. Suffering comes to an end at this stage as one enters the bliss of emptiness.

Is an Anagami someone who has opened four chakras, and has thus entered the Fifth Chakra?

Yes.

What about Arahants? Some of the scriptures say that Arahants are fully enlightened, and others say that they are not. Are Arahants *ascended beings* with all seven chakras open?

Arahants are those who have opened *at least* the first five of the seven main chakras. The majority of Arahants did not become ascended beings during Buddha's time.

Oh, really?

The awakening through the opening of the first five chakras is so profound that it feels like complete enlightenment. So, at first, an Arahant would think of themselves as a Buddha, or as an ascended being, *as if there was nothing more to attain.* Most enlightened ones reach up only to this stage in their human incarnation because reaching this stage is so blissful that there is little desire to move further. Since full enlightenment of an Arahant is assured after their passing, the distinction between an Arahant and an ascended being is not so crucial from the perspective of final attainment. This is why Buddha did not explicitly differentiate between Arahants and himself. In Buddha's presence, many Arahants realized that the journey continues even further. Upon this realization, they surrendered even more to attain higher enlightenments, and with Buddha's grace many became ascended beings with the opening of all seven chakras. This is something only an ascended being like Buddha or higher divine beings can show to an Arahant.

I find it hard to believe that so many became ascended beings like Buddha. That would be like saying that many became like Jesus during the time of Jesus.

It is true! While there was only one Buddha and only one Jesus who discovered those beautiful paths of liberation, hundreds became like Buddha in Buddha's lifetime.

And how many became Arahants but did not become ascended beings?

Thousands! The whole region was aflame with divine light. A few transformed within minutes of meeting Buddha! They had worked on themselves for many lives in both the physical and the spiritual realms and were on Buddha's path for attainment. They were fully ready to receive when they met Buddha.

Many more humans will become Arahants in the next Yuga that we are entering into now.

Really?

Yes. Humans are entering the most glorious period of spiritual evolution at this time. Let's say hundreds, and perhaps thousands, will be enlightened in your lifetime. It will gather pace over this century and the next century and billions of humans will be enlightened by the time this spiritual cycle reaches its peak.

Will a specific religion be more important than others in this grand spiritual transformation on Earth?

If you think of each religion of the world as a river that flows through and unites many lands, then spirituality would be like a vast ocean that unites the whole Earth. *The ocean simply rests where it is.* Organized religions, as you know them now, will not exist in the glorious matriarchal period that we are entering into in the near future. Like the ocean, there shall be a spiritual awareness that embraces all of humanity.

So, are you suggesting "one" spiritual path for all?

No, we are not suggesting one path for all. We are simply observing that spiritual awareness will be felt as real as the awareness of your senses. You will know yourself as the *spirit* and feel the *oneness with the spirit*, which is the true meaning of *spiritual* awareness. Only the blind carry beliefs about the sun; those who can see the sun do not argue about its existence. As the collective emphasis shifts from fighting and survival to love and joy, the spirit will shine forth again for all to see. Strong patriarchal beliefs of organized religions will slowly lose their grip over the masses.

22

Ananda and Devadatta

Earlier you said that thousands of people became Arahants and that hundreds were fully enlightened during the time of Buddha. Yet, Buddha also had two cousins named *Ananda* and *Devadatta*. Ananda became his personal attendant and Devadatta became his archenemy. Neither of them got enlightened during Buddha's lifetime.

Both were too attached to Buddha. Ananda was attached positively and my brother, Devadatta, was attached negatively. They both focused their mind on Buddha so much that they forgot about themselves.

But wasn't Devadatta too ambitious and very self-centered?

Yes: almost all of Devadatta's thoughts were about comparing himself to Buddha. Due to the gift of his siddhis,[20] he had a big "spiritual" ego. So even when he thought about himself, he mostly thought about Buddha. He had a big imbalance in his lower two chakras. Extreme negative emotions of jealousy, envy, and hate arose from his Second Chakra because he could not measure up to Buddha in his own mind. The imbalances in his first two chakras manifested as delusions of his ego in his Third Chakra. He forgot that he was his higher self and fell under the spell of his ego.

This is the main choice in the Third Chakra; one either surrenders to the soul path or to the ego path. It is hard to be on one's soul path if one feels lack and fear from the First Chakra and emotional turmoil from the Second Chakra. Much surrender is needed to open the first two chakras so that one may surrender one's egotistical worldview in the Third Chakra and begin to receive guidance from one's higher self—what Buddha called becoming a Sotapanna.

So, did Devadatta not even become a Sotapanna?

He did not.

How was he able to be so influential in the Sangha if he was not even a Sotapanna? The scriptures say that he created a schism in the Sangha and persuaded many monks to leave Buddha and go with him instead.

The name Devadatta means "given from God." He was born with the gift of psychic powers. As he experimented with meditation, he soon realized these psychic gifts; he could change his body at will; he could sense what others were feeling; and he could read into the future. He deluded many about his spiritual attainment using his psychic powers.

Did he not see his own downfall if he could read into the future?

This is the danger of having a psychic ability without having opened the lower chakras. Psychic powers by themselves give you neither wisdom nor enlightenment. They are a gift, and one must know how to use the gift properly. One has to either open one's lower chakras, or, if one has not fully opened the lower chakras, then one must work to keep these chakras dormant—like what the great Shamans do with much prayer, meditation, and seclusion. Otherwise, one sees selectively into the future using the filter of one's ego to delude oneself.

Devadatta saw through his Third Eye that many disciples of Buddha would become his disciples, but through the filter of his ego he could not see that soon after leaving Buddha, they would leave him and return to Buddha.

Is the future deterministic? With perfect foresight, could Devadatta have seen that the monks would leave him and go back to Buddha?

There are quantum choices that arise out of your free will and you can co-create alternative realities based on these choices, but once you have made these choices you are on a deterministic path based on the law of Karma until you are faced again with more quantum choices. Some choices put you on your soul path, while other choices put you on your ego path. Ultimately, both paths reach the same destination. As you get closer to the destination you have fewer detours, because you are more familiar with both paths and more in a state of surrender to your soul path.

Did you say that both paths reach the same destination?

Every person, including Devadatta, is destined to be fully enlightened.

Oh, I see! That explains Buddha's prediction that Devadatta would be fully enlightened and become a great future Buddha himself, despite the fact that he made multiple attempts to kill Buddha.

Yes, that is true! While the ultimate destination is the same for all, some will get there sooner than others who may take a detour.

So, has Devadatta since reincarnated and become enlightened?

No, he has not. Let's say that he is in a limbo, waiting to be reincarnated.

But it has been almost two and a half millennia!

Laughter! The compassionate Buddha gave him many opportunities, but he insisted on a longer detour.

Okay! I have another question about one's psychic abilities. There are many who go to spiritual healers and psychics who have abilities similar to those of Devadatta. Is this a good thing for people to do?

Many hold space for ancestors, guides, angels, and divine beings to communicate with humans. We do not have a judgment regarding this. The best advice we can give you is to surrender your ego and open up to the higher self so that you can be your own healer and your own psychic. When we say, "be your own psychic," we do not mean that you listen to your ego. What we mean is that you connect with your ancestors, angels, guides, divine beings, and your higher self. Know that each one of you on Earth can receive guidance from the Heavens through the opening in your Third Chakra.

Buddha's cousin, Ananda, did not have unusual psychic abilities but he was spiritually far ahead of Devadatta. Ananda remained a Sotapanna for most of his life and became an Arahant only after Buddha's death. Yet, Buddha trusted Ananda to lead meditations and give wisdom talks to the entire Sangha because Ananda was open in his Third Chakra and received much from that space. He practiced dharma with great humility, devotion, and compassion towards all. In contrast, Devadatta stayed in his ego and eventually lost his psychic abilities because of the Karma he created from that space. Ananda received more wisdom from his Third Chakra than what Devadatta received from his Third Eye.

The scriptures say that Buddha had two chief male disciples named Sariputta and Moggallana. Sariputta was known for his wisdom, and Moggallana for his psychic abilities. Similarly, Buddha had two chief female disciples named Khema and Uppalavanna. Khema was known for her wisdom, and Uppalavanna for her psychic abilities.

They were chosen to create a balance together. You and Jade have wondered at times why we have asked *both* of you to help bring our words to the world. It is for the same reason.

Interesting! What prevented Ananda from becoming an Arahant while Buddha was alive? I find it strange that he remained only a Sotapanna while thousands became Arahants around him.

Think of many who spent their whole lives serving others but were not enlightened until their very end. We told you earlier how Mother Teresa had a profound awakening the month before she crossed over. Ananda's story is not so different from Mother Teresa's. Unlike other disciples in the Sangha, Ananda did not have extended periods of solitude in which he could let go of everything and totally empty his mind. Let us say he became attached to serving Buddha.

Are you saying that our service to Buddha can become an attachment too?

Yes, but do not judge this, for it is a part of the divine timing to let go of an ascended one like Buddha. The danger of letting go of the attachment to the ascended one too early is that your ego will attach itself to something else, which will again become a trap. So serving the ascended ones like Buddha or Christ with an *awareness* of our attachments to these beings can be a much easier path to move beyond all attachments, including the attachment to these divine beings. When you serve without any attachments to your *ego*, the will of the divine becomes your will. *This is true surrender.*

Both Ananda and the Mother Teresa were Sotapanna for most of their lives. But unlike Devadatta who died unenlightened, both Ananda and Mother Teresa attained the highest levels of enlightenment in the final stages of their lives as they let go of all attachments and surrendered completely. As I said earlier, there is also a timing issue in this. For example, in my lifetime as Yasodhara I was able to let go of my attachment to Buddha as I *surrendered all* before he returned to the palace after his enlightenment.

23

Beyond Within and Without

It is interesting that as Yasodhara you found enlightenment in whatever unfolded, but Siddhartha went to the extremes to find enlightenment.

> He was back at the beginning rediscovering himself. Just as Vishnu was always *within*, Siddhartha was always *without* to the extreme. As Siddhartha, he kept looking without in order to find himself within. But he simply needed to surrender to what was right there in front of him, which was something beyond "within" and "without."

So, initially, he was looking "without," meaning he was trying to escape from his princely life, and then later he continued to look "without" as he denied his needs in the jungles.

> Yes, and in both ways he was searching outside of himself in his mind. He had to surrender

to what he had *here and now,* as both extremes represented different aspects of his ego.

So, all he had to do was be here and now, wherever he was?

Yes. That is always the answer.

And is that what he found in the end, when he found the *middle way*?

Yes. Laughter!

You said Lord Vishnu was always within. So is that the "here and now?"

No. He was absorbed *within.*

Is this when you chose him from all the angelic beings to be your husband?

Yes.

So, are you saying that Siddhartha was too *without,* and Vishnu was too *within*?

Yes.

Are you saying that the center that we are all searching for is beyond both within and without? In other words, going within can be as much an illusion as staying without?

Laughter! Everything is an illusion. Even when we look at a rainbow, it is an illusion. So you have answered the question.

If you think of a child, they do not determine what is *in* or what is *out*. They have no decision about life or death, within or without; they just are. Laughter!

That is a beautiful insight. So, the whole judgment of within and without comes from the mind. And when we get out of our minds, we go beyond the duality of within and without.

Exactly!

But don't we begin our spiritual journey by going within, and not without?

Spiritual journey begins as you stop seeking outwardly, which feels as if you are going inward because that is how the mind interprets it. So, when the spiritual teachers say, "go within," what they really mean is "stop seeking without." One reaches a point in one's journey when any distinction between within and without is also seen as *without*—a part of the duality of the mind.

Aha, I get it now. When Vishnu was so within, how did you get him out of that place within?

Get him out? Laughter! This was the purpose of my seduction, which was no seduction at all. Most who came to him were in a quest seeking to disturb him because they could not find within themselves what they desired. When I came to him, I sat and manifested what I desired myself. This is what caused a curiosity in his heart that drew him to me. He saw in me that which he sought to manifest in himself and he simply opened up to it. As he surrendered to me in our sacred union he ascended to his Seventh Chakra.

But was he not fully ascended when you chose him?

I came to him as a Goddess when he identified himself as the preserver of the worlds. He was all of existence and all of time—past, present, and future, which was his experience of being in the Sixth Chakra. He was everything that ever existed or exists now or will exist in the future. As he opened his Seventh Chakra he dropped his identification even with existence, which he finally saw as an illusion.

So, when Vishnu saw himself as "all of existence and as the preserver of the worlds," did that also represent a very subtle attachment?

Yes. This is not always what the world has understood but that does not mean that no one has understood it. These things that we teach are for those who want a fuller understanding of their infinite higher selves.

So, is he no longer the preserver of the worlds?

From the illusion of mind, it is not possible to imagine the final liberation. When that moment arrived, he became both existence and non-existence, and went beyond both. He was no longer identified with his role as the preserver of the worlds, just like Lord Shiva in the moment of his liberation was no longer identified with his role as the destroyer of worlds. After their liberation and ascension, they both continue to play their roles but without any attachments. Know that the subtlest attachments to the roles make up the invisible tail of the mind.

24

Flowers of Joy

Listening to you feels so nourishing to my soul.

The essence of a flower heals the one who partakes of it. The fragrance of a flower raises the vibration of the one who smells it. So, think of us divine beings as *flowers of joy* that you may use to heal your soul. The more you drop your limiting beliefs about us, the more deeply you shall connect with our essence.

Think of Buddha: was he an atheist? Did he reject divine beings, such as angels and Gods and Goddesses? Let me tell you that Buddha rejected the limiting *beliefs* about divine beings but not the *experience* of being divine or fully enlightened. It is the limitation of beliefs that takes one away from experiencing the divine in different religions.

Hmm....what kinds of beliefs take one away from experiencing the divine?

> *The belief that you need God.* You can raise your vibration with the sweet nectar of divine beings. You can also raise your vibration by simply surrendering to your own higher self. All divine beings are manifestations of the deepest part of your higher self. While divine beings can help much with your spiritual journey towards enlightenment, you do not need them.
>
> *The belief that God is male and singular.* Know that in this great garden of universes, divine beings blossom like flowers of joy. Divine beings may express themselves as Gods, Goddesses, or androgynous forms, all joined in oneness with infinities merging into larger infinities. Know that the source of the highest infinity is within you. It is your infinite higher self, made up of nothing but the ever-expanding emptiness.
>
> *The belief that God judges you.* Love is life vibrating at a high frequency and divine beings are love vibrating at infinite frequencies. All judgments dissolve in such divine love.
>
> *The belief that God wants to control you.* Divine beings exist in a purposeless ecstasy. Why would a flower that is so complete in and of itself have any desire to control you?

Wow! This really lightens the word "God"!

The word "God" represents the deepest expression of your higher self in many religions. But the word is not the experience of your higher self. The patriarchal religions have repressed the experience of God and perverted its meaning for political reasons. The experience of God transcends the mind and shines through even the smallest spaces of emptiness that lie between thoughts.

How do we transcend the mind to experience our higher self?

Think of the beautiful resplendent sun. The sun just *is*. It is a transformative energy beyond the concepts and beliefs of the mind. There are many beliefs attached to even the sun and the elements. As you make a discovery of each new belief, you in your choices as a human may say, "I release that, and I see more clearly." So, your thoughts about the stars are like little beliefs in the sky. As the human race allows itself to discover more, it shall see that stars are much more than little twinkling lights or big burning suns: they are the heart-essence of a vast and mystical spiritual reality. So, if you look up in the sky on a clear dark night and consciously release every belief you have about the stars, something very immense will open up within you. We are not saying that the scientific beliefs about the stars are not true. But a mind attached to beliefs does not feel the incredible beauty and mystery of the stars. In order to feel the beauty and mystery one has to surrender to the emptiness that transcends the mind.

As a Goddess, can you share a little of what it feels like to live in this emptiness that transcends the mind?

Laughter! Let us look again at the experience of making love. My beloved and myself were joined in that primordial joy and it went on forever until someone brought our attention to our minds. I have shared this with you before, and I will share it again. As soon as our attention was brought to our mind, there was a thought which manifested an entire new creation.

Of the universe?

Of a universe.

Oh, I see! So, there are many universes...?

Infinities exist within infinities in an ever-expanding play of consciousness.

So, even our universe may have been created by the love-making of Gods?

Yes, it was.

...And there may be an infinite number of universes?

There is a lot more going on here than what your mind can comprehend. This is why it is important for you to clear the lower three chakras so that you may begin to explore those universes within.

Is it literally true that there are universes within us?

Yes. Your higher self is truly infinite. Those who have been on the other side have occasionally come back to share these experiences.

You described the forever nature of the experience of making love when you and your beloved were in this primordial joy beyond mind. Can humans, who are in the mind, reach this place through love?

The love between my beloved and myself was beyond our bodies; it was the merging of our higher selves. To come to this place in a human body, the sexual energy must transform into Vajra energy that joins all chakras into oneness. There are many writings on this from the ancient times, but one needs much surrender to be on this path.

Is this the path of Kundalini Yoga?

There are many paths that seek to unify the physical with the spiritual including Kundalini Yoga, Shaktism, Vajrayana, Tantra, and such. One has to be careful, however, as these paths require much integrity and balance for spiritual awakening. There is also the danger of Kundalini energy rising too quickly before the energies of fear and ego are completely clear from the lower chakras, so it requires an enlightened teacher to be one's guide.

Does an enlightened teacher have the same level of realization as a God, a Goddess, or the Infinite Source?

Laughter! The first explosion into bliss feels so complete that some enlightened teachers feel that they have merged fully with the Infinite Source. However, the idea that one has attained the highest level with the first explosion becomes an impediment in one's realization of higher enlightenments. Infinity never ends!

So, there is growth even for enlightened teachers?

Yes. Enlightened teachers are on a strong path to become *ascended beings* by opening all of their seven chakras, just like our beloved Buddha. It begins with the emptying of the mind through the opening and aligning of the lower three chakras. The death of the ego in the third chakra awakens the primordial joy in which everything becomes one. Then, the opening of higher chakras lead to higher levels of enlightenment and deeper experiences of oneness: a blossoming of love for the trees and the stars occurs with the opening of the Fourth Chakra; the *expression* of joy and love into the world occurs with the opening of the Fifth Chakra; a complete opening to all there *IS*—the past, the present, and the future occurs with the opening of the Sixth Chakra; and the ultimate flowering that is beyond existence and non-existence occurs with the opening of the Seventh Chakra.

Do the higher chakras open in a linear, sequential manner?

No, many chakras open and close together in a non-linear manner, and often enlightenment happens with many chakras opening simultaneously. After the opening of the first three chakras, each higher level of enlightenment can feel like one has arrived at the final destination from the perspective of the mind dissolving into emptiness. However, while the mind no longer occupies the infinite center of one's being, it still exists on the finite surface and it tries to protect that which has been attained, creating an almost invisible ego in the lower three chakras with each higher level of enlightenment. As one moves higher, the mind surrenders more of this residual ego, the tail of it that was left, until everything is gone with the opening of all seven chakras.

So, what you are saying is that even the enlightened teachers have a tail of the ego that creates illusions.

Yes. *The tail is the illusion.* As they say, the whole body of the elephant passes through the eye of the needle, but the tail gets stuck. One needs to move deeper into emptiness to see the almost invisible tail. The residual ego cannot see this tail *because it is the tail.*

Okay, so what should one do?

Meditate and be open to receiving divine grace. Even enlightened teachers can meditate until they become *fully enlightened* Buddhas with the opening of all seven chakras.

What happens after all seven chakras are open?

At this point one has surrendered all one is able to as a human, and one has ascended beyond the Earth and the Heavens.

Is there growth beyond even the opening of seven chakras?

Growth is forever! One may choose to come back as an ascended being in other universes to know the play of consciousness in these universes. The journey continues even for divine beings. The infinite expansion continues forever as infinities

dissolve into emptiness, which then keep opening to deeper infinities. The merging happens
in multiple dimensions as Gods and Goddesses
merge into higher Gods and Goddesses.

Oh, so it is truly forever! And you are growing too, even
as a Goddess?

Yes.

There was a point that I came to in my journey where a
book by Jiddu Krishnamurti helped me tremendously. Can
you tell us more about him?

He reached up to his Fifth Chakra, more than
most enlightened teachers have attained in these
times. He spoke much about *how the mind can
see its own prison* and be liberated beyond mind.
However, his message did not reach the world in
the way he had imagined. So, even though he had
many followers around the world, only three were
enlightened by following his path.

Are you saying that more people could have been
enlightened if his message had unfolded differently?

His message was his message. It is a beautiful message about healing the mind for those
who are too much in the mind. This being said,
his belief about how this message would enlighten
many humans was incorrect. For much of his life

he carried the belief that his path would enlighten many humans, though less passionately as he grew older. He was often in tears because his listeners would get much in their minds trying to understand his message about getting out of their minds. Laughter!

Don't we understand any message using the mind?

Instead of thinking how to get out of a thinking mind, one can directly engage in practices that use one's body, soul, and higher self to dissolve the mind. Devotion to divine beings with prayers, chants, and mantras can also help dissolve the mind.

Why did he not consider other ways of freeing oneself from the mind?

There was potential for him to reach higher as a world teacher like Gautama Buddha, but due to certain events from his childhood he became skeptical of the teachings based on faith and devotion. He rebelled against these and became, instead, a teacher of *inquiry* and *doubt* as practices to reach enlightenment. His was a path of negation of the mind, using the mind.

Aha! So, can faith and devotion enlighten also, unlike what Krishnamurti preached?

The path of negation and the path of affirmation can both open and align the lower three chakras in order to experience the first big enlightenment. But higher enlightenments with the opening of the higher chakras happen mostly by divine grace!

Oh, like Sri Ramakrishna's surrender to Goddess Kali?

Yes. Or like hundreds who became ascended beings by the grace of Buddha, including Angulimala.[21]

Aha! And only three were enlightened on Krishnamuti's path?

Yes, and even those three did not become *ascended beings.*

Are there ascended beings on Earth at this time?

No, but some have opened six chakras and are on their way. While an enlightened teacher may help millions open their lower chakras, an ascended being can recognize and enlighten those who are completely ripe like Angulimala. An ascended being is also a pathway for the enlightened ones to ascend fully with the opening of their Seventh Chakra.

Some Buddhist scriptures say that Gods and Goddesses are *lower* than ascended beings, such as Buddha.

> Buddha spoke of those enlightened souls who had the first four or more chakras open and chose to remain in the heavenly realms instead of incarnating on Earth at that time. While these enlightened beings had many psychic powers, which made them appear like Gods and Goddesses to humans who meditated upon them, they were not fully enlightened and did not have all seven chakras open like the Buddha. During the time of Buddha's life, there were many such Gods and Goddesses in the heavenly realms. However, when we speak of Gods and Goddesses in this book, we mean *ascended* Gods and Goddesses who have opened at least the first seven chakras. For example, the ascended Goddess *Tara* came from another universe with many more chakras open, and her infinite compassion blesses many worlds and universes.

Are these "Gods and Goddesses" who are not *fully* enlightened still in the heavenly realms?

> Some have chosen to remain in the high Heavens like the great Bodhisattvas. Others have chosen to ascend fully into the expanding realms of infinite emptiness. And yet, others have chosen to descend to experience more contrast on Earth before returning home. Some who chose to ascend

did so by birthing into the heavenly realms. Others chose to incarnate on Earth and ascend from that place, knowing that doing this would allow their light to touch humans more directly.

Many of these "Gods and Goddesses" that you speak of are from the same soul tribe that Saraswati spoke about in the first part of this book. This was a very large soul tribe with a specific spiritual mission to allow billions of souls to descend into contrast and then help them ascend back into an even greater emptiness.

25

Secrets of a Soul Tribe

Can you tell us more about soul tribes—what are they and how do they manifest?

The easiest way to experience contrast is through incarnations in the physical realms. Members of a soul tribe incarnate with one another in both meaningful and challenging relationships, creating karmic ties with one another over many lifetimes. Initially, the relationships are joyful as the souls begin their journey from a place of high spiritual awareness. Slowly, as the soul continues to incarnate and descends into karmic ties with the members of its soul tribe, it experiences pain, fear, and other negative emotions. After experiencing enough contrast, the soul reverses its journey on the path of ascension, remembering what it had intentionally forgotten. The compassion between the members of the soul tribe allows them to create contrast for one another, and then ascend back into greater emptiness. Some members of a soul tribe may get enlightened and ascend at similar times as they resolve and release their karma together. This is what happened with our soul tribe: some of us chose to ascend together in the lifetime that Saraswati spoke of.

Is this the same lifetime in which Saraswati ji spoke the words that helped manifest your incarnations as Sita, Radha, and Yasodhara?

Yes.

What occurred after your ascension in that lifetime?

Some of us chose to incarnate at different times on Earth to help with the unfolding of the new soul cycle. Remember, the words Saraswati spoke came from a great knowing, which included the agreement that we had all made with our higher selves. So, even as she spoke, her words were based on the *choices* that all of us had agreed upon already from a higher place. Since some of us opened all seven chakras in that lifetime, we ascended each time we incarnated again, and returned to an even greater emptiness of our higher selves. As divine beings, some of us birthed new universes in order to create the contrast that expanded our emptiness even more.

...you birthed new universes?

Someday you shall also realize yourself as a divine being and perhaps birth universes. Laughter!

Really? Even my soul could birth universes?

If you choose to do so. Creation of contrast by birthing universes expands emptiness to an even greater infinite version of itself.

So, we are equal in some sense?

Yes, we are equal! The curtain is being pulled back, finally. You simply have to see yourself as that emptiness in which we are all *one*. A portion of your infinite soul falls to experience *that which it is not* in order to create contrast. Falling into the suffering of body sensations, emotional turmoil, and egoic delusions is part of the path of each and every soul. Some souls may experience less contrast, while others may experience more in a given lifetime, but all souls experience enough contrast over many lifetimes. Experiencing contrast allows a soul to experientially know that which it is not, and to rediscover all of the *soul feelings* it will need when it ascends back to its higher self and creates its own worlds.

Not only are you divine beings, but you will also grow into even higher divine beings, as expansion into emptiness continues forever. As one grows more, one has a more ecstatic experience of the primordial joy, a more unifying experience of oneness, and a deeper experience of emptiness. You may say that one has a deeper embodiment of the emptiness that pervades the universes within and without in many dimensions. The time has come for humanity to let go of their illusion of being anything less.

If emptiness is everywhere, why do we not sense it in our everyday life?

You are always connected to emptiness because you are made up of emptiness and live in it, but the connection is so subtle that you cannot feel it. Searching for it is like the fish searching for the water they live in. Searching hides what you are looking for, but it is the nature of the mind to always search. You have to keep surrendering in this journey. Since the journey is infinite, there is no reason to hurry.

You said earlier that some members of your soul tribe chose to reincarnate together when the new soul cycle unfolded. Could you say more about this?

Yes; as I said, it was a plan that we all agreed upon even before Saraswati uttered those prophetic words that co-created our paths as her soulmates. Some of us chose to work together more closely than others. While a few of us incarnated, others held the space from above. We took turns doing this growing both in the physical realms and the spiritual realms until we fully realized our higher selves.

Did your soul tribe realize its mission?

We took births to create new paths, which in turn created what the world now sees as the Hindu and Buddhist pantheons. Shiva incarnated frequently to keep the flame of Vedanta burning in India. After ushering in Kali Yuga in the form of Krishna, Vishnu incarnated a few more times to create new paths that formed and shaped Buddhism, which balanced and complemented Shiva's work in Vedanta. Parvati, Saraswati and I incarnated *both* in Vedanta and in Buddhism at different points.

Really? Why would you all incarnate in *different* religion*s*?

From the larger soul perspective, we do not see the separation between religions as humans do. The feminine paths associated with different religions have more in common with each other and less in common with the masculine paths associated with these religions. We incarnated both in Vedanta and Buddhism to balance these paths with our divine feminine energies.

For example, consider the incarnations of dear Saraswati. She incarnated in many lives that have not been written about. Sometimes she came with a partner to simply hold the feminine space. They would be like two high-energy human beings, very good, angelic types of people, but not so angelic that they would not be human. Her work was not always scholarly in these lives, but rather it was to change the energies of the harsher, negative emotions into the lighter soul feelings.

While she chose to incarnate over and over again, let me tell you about three incarnations of hers that helped in the creation of some new paths of spiritual wisdom. In her first incarnation that she has spoken of already, she manifested the causes and conditions for the creation and expression of the great wisdom of Vedanta. These causes and conditions allowed her soulmates to fall into contrast and then rise above it, manifesting the human incarnations of Vishnu, Shiva, Parvati, myself, and others.

In her second incarnation, she came as a partner of the Bodhisattva, *Manjusri*, who founded the *Mahayana* path in Buddhism. In this incarnation, she scribed and composed many scriptures of the Mahayana path.

In her third incarnation, she came as a friend and consort of *Padmasambhava*, who established the *Vajrayana* path in Buddhism in Bhutan, Nepal, and Tibet. In this incarnation, she scribed and composed many scriptures of the Vajrayana path.

Oh, really? Saraswati ji incarnated as the great female Buddha, Yeshe Tsyogal, with Padmasambhava (also known *Guru Rinpoche*)?

Yes! Her path in this life was to support Padmasambhava by writing about the feminine side of Buddhism. This path *unifies* tantric body practices, soul feelings, and meditations on emptiness to bring a faster enlightenment. Many have become fully enlightened in just one lifetime following the Vajrayana path, which creates an exalted union between the energies of the divine feminine and the divine masculine, allowing the mind to quickly dissolve into emptiness. Know that with each new incarnation on Earth, Saraswati's higher self expanded into an even greater realm of emptiness. The same happened with Vishnu after he became *fully enlightened.*

How did Vishnu become fully enlightened?

As Vishnu's heart melted when he gazed upon countless realms of suffering, he surrendered even more and became a Bodhisattva with 'six of his chakras open. He became fully enlightened after I chose him from the assembly of many Gods who desired to be with me. As a result of our sacred union, his Seventh Chakra opened and he dropped his identification with all of existence, which was his prior experience of enlightenment with only six chakras open. In this state of pure emptiness, nothing *real* is ever created, preserved, or destroyed. This occurred at the end of the Vedic period.

We birthed new universes after his ascension, and he sent many manifestations of himself, both as emanations in the heavenly realms and as incarnations in the physical realms, to end suffering in different world systems. In your world, Vishnu manifested as Rama, Krishna, Sugata Buddha, and Gautama Buddha. After passing over as Sugata Buddha, he merged with Saraswati and realized himself as the primordial *Adi Buddha*. From this place of emptiness, he sent numerous emanations of himself that created spiritual *pure lands*.

Oh, so Saraswati ji helped Lord Vishnu realize himself as *Adi Buddha?*

Yes. Vishnu became Adi Buddha after he passed over as Sugata Buddha and merged with Saraswati in her manifestation as *Prajnaparamita*— also known as the mother of all Buddhas.

Is *Prajnaparamita* none other than Saraswati ji?

Yes—she is the divine mother, the Goddess of primordial wisdom. She inspired the *Prajnaparamita sutras* on the Mahayana path and tantric practices on the Vajrayana path. From her spiritual abode, she offered the transcendental wisdom of emptiness to Gautama Buddha, Bodhisattva Manjusri, Bodhisattva Avalokitesvara, and others, with Sutras such as *The Diamond Sutra*, *The Lotus Sutra*, and *The Heart Sutra*[22]

Oh really? This is truly fascinating! I am surprised that Saraswati ji is so deeply present in Buddhism, but this is not how she is seen in Buddhism. According to the Buddhist scriptures, Prajnaparamita and Yeshe Tsyogyal helped inspire and create the main scriptures of *Mahayana* Buddhism and *Vajrayana* Buddhism, respectively. Can you tell us more about these two paths in Buddhism?

The *Mahayana* path provides a radical way to free the mind from self-nature, including the subtlest attachments of the ego. The true meaning of *emptiness* is not the absence of phenomena, but a complete dissolution of self-nature, or ego. In order to help dissolve the self-nature, the Mahayana path uses the Bodhisattva vow of enlightening others *before* enlightening oneself. Feeling the primordial joy of enlightening others before one's own enlightenment melts the boundaries between the self and the other. While the bodhisattva vow creates infinite compassion, a subtle distinction between the self and the other remains, *for the vow is based on this distinction*. However, by repeatedly feeling the primordial joy of enlightenment for others, a point arrives on the Mahayana path when *even the self is seen as the other*. As the infinite compassion reaches out to the self, *which is seen as the other*, the boundary between the self and the other melts away completely, and the Bodhisattva realizes themself as Buddha.

The *Vajrayana* path is built on the Mahayana path and is even more holistic because it uses the whole range of body sensations and the diverse set of soul feelings, from sensuality and joy, to faith and devotion, which allow the mind to surrender to emptiness. The Vajrayana path is closest to the divine feminine path of joy that Saraswati and I bring to you through this book.

Most Hindus think of Saraswati ji as the partner of Lord Brahma and you as the partner of Lord Vishnu. However, from what you have shared earlier it seems that *both* Saraswati ji and you were Lord Vishnu's spiritual partners in either the physical realms or in the higher realms. Could you speak more about this?

Yes. Vishnu's surrender to Saraswati and myself expanded his emptiness greatly. Souls evolve spiritually with different soulmates. This is true for human beings as well as divine beings. In another lifetime, both Saraswati and I were the wives of the great Bodhisattva, Manjusri. Saraswati composed additional teachings of the *Prajnaparamita Sutras* in that incarnation.

Really? Both Saraswati ji and you incarnated with *Manjusri?* This might be hard for both the Hindu and Buddhists to believe.

You will find evidence of this in the near future.

What is Saraswati ji's relationship with Lord Brahma? Some say she is his daughter, and others say she is his wife.

Brahma and Saraswati arose together as twin flames. They both help in the creation of new soul cycles on Earth.

Saraswati ji is recognized in Buddhism as a fully enlightened being. However, the Buddhist scriptures do not speak of Lord Vishnu as a fully enlightened being. Why is this so?

In the initial Vedic period, Vishnu was an enlightened being and was considered a God by his followers because of his psychic powers. However, only his first four chakras were open at that time. With higher enlightenments, the opening of more of his chakras, and his subsequent incarnations in Vedanta and Buddhism, Vishnu transformed into a Bodhisattva, a Buddha, and then into an ascended God. Remember that even Gods and Goddesses are expanding forever into deeper realms of emptiness.

What is the difference between a Buddha and an ascended God? Is one state higher than another?

Is a sunflower higher than a rose? Some might say it is! But truly, are not all flowers equal? Are they not all joined with Mother Earth in their profound bliss, which is felt by all who care to look, touch, and smell them?

After the first big enlightenment with the opening and aligning of the lower three chakras, all beliefs about lower and higher dissolve with the dissolution of the mind. All comparisons about states of enlightenment arise from a dualistic mind, which does not exist after enlightenment. There is great joy even if one chooses to remain in the same place for eons. While there is always spiritual progression, the progression serves the whole, and not just the ego, after one's enlightenment.

You may think of spiritual progression as follows: A God or Goddess is an enlightened being in the heavenly realms with at least the first four chakras opened. Such a being feels profound compassion and seeks to end the suffering of all sentient beings. A God or a Goddess does not have to incarnate in the physical realms to get fully enlightened, but he or she may *choose* to incarnate to help heal sentient beings.

A bodhisattva is a God or Goddess in the heavenly realms *or* an enlightened human being in the physical realm who dedicates their life to enlightening others before becoming fully enlightened.

A Buddha is a fully enlightened being—also called an ascended being—with all seven chakras open. Numerous emanations and incarnations of a Buddha reach out with compassion in different world systems. The state of Buddhahood is not static because even Buddhas grow into deeper realms of emptiness with the opening of more chakras, forever.

An *ascended* God or Goddess (whom you may call a *Mahadeva* or *Mahadevi*, respectively) is a fully enlightened being *who chooses to birth new universes* after having served in the different universes with numerous incarnations and emanations.

So, is an ascended God or Goddess vaster than a Buddha?

You have chosen to not have your own children in this lifetime. Do you feel another human being is vaster than you simply because he or she has chosen to have their own children, and you have not?

No!

So, it is similar to this. Not having your own child does not prevent you from feeling oneness with all children of the world. There are Buddhas who are much vaster than ascended Gods and Goddesses, and there are ascended Gods and Goddesses who are much vaster than Buddhas. The expansion in the deeper realms of emptiness has nothing to do with whether one births new universes or not. It is an endless journey into infinite realms of emptiness that exist already and are expanding forever.

Aha! All of this information is so different from my previous understanding of Hinduism and Buddhism. It is fascinating that so many beings from your soul tribe, including Saraswati, Vishnu, and you, created so much of what we know today as Buddhism.

Know that many who have attained Buddhahood in this Yuga are incarnations of Gods and Goddesses from our soul tribe. The time has come to reveal this secret to the world. These Gods and Goddesses had accumulated merit from their previous lifetimes, which allowed them to be born into the heavenly realms. Some have chosen to become Bodhisattvas and have become fully enlightened in these realms, while others incarnated on Earth to get enlightened and to spread the teachings.

I have shared the stories of incarnations of Saraswati and Vishnu from the Vedas and Vedanta in order to teach you about the spiritual progression that is available to every human as we transition into a new Yuga at this time. Also, let me share that even Goddess Parvati incarnated on the Buddhist path in one incarnation.

Oh, really? When?

Parvati incarnated between 4th and 5th centuries CE in a place that is northwest of India. She was born as a male child, and the mother of this gifted child took him to a Buddhist monastery at a very young age. As the child grew older, he dedicated his life to the Buddhist path in this monastery. He was fully enlightened by the age of thirty. Through the body of this male Buddha, Parvati dedicated this lifetime to writing a vast number of Akashic records that are in print even today in many parts of India. As a fully enlightened male Buddha, Parvati meditated and received information from Shiva day after day, month after month, and year after year for forty-seven years.

Often this is how soulmates, even ascended ones, do their work in the physical realm. One soulmate holds the space from above and guides the other soulmate to accomplish their particular mission on Earth.

It is fascinating that Goddess Parvati incarnated as a *male Buddha* and received Akashic records from Lord Shiva! It all seems so interconnected—as if Hinduism and Buddhism are really one stream, and not two.

This is true! Many who realized Buddhahood even during the lifetime of Gautama Buddha were the Gods and Goddesses from our soul tribe who incarnated in order to ascend into emptiness. It was useful for Hinduism and Buddhism to be seen as two separate streams in the external world, until now. Up until this point their perceived separateness allowed a balance between the acceleration of contrast at the end of Kali Yuga, and a gradual awakening into enlightenment as we transition into the Satya Yuga. But as the contrast plays itself out fully with the transition of Yugas, different spiritual streams, including Hinduism and Buddhism, shall again join into oneness.

Can you tell us more about the Akashic records?

Think of how a computer can store vast amounts of information on a very small chip. Similarly, every thought, emotion, feeling, action, and event in the universe is recorded in the infinite spaces of the high-dimensional realms. The information that is of most interest to any soul is the mission the soul has agreed to accomplish on its soul path when all came into existence. Akashic records allow souls to know how their past karma supports or impedes their journey on their chosen soul paths. These records can be helpful when a new soul enters the contrast of physicality, or when an old soul desires to ascend back into emptiness. The information matrix of the Akashic records is so vast that it takes great surrender and skill to receive only the information relevant for one's soul path. While full Akashic records of each and every soul exist in the non-physical realms, summaries of many from our soul tribe were written by Parvati and a few other enlightened beings from our soul tribe.

Where can we find these records?

Did you not find your own Akashic record a few years ago?

Oh, you mean my *Naadi* reading?[23]

Yes, that was your Akashic record written by Parvati when she incarnated as a male Buddha.

Oh wow, this is truly amazing! You are saying that Goddess Parvati herself wrote my Naadi scroll?

Parvati wrote the Naadi scrolls of thousands of members of our soul tribe, including yours. Before incarnating on Earth as a male Buddha, she had already channeled many more Naadi scrolls from the heavenly realms to different Vedic sages. These channeled Naadi scrolls are about the life histories and alternative futures of most members of our large soul tribe.

What is the purpose of Naadi readings?

The most divine purpose of the Naadi readings is to help many awaken to their *soul paths* at this time of accelerated contrast during the transition between Kali Yuga and Satya Yuga.

If you desire, you may share your experience of your Naadi reading.

I was completely blown away by my Naadi reading in Delhi on August 7th, 2013. Only using my thumb-print, the reader knew my name, the names of *both* my parents, and my birth date of October 11th, 1963. Knowing how rudimentary this center is in terms of technology, there was not a chance in the world that the people working there had somehow obtained my information before I arrived. I work as a professor in Amherst, Massachusetts, in the United States. I hardly know anyone in Delhi because I grew up in Mumbai. I took a taxi selected randomly from my hotel to the *Sri Agasthiya Mahasiva Adhi Sukshma Naadi Astrological Centre* without giving away any information prior to my arrival at that center. The only *specific* information I provided them was my thumb print.

That particular reading was one out of the seven Naadi readings that Parvati wrote about alternative soul paths for you in this lifetime. Two paths did not come to fruition because you did not pursue them by your own free will. So, you were not directed to those Naadi readings. In most likelihood, you will choose two of the four remaining paths that lie ahead of you, though you don't have to.

Aha! So there is choice! Thank you! This Naadi reading specifically mentioned you as blessing my life in your form as *Ashta Lakshmi*, which represents eight manifestations of you as an ascended Goddess. The reading also mentioned that I have the blessings of Lord Shiva and Lord Vishnu, and my life being devoted to spiritual work. I still have a recording of this reading.

Through your devotion to me and other divine beings you have dedicated this life to the spiritual transformation of yourself and the larger world. While I am your *root* Guru, you have many divine beings as your teachers in this life.

Also, your mother was your very first teacher, as every mother is to her child.

While your Naadi reading had some very specific personal information, much of it pointed to a path that can play out in many different ways. You always have much freedom in how you wish to walk on your soul path.

The Naadi reading mentioned that I will take an important spiritual journey in the north of India when I turn 54.

Yes, you may go to Nepal, Bhutan, and Tibet to be with the energies of Saraswati, Parvati, and myself. Parvati received and wrote many futures for you to help you with your journey towards enlightenment and to serve the larger mission of our soul tribe. Many such as you from our large soul tribe are awakening to their soul path at this time. The same is happening in other soul tribes on Earth as all of these tribes awaken to their shared spiritual destiny.

Based on your earlier teaching I am guessing that the soul paths of those who are awakening at this time *are diverging from their ego paths.*

Yes! At any given point of time, there are literally an infinite number of futures in this quantum universe. Making choices using only the mind keeps you stuck in your ego path. Letting the mind surrender to your body and soul allows you to awaken to your soul path.

You picked specific futures that Parvati wrote about because your soul, like most other souls, desires to harmonize your soul path with that of our soul tribe at this time. In fact, your *higher self* co-wrote your Naadi reading with Shiva and Parvati.

You may think of your Akashic record as a spiritual GPS that allows your soul to coordinate its mission with the mission of the larger soul tribe. Numerous soul tribes align themselves in a larger *soul constellation* guided by intergalactic divine beings in order to dive into contrast and rise into enlightenment. Billions of souls have come together on Mother Earth at this time to rise into enlightenment as we transition into the next phase of spiritual evolution.

Can you tell Jade and I more about our soul paths in this life?

You and Jade have chosen this life to rediscover and reunite the divine feminine teachings of the ascended Goddesses of many pantheons. The two of you are strong soulmates who desire to awaken and empower the divine feminine in all humans. You are bringing forward the teachings of the Eastern Goddesses, and she may bring forward the teachings of the Western Goddesses. As you join these paths together, all of humanity will come together into more oneness. Our messages of joy, love, and other soul feelings shall bring great blessings to many.

Namaste!

Namaste Lakshmi ji!

PART VI

SELF-TRANSFORMATION WITH JOY

SELF-TRANSFORMATION MANTRA

So Hum

सो sहम्

26

Dark Night of the Soul

Namaste Lakshmi ji!

Namaste!

Today I would like to share my own experience of *contrast.*

Go ahead! We already know everything about you!

My childhood in India was magical. I remember the heartfelt connection that I had with nature, especially with the trees and the mountains. These "wonder years" only lasted until I turned 18, however, because of my journey through a painful mental process. This difficult journey affected my mind in all waking hours for nine straight months. It literally destroyed every shred of happiness I knew. If there was hell on Earth, this time was that for me. Much to my surprise, this process ultimately became an "awakening" for me in that the pain dissolved with a single insight from a Zen book named *The Sound of the One Hand*. My suffering was wiped out in a flash when I was prompted, through this book, to *accept* the painful thoughts. As I moved my energy into the feeling of *acceptance*, I realized that I had been running away from these painful thoughts with much fear for nine months. The more I tried to run away with fear, the more these thoughts multiplied. The key was to look straight into the fear and accept these thoughts fully. As I did this, the fear and pain dissolved in a flash. Not only did my hellish experience end, but I also had discovered a key that unlocked even other areas of my life. As I fully embraced other fearful sides of myself without any judgments, the fears dissolved. This process of total acceptance allowed me to integrate deeply with all parts of myself by dissolving my fears. Since then, my journey has been simply one of expanding my consciousness by surrendering more and more.

> This was your dark night of the soul. The complete surrendering of your ego opened you up to your soul path. It is like a difficult birth, which puts the mother through much pain and anxiety, but as she releases these, the child bursts forth. This was a process that you had contracted to experience before you incarnated, a process that you had experienced in other lifetimes, and each time it had led you to a higher aspect of yourself. Had you not gone through this process at the age that you were, you would have grown into a closed-minded human being in this lifetime, looking only to the mind for answers. It would have created a terrible

anger that would have disrupted your path in this lifetime. Your heart would have been so harmed that it would have been difficult for you to make the journey to where you are now. The process also helped you free yourself more quickly in your human relationships.

Angels were in attendance with you during this difficult journey to guide you, along with our dear Saraswati, and assisted you as you sought the most purposeful knowledge related to how to bring yourself into the light. I was not assigned to guide you at that time, as Saraswati was your patron until you turned 18. Your guides and angels also helped you to cross this path, knowing that you would be able to recreate joy in your future. Your higher self was aware of this and made preparations during your non-waking hours with the help of your guides. You made a plan with stepping-stones, coincidences, and signs to assist you through this process. That is not a necessary process for you to go through again. So I will say to you that future incarnations for you will not be so horrendous with a test as painful as this again.

Thank God! Why does such pain exist?

It was your soul path to experience it all. There are many that go through this most holy process, as you have ultimately found it to be. It allowed you to free yourself from the mind by opening your lower chakras.

Until my awakening, the pain followed me during all waking hours of the day for nine months.

Through that blessed awakening you glimpsed the emptiness in your First Chakra, and then each time that painful process would return due to your mind going back to the old pattern of resistance, you would catch yourself and surrender again. Slowly, you discovered the knack of dissolving the mind around your First Chakra and the painful process was wiped away from your being. However, your mind around the Second and the Third chakras was yet to be liberated from emotional and egoic processes. It took many more years for you to open the Second Chakra by resolving the emotional attachments you experienced in different relationships through love and forgiveness. Now with your connection to us Goddesses, you are releasing the mind around the Third Chakra and moving into your heart. As you are finding much joy being with nature and simple day-to-day living, you are rediscovering the magical awareness of your childhood and reuniting with your higher self.

Do such painful processes happen to everyone?

Everyone passes through the dark night of their soul. Think of Christ, for instance. As he walked into the desert, he faced his first test: just for a moment he became of a *lower* energy simply because he was lacking in food, water, and those things that sustain the human body. As his energy attracted the negative energy around him, he became *aware* of it. From this awareness he had no fear of that energy taking him down. He simply stated that he was not of that energy, and it left him. You might ask how these fallen angels could have tempted someone as high as Christ. They do because they themselves came from higher realms but fell into the lower realms because of the choices they made. I am not saying that Jesus had low energy at any time. Rather, this is simply a metaphor for him feeling *lower* than what he actually was. But, because there was nothing in his nature that would make him desire to speed up his process, he rejected this negative energy immediately without fearing it. Not everyone will experience the extreme depth of what he had experienced, but all go through their dark night of the soul.

I have always been inspired by how Mother Teresa surrendered her whole life to Christ by serving the poor and the sick. However, I read recently that even Mother Teresa had her own dark night of the soul. Is this true?

When someone with an open heart is walking on the Earth, there is a great healing in the areas where they walk just by their essence being there. Despite her intense spiritual longing for Christ, which became the dark night of her soul, Mother Teresa did not think or say to herself, "how is it that

I can be enlightened?" Instead, she said, "how is it that I may bring joy to others?" In this way, her actions said everything that needed to be said. It was her choice to cross over to the other side. She knew approximately thirty days ahead of time that she would make this choice. She laid herself down like all enlightened beings lay themselves down. She knew that there was much still left to be done on Earth, but she felt the energy of her body wearing out, and so she chose to pass over and create a space for others to take her place.

Did Mother Teresa get "enlightened" during her lifetime?

She had a great opening in her lower chakras in a blissful moment of prayer and surrender when she was in her 30s. It was like a mini enlightenment, but she did not stay with that opening long enough and moved back to her day-to-day responsibilities of caring for others. She gave so much of herself to others that she did not have the time to clear her own pain during most of her life. When she got sick around the time of her transition, she was free of her responsibilities to others and so was able to go deep within with the knowing of that mini enlightenment that had happened before. This journey inward reactivated the dormant lower chakras and this time she completely surrendered whatever remained around those chakras.

As she did this, she had enlightenments upon
enlightenments reaching all the way to her Sixth
Chakra. Jesus came to receive her as she passed
over to the other side.

Oh, really?

She walks with Jesus!

So, it sounds like her sickness became a gift that helped
clear her Karma!

Yes, more than people realize. Many people
heal their Karma through sickness. Did you not go
through a long sickness yourself?

Oh, yes! I was 24 years old when I got extremely sick
and almost died. After that incident my body did not
feel healthy for many years. At one point I was having
difficulty even walking properly. Interestingly, this physical sickness allowed me to have the most magnificent
spiritual experiences over the next 14 years. These experiences would begin at night with me feeling as if I was
dying. As I would begin to go out of my body, a great
healing energy would envelop me and I would feel great
waves of bliss that I have no words for. In fact, there is
nothing that I have experienced in ordinary human
realms that come close to these ecstatic experiences of
oneness with everything. Interestingly, these experiences do not happen as much anymore because my sickness
went away.

That sickness prepared you for the life that lay in front of you and for the work you are doing now. It taught you humility and surrender and how to take one step at a time when you were having difficulty walking and moving forward. If you look around, you would find many who give too much of themselves either to work or to their ambition, and then they get sick from the unbalance. They give themselves the gift of sickness in order to *turn inward*. This gift also allows the loved ones to come together and heal their Karma with the one suffering from the sickness.

If people understood sickness in this way they would not hold such negative beliefs about it and would surrender more easily.

Surrendering would allow them to heal quickly, for the chakras would open and align more easily. There is much clearing of Karma by surrendering during the time of sickness. The surrender allows many who lead a simple and humble life—such as your own father—to have a great opening during the time of sickness around their death.

My father?

His lower three chakras opened as he lay in a coma for three days before he passed over. In that most holy period before he left his body he visited with his higher self, and since he was still in his body, he was able to clear the lower chakras and enter his Heart Chakra. Though he no longer needs to incarnate in the physical realms for higher enlightenments, his intention is to revisit the Earth with your mother in his last incarnation.

Oh, I am really happy to know this.

Many have ascended through dying, so death is a great equalizer. Think of two people. One is a spiritually realized person and the other leads an ordinary life. If the one living the ordinary life *surrenders deeply* around the time of their death, then both may find themselves at a similar level of enlightenment after their death. This is why the time around one's death was welcomed as the most transcendent period of one's life. It was celebrated with great joy in many ancient cultures.

27

From Ego to Primordial Joy

I am intrigued by the fact that death was seen as a time of celebration and joy in many ancient cultures. Did the people of ancient cultures not suffer when a loved one died?

They did not suffer as much as people do now. They knew of the soul feeling of *primordial joy* that lies beyond birth and death. Embracing death with this joy helped the dying one get enlightened in those precious moments preceding one's death.

Can you tell us more about primordial joy?

Unlike the finite joys of the mind and body arising from the lower two chakras, the primordial joy has no beginning and no end, expanding forever into the formless, infinite emptiness. The primordial joy opens the door to *who you are*. A window to this joy opens up as one surrenders one's ego around the Third Chakra.

Does the Third Chakra have both the ego and the primordial joy?

> Ego is part of the mind. The mind exists not inside but *around* the lower three chakras— similar to how muddy water exists around those beautiful lotuses. Around the First Chakra is the instinctual mind related to the earth element; around the Second Chakra is the emotional mind related to the water element; and around the Third Chakra is the thinking mind related to the air element. The ego manifests as the culmination of the thinking mind around the Third Chakra. The emptying of the mind around the lower three chakras starts with the dissolution of the ego, which in turn leads to a major enlightenment. As the mind dissolves from the center of one's being, one experiences a radical emptying of all thoughts and beliefs and awakens to the primordial joy. It is easiest to surrender to this joy from the Third Chakra as one dissolves the ego and receives guidance from the higher self from this place, but searching for this joy is like the fish searching for the water they live in.

Does all suffering come to an end after this enlightenment?

> Like a child, one may still have occasional tears of sadness or moments of anger, but these dissolve as soon as they arise. One may still experience physical pain, but there is no psychological suffering anymore. The realization is so deep and profound that

one remains in divine rapture for some time not wanting to even speak. From the space of emptiness, one sees the limits of the mind for the first time. One feels great wonderment at how a single thought arises miraculously from the void and then disappears back into the void. And again, another thought arises, and again into the void. One rests in bliss in the spaces between thoughts, and over time these spaces become longer and longer. Every thought, idea, concept, and belief—including the sense of identity—is now seen as an illusion because the mind is emptied of itself. As more chakras open, the sense of identity dissolves in stages from *I-ness*, to *am-ness*, to *is-ness*, to even beyond existence and non-existence. Those who have attained these enlightenments do not experience a sense of identity that separates them from others. However, most learn to say, "I," like I do as a goddess, in order to relate with others still caught up in their minds.

Can you tell us more about the ego around the Third Chakra?

The ego around the Third Chakra is connected to our psychological identity and worldview, including our self-esteem and personal power. This is the place where we build the illusion of our life and how we might play this life out. Though a little ego is needed for our safety as physical beings, much suffering is created by the disproportionate growth of

the ego around the Third Chakra. Since karmic patterns are *assimilated* in the Third Chakra, the possibility of transformation is also greatest here. There
is always a choice whether to create more suffering
by strengthening the ego *or* to surrender to the primordial joy in this chakra. As one clears this chakra
and opens to receiving the primordial joy, one experiences a monumental change within oneself. When
one surrenders to this joy, one can receive guidance
from one's personal guides and the higher self.

Why are our karmic patterns assimilated in the Third
Chakra?

Well, it is a culmination of the lower two chakras
that get expressed in the Third Chakra. It is not just
one chakra in and of itself, but also the Karma that is
synthesized here, so it is a place where one wrestles
the most, and the place where the possibility of transformation is the greatest. Overall, this is a very important chakra to keep clear and free of grief in order to
clear Karma. It is also important to keep this chakra
free of egotistical work that makes one a workaholic.
Overindulgences in physical substances such as too
much alcohol and drugs can make this chakra very
murky. If this chakra gets very clouded, one could
get entangled with negative energies. This is where
it is advantageous to ask angels to assist and protect.
They can replace one's sorrow with joy. One becomes
of a higher nature as one clears this chakra.

Would you say someone like Hitler had a big imbalance in his Third Chakra?

Yes. As Hitler's Third Chakra began to close, the higher voice within him became faint. He reached a point when he became completely deaf to the higher voice within, after which he had no reference framework left to even recognize his ego. When someone succumbs to such depths of unawareness, the higher divine beings may sometimes appear in the world to maintain the balance in the universe, for all are subject to the law of Karma.

Oh, like Lord Shiva?

Yes, or Durga, Kali, and other Goddesses.

This explains why there are divine beings of *destruction*. Sometimes evil has to be removed like we remove cancer.

Except that divine beings have no judgments and do not see anything as *evil*, just like you do not see cancer in your body as evil. You simply remove the cancer, so that there can be more harmony in the body. If you do it with much love and care, the cancer is less likely to come back.

I have discovered that ego manifests not only in extreme ways—like in Hitler—but also in more subtle ways, even on a *spiritual* path; for example, the ego of having *great humility*, or the ego attached to having *great siddhis* (psychic powers), etc. So, how does one surrender these subtle aspects of ego?

By embracing the ego gently and then letting it go instead of fighting with it. Know that there is nothing wrong with a little ego, and fighting with it only feeds other aspects of the ego. The important thing to remember is that *you are not your ego*, and a little ego is needed for your survival until you are fully enlightened. However, the ego should remain on the surface and not become the center of your being. What humans think of as evil is simply the ego overplaying its role. Take certain kinds of cancer, for instance: they are invasions of tumors, which are not in harmony with the body. The invader says to itself, "I will grow big and become different from the body," and then there is a war within. The war ends when the ego surrenders, and then the door opens to the primordial joy that was always there.

Does the ego arise from early childhood?

Yes, and the process accelerates with the closing of the lower two chakras by the onset of puberty. At that time in their lives children begin asking about their path; they are already wondering, "what will I become?" As fear and other emotions grow around the first two chakras, the ego is triggered around the Third Chakra to deal with these lower energies. The rising of ego begins to close the Third

Chakra. You could say that it is like pollution rising up from around the first two chakras, and then getting expressed as the ego around the Third Chakra.

It seems as if the primordial joy is the pure creation of the Third Chakra, and ego is the psychic pollution expressed around the Third Chakra. It is how the industrial world produces both goods and pollution.

Yes. Except that primordial joy was *never created*. It has no beginning and no end.

Oh, yes! So, it seems that we need to learn how to have less psychic pollution of the ego. Maybe we need environmentally-friendly chakras. Laughter!

Laughter! Yes, environmentally-friendly chakras!

Can you tell us how to recognize when our Third Chakra starts closing because of our ego?

Have you noticed that much of the emotional pain is felt around the Third Chakra—in and around the Solar Plexus and the surrounding organs? Though most emotions originate from the Second Chakra around the pelvis, people don't hold their pelvis as much as they hold their stomach because emotional pain is expressed in the organs surrounding the Third Chakra. When people hold their stomach, they are attempting to hold in the energy that pours out of the Third Chakra. They are attempting to nurture themselves in that place and give themselves hope. The judgments about right and wrong, success and failure, holy and unholy, and all such opposites about one's identity and worldview are created around the Third Chakra. The ego enmeshed in these judgments creates much stress, worry and sorrow around this chakra. Think of the ulcers many people get because of overworking and overthinking, all of which occur mostly around this chakra. As this chakra gets very clouded, one may have thoughts of being a complete failure without any hope. When this happens, the energy pours out of the Third Chakra as if one is tossing one's life away. Also, some emotions leak into other chakras; for example, hate rises to the heart and anger rises all the way to the head. If all of the pain were to be experienced only in the Third Chakra, the organs around this chakra would collapse. It may be too much! By absorbing most, if not all of the emotional pain in the Third Chakra, the body prevents the heart from shutting down. Before experiencing a heart attack, one would get signs that something is not right in the Third Chakra.

I see. Okay, can we now talk about how to open the Third Chakra?

The journey in this chakra begins before birth. The connection is more from the mother during pregnancy and childbirth, and it is her duty to think higher thoughts at this time. When the mother speaks to the child in the womb there are things that she can say or tend to that would assist the child in feeling loved. She can invite guides or the angels to stay connected with the child. There are those who would not understand this and will question it, but the mass belief regarding guides and angels will shift as time goes on. As more and more people connect with the Heavens, this will seem as normal as it once was in the ancient past. During those times, one would hold a newborn to the sun to build that connection with the universe. The father or the co-parent would provide the space for the mother to be more contemplative and meditative.

As the Third Chakra begins to open, it creates the highest hope, the truest of hope. Not the hope with a fear attachment, but the hope rooted in joy arising from this chakra. One may wonder, "well, is hope not located in the Heart Chakra?" It is not. It is felt most deeply in the Third Chakra. It is important to have joy and laughter each day to keep this chakra open, especially as we get older. Having good rest, eating healthy, listening to soft music, dancing with nature, and all things that create balance in one's life keep this chakra open. One is connected in joy with the Heavens when this chakra is open. This chakra is connected strongly to the Sixth Chakra, or the Third Eye, where we receive our inner vision. When a person says, "I had a great insight," that comes from the Third Chakra through the Third Eye.

Can you share an experience about opening your Third Chakra from one of your human incarnations?

Let me share with you how I kept my Third Chakra open when I was sequestered alone in my incarnation with Rama. My life transformed in that incarnation as I surrendered the little remnants of my ego around my Third Chakra. As I did this I accepted the hard times and moved into joy. I had many talents that I could use in this lifetime. I was able to access my guides easily from this place, and this is where the teachings came from. There were many channelings and messages I received at that time. I was not required to have any wifely duties at this point. To maintain this opening in my Third Chakra I would meditate during different moonlit times during which I would visit sacred places and sacred waters. I would eat very sparingly. This opening gave me opportunities to connect with nature and receive profound lessons. I wrote many things and I was able to use these teachings to have joy in my life. This chakra was clear at all times, which gave me balance in my creativity and sensuality. Even you are choosing to do some of these things. You are in the world and not of the world. You are choosing to eat in a very simple way. You are choosing to do much meditation. Have you not noticed a great change in yourself?

Yes, and the change seems to have accelerated in the past few years.

At one point did you not think that your life was hard?

Yes, but a lot has shifted and opened with my surrender to you.

> Asking us for guidance can be of much assistance in the opening of this chakra. Your guides can also channel information through this chakra. Much spiritual communication happens through this chakra, as this is the entry point for the life itself. The soul of the child enters through this chakra and the body of the child is nurtured in the mother's womb through the umbilical cord around this chakra. This is also the place of exit when one crosses over to the other side. This is the most creative place. And, since it is connected to the sun, it is also the clearest place.

Is that why they call it *Solar Plexus?*

> Yes: you may see this chakra as a bright yellow sun, almost like a coppery golden yellow. As you receive from this place you will become more creative. Your ideas will be easier to receive, and your love will expand. Located in the mid-part of the bottom of the foot is the Solar Plexus point, which is your direct connection to the Earth. If you lay upon the Earth, which you have been asked to do at certain times, it can help you get reconnected with the Earth. You may have noticed that while we invite animals upon our beds, and they may rest for a time in our beds, all in all, they prefer the floor. They prefer to be on the belly of the Earth, connected to the Earth. If you go to sweat lodges, they will encourage

you to put your belly upon the Earth when it gets hot. Not your back, but your belly. When one lays with another, which is the closest two humans may experience being with each other, these chakras come together even more than the hearts. When mothers lay their newborns upon their stomachs they create a deep connection of primordial joy with them. A mother surrendered to this joy in the Third Chakra is a great blessing to the child.

You told us that even you had many good mothers in your human incarnations.

Yes. Not only is a good mother a great blessing for the child, but when the child comes into the arms of a mother, it is also an opportunity for her to clear lifetimes of Karma by holding the child close to her.

Aha! So, the child can heal the mother?

Yes. The heart and the higher chakras of the child are clear, which allows the healing of the lower chakras of the mother. However, it is important for the mother to not become attached to clearing her own pain, and to love the child unconditionally. There are many mothers who are raising their children this way so that the children blossom without much conditioning and expectations. As we become one with a child who has incarnated, we experience one of the greatest bonds through which we can become one with ourselves.

That is so true—when we look at very young children our hearts melt.

> When we say that our "hearts melt," what we are saying is that we have an experience of the lower three chakras *opening and aligning*, which makes the heart available to us. This is something everyone can feel, as it only happens in the presence of children. Even the most serious people begin to smile as they interact with children. The energy that we are feeling from the child is from the upper chakras and not from the lower chakras of the child.

What about the lower chakras of the child—are these not open?

> The Karma of the child from previous lifetimes is carried around their lower three chakras. The mind around these chakras is not activated at that time, so the karma lays dormant. Even Shamans and Yogis with great Siddhis learn how to keep their mind around the lower chakras dormant. Little children are naturally in a state of surrender to *what is*, so the mind around their lower chakras remains dormant. However, with the passing of time, the mind around the lower chakras of the child becomes activated, and then the chakras start closing, especially as the parents impose their own fear-based beliefs on the child. By the age of five, it happens enough to affect the spiritual choices the child would make in his or her life.

Can parents learn how to not impose their beliefs on their children?

It is very subtle and almost impossible for parents not to do this at this time because of their own conditioning. Many parents do not connect with their children from the silence of their own hearts. They pay attention to their children only when they are in some need. Though children must be fed and protected, it is very important to nurture their higher chakras so that what is open may remain open. Parents can nurture the higher chakras of their children by spending more time in nature and living in the present moment with them. But instead, the parents activate fears and insecurities around the lower chakras of their children by laying their own beliefs upon them. Soon, the children forget their divine nature, their great inner gifts, and their ability to laugh in joy at everything.

Think of those children who start playing musical instruments at young ages. They have chosen parents to assist them so that they can remain in joy. In return, they affect the DNA of their parents. However, parents have to be careful. While they may receive the gifts of their children, they should not see their children as a "means" of healing the weaknesses in their own chakras. If the parents help the child by not imposing their own beliefs on to them, then opening and aligning the chakras becomes a choice for the child. It allows the child to grow the seed of joy instead of the seed of ego.

Can you define more concretely what you mean by the
"opening and aligning" of the chakras?

The opening of a chakra means the emptying
of the mind around that chakra. The mind exists
only around the lower three chakras, so the upper
chakras are always open. If all three lower chakras
are fully open, they naturally come into alignment
in one's enlightenment. So, the choice between
alignment and misalignment exists only when the
lower chakras are *partially* open. Let us explain
with an example: let us say that you go for a walk.
You are feeling the wind, listening to the sounds
of nature, and embracing the tender Earth with
your bare feet. Your senses are fully alive and you
have surrendered your fear-based instincts around
your First Chakra. Let us say that you are also able
to drop your emotional pain in those moments by
feeling a heart connection with those splendid
trees that know nothing of suffering; also, let us
say that the feeling of communion with the trees
also sheds your ego of being human and superi-
or to the trees in those meditative moments; the
opening in your lower three chakras also allows you
access to some of your higher chakras in those precious moments. Since you are in emptiness from
the three lower chakras and the upper chakras are
always open, all your chakras are open and aligned
in those moments. From this place of emptiness
you experience the primordial joy that unites all of
the chakras. Most humans experience such states

only momentarily until the mind enters again into one or more of the lower three chakras.

On the other hand, let us say you go for a walk but you are unable to drop your loneliness and are also feeling angry with someone who has offended your ego. The loneliness in the Second Chakra makes the insult to the ego feel more acute in the Third Chakra, and vice-versa. Though being with nature would have allowed you to experience the emptiness from your First Chakra by surrendering to your senses and being nurtured by nature, your Second and Third Chakras have closed, so a misalignment occurs between the lower three chakras. Because of this misalignment, you also cannot access your higher chakras. This clouds the totality of your experience and now even the trees become cold, hazy, and distant.

Oh, so the misalignment is due to some of the lower three chakras being affected by the mind.

Exactly! The misalignment makes the mind around one or more of the lower chakras inflame the mind around the other lower chakras, while the alignment allows the emptiness to expand in all three lower chakras. Your chakras are misaligned most of the time except during sleep and during a few precious moments of meditation, as some open and others close, making it difficult for you to experience the primordial joy of emptiness. This is why some people take complete breaks from family and work and go on retreats where they can become aware of their body and breath and simply sit with nature in silence. Such breaks give them opportunities to empty the mind around *all three* lower chakras and experience the primordial joy. A daily spiritual practice can also help in opening and aligning these chakras. It would be like a daily mind cleanse, similar to how the body must clean itself daily to stay healthy. Spiritual progress is rapid when your lower chakras get aligned, i.e., the mind is emptied around these chakras in the *same* moments. This allows you to have momentary glimpses of the primordial joy that becomes the door to enlightenment.

So, for now I ask you to think of a color wheel. It may start with the darkest color, which blends into the next color, and then the next color, and so on, with great synchronicity. The primary colors blend into secondary colors, which then blend even further into colors of higher vibrations; this is similar to what is going on with the chakras. As they blend they become like colors of higher vibrations creating the most exquisite experiences of primordial joy.

28

Joz-Laughter-Creativity

I am curious about the different dimensions of primordial joy. For example, how is this joy related to laughter?

As joy deepens into primordial joy, one realizes that joy *is* laughter and laughter *is* joy! That is why belly laughter is such an authentic, pure, and creative energy. Obligation to laugh comes from the desire for approval, and therefore such laughter sounds fake to everyone. You may hear such laughter in those meetings of people who think they are very important. Even those dedicated on spiritual paths do not always laugh as much. Think of stoic priests or religious teachers who are trained not to smile at all. How could they teach joy when they are taught not to have it? Laughter! So, remember to incorporate moments of laughter in your life throughout the day.

Is that why we have the Laughing Buddha?

Yes. And this is why I laugh so much! You could say that I am a Goddess of laughter, a Goddess of joy.

Sometimes jokes can seem a bit disrespectful and is that why I do not crack more jokes with you.

You should crack more jokes. Of course, there is a time and a place.

Right—one cannot always be cracking up because that may be inappropriate in certain situations.

Well, we could laugh more if we received one another as we are. Look at little children: they find the simplest things very funny. But, as they get older, they get conditioned about when to laugh and when to not laugh.

I used to laugh so much as a young child, but my laughter became less frequent as I grew older. I have rediscovered my laughter in recent years, and I am happier.

That is why I would like more laughter in this book—to encourage more laughter in the world. When Jade is working she laughs much, and her coworkers can feel the joy that pours out of her laughter. They see how laughter heals them. She shows them how to not take their issues so seriously by looking at them in a different light. Once they see that, they let go of the sorrow and the suffering and start smiling again.

Do we have much laughter in this book?

Oh, I think there are a few funny things here and there; however, it is quite a serious book! Laughter!

Laughter! When I go home to visit my brothers and my parents, I have the whole family in much laughter most of the time. My mom especially laughs a lot!

That is affecting their DNA. It helps your family very much. When you visit your mother this time you should remind her to have more laughter in her life.

She tells me that she does not laugh so much without me.

You can say to her, "yes you can." There are so many things to laugh about. She can be with children and laugh with them. She's trained to laugh a certain way because of the patriarchal norms of the society in which she grew up. It is almost like laughing behind her hand. So, you can help her to have joy, to laugh without caring so much about the societal norms.

There is this Zen painting I really like in which there are two monks who are getting blown away by the wind while they are looking at a leaf that is inexplicably hanging there, unmoved by the gale. And the two monks are busting out laughing because they have this realization: "Who do we think we are anyway, when we are no different from this little leaf?"

It is true! The monks are in such great joy that laughter is arising from within, from that place of emptiness. The painting is the metaphor for knowing that *joy is laughter.* And more things are created from joy than anything else. Think about why Disneyland is so amazing: people go there and have much fun with their families, and great healing happens. Who would have thought that the creator of Disneyland was a genius who was actually assisting people in changing their DNA by creating a place of joy and laughter?

Really? Laughter can change even our DNA?

Yes, because laughter creates new pathways in the cellular make up of our bodies.

Oh, so would you say even Disneyland is a place of spiritual healing?

Yes, because families go there and have much joy and laughter. The energy is the same whether one feels laughter through a funny Zen painting or by being with Mickey Mouse.

Earlier you said that *joy is laughter* and *laughter is joy.* What makes joy into laughter, and laughter into joy?

They are the same. If one is feeling the primordial joy, one is also smiling from within.

So, if joy has no smile in it...?

...there is no joy! The primordial joy is a pure creative energy in the Third Chakra, and as we completely embrace this energy, we always find laughter in it. There is no thought in such laughter, as one does not think about how to laugh; it is our very nature!

Can we feel this joyous smile all the time?

It is your nature, so the more you surrender to your emptiness, the more you will have this joyous smile. However, you are conditioned by society to not have this joyous smile all of the time. But you can change that. For example, when you do yoga, do your practice with a joyous smile, and you will have a different experience. When the Third Chakra is in a joyous smile, it not only nourishes the First and the Second, but also the upper chakras as well. It is like "as above so below," and so meets in the middle. One would think that in the "middle" is the Heart Chakra, but the middle one is the Third Chakra. So, if you were to ask, "which chakra should I begin with on my healing journey?" I would say, begin with the Third Chakra. When you throw a rock into a pool of water, does it say that "you did not start at the edge of the water?"

No.

You are supposed to laugh! Laughter!

Laughter! I think I am trying to understand this wisdom about laughter very seriously!

You will understand it better if you breathe and feel the laughter within. Think about it. *If you throw the rock in the pond, it expands outward.*

(After five seconds)

Oh, I get it! If we begin with the First Chakra, it is like throwing a rock at the edge of the pond. Doing that creates hardly any ripples. But when we begin with the Third Chakra, it is like throwing the rock in the middle of the pond, which creates expanding ripples that reach both the lower chakras and the higher chakras.

Exactly! So, as you open your Third Chakra with joy and laughter, it will help you open your lower two chakras. This is why we have a laughing Buddha instead of a solemn Buddha.

Oh, this is profound! I love this wisdom.

Joy and laughter has helped you understand this wisdom quickly.

Okay, going back to joy and laughter, I am still amazed that these two are the same. Would you say that when you are dancing in joy, you are in laughter too?

Dancing brings a smiling joy; drumming brings a smiling joy. The smiling joy is bound to be there if you are totally immersed in your dance. But if you are doing it for the approval of another, wondering, "gee, am I the best one on the dance floor?" then you are not experiencing a smiling joy.

Aha!

Think about people who go out, and there is a lot of smiling on the dance floor. It is the smiling Buddha joy. Depending on the level of immersion, there may be a tremendous amount of joy in the dance. You may even picture the Flamenco dance with its intricate movements and complicated steps that make it such a beautiful dance. It may seem serious and intense but the great Flamenco dancers are actually drumming to the Earth with a joyous smile in their feet. Similarly, many indigenous people from different cultures dance with much celebration, joy, and laughter.

This smiling joy is the Holy Grail that people have been searching for. To be in this joy is the most creative state to be in. Your whole body and heart can smile with this joy. When you cradle a child, you are in this joy. When you take a walk and are just "people watching," you are in this joy. Interestingly, when you look at someone and find something funny and laugh, you might wonder, "are they feeling judged?" Yes, at times someone may feel judged and so you have to always act from a place of compassion; however, it may be a moment of innocent laughter as well. It is like two little kids getting together and laughing about nothing.

Okay. While I am listening to you I am beginning to feel this laughter arise within me. It seems very creative, almost as if it is coming out of nothing.

Laughter! Well, that is the purpose. We want people to let go of the idea of what laughter is and what laughter is not, so that they can freely embrace this joyous energy, rather than analyze it. This is the easiest door from the mind into emptiness. When you look at someone such as Sri Sri, you can definitely say that the one thing everyone wants is what he has. He is always smiling and laughing! He sees the whole world as funny.

Does he actually see the world as funny?

Yes, he does. Laughter! Because it is!

Right now I am talking with you upside down. It began with some laughing, and then I somehow got on the floor, and then somehow my feet climbed up the wall next to me. I have never been like this before talking with you!

> It is very good for you.

Hmm...it feels like I am generally serious when I am talking to you. I need to...?

> Okay! You are not always serious.

But I need to be more...?

> You have to allow yourself to be *you*. I appreciate everything that you do for me with great devotion. To allow laughter does not mean that you are disrespecting me. That is a learned behavior. It is like children sitting on a bench in a church and their mother elbowing them on their side asking them to be quiet. Yes, there is a time to be quiet, but even during that time you can have a smiling joy within.

This feeling of smiling joy is getting deeper now. I think having two words, *joy* and *laughter*, divides the energy.

> It is one energy that is also *creative*. Now, when you speak of *joy*, know that it always includes *laughter* and *creativity*, for joy becomes *joy-laughter-creativity* as you reach deeper into it.

I feel that if I had allowed the oneness of joy-laughter-creativity in all those happy moments in my life, I would have felt even more alive. So, in reality, these moments were always more alive, but I did not see them like that.

> Well, I am glad you completely learned something today. This wholesome joy is very healing! If you went to a hospital and you saw children in the cancer ward, knowing then that they may decide to cross over within a day or two, would you not prefer to spend time with them laughing in joy? Or, would you prefer to be in quiet solemnity?

Laughing in joy.

> Good! And that joyful laughing would be creative! So, now when you go dancing, or are doing yoga, do it with joy-laughter-creativity, and you will have a fuller experience.

I am recalling a very vivid experience from my childhood when I was young, like around 12 years old. This was during the mid-70s in India when children of my age were generally not allowed to go out late at night. But I had this adventurous friend with whom I would sometimes sneak out in the middle of the night. I remember some of the experiences very clearly. He and I would be walking together and every now and then we would look at each other and the joy of being out so late and the feeling of adventure would lead to bursts of a joy-like laughter from deep inside us. Then, we would be quiet for a few moments, but every time we would look back at each other, we would both find it very hard to hold the joy inside. We would have these huge smiles on our faces as we tried to control the laughter within ourselves. It was such a completely overwhelming feeling that I would often wonder about it during the daytime—wondering why we only felt this amazing joy in the night: what was so special about the nighttime? The joy we experienced had a distinct quality of laughter to it, which was so hard to hold within that we would smile at each other again and again, to the point of getting very conscious about it. We would try to stop the laughter that was coming from within, but as soon as we would look at each other we would again have these big smiles on our faces again.

> This is beautiful! It brings great joy and a smile upon my face that you would remember yourself in such happy moments. You are all these moments and much more as you step out from your mind and surrender to the emptiness of yourself. Remembering such moments from your childhood will bring great healing to you. This is what the enlightened ones, or the ascended beings, teach—that all moments are always of a deep, smiling joy. Everything is speaking to us in this joy, and the joy would expand even more if we would receive all in joy. Even sorrow would transform into this joy quickly if the ego would not hold onto it.

This discussion of joy-laughter-creativity also reminds me of the *Flower Sermon* story in Buddhism. One day

Buddha came to his sermon holding a flower in his hand, but instead of speaking to his disciples, he simply looked at the flower for a very long time. The disciples were unsmiling and solemn and became somewhat restless waiting for him to speak, but Buddha continued to look at the flower with total calm. Mahakasyapa could not hold anymore— finding the whole situation comical, he smiled. Buddha gave the flower to Mahakasyapa and picked him as the one who understood his message that could not be conveyed by words. They say that the Zen tradition of "special transmissions" began with Buddha's gift of the flower to Mahakasyapa.

Zen teaches about surrendering to the primordial joy. From the place of joy one cannot be so serious like some of Buddha's disciples were in that gathering. Mahakasyapa's mind dissolved as Buddha looked at the flower for such a long time, and then he simply smiled with a mysterious laughing joy he felt in his Third Chakra. That is the primordial joy! With that smile, Mahakasyapa glimpsed the emptiness within himself, and this is what I have to say about this story. It is simple, and there is no ego in it. It is similar to your story when you would go out with your friend at night and you could not hold your laughter inside. The next turning of humanity toward enlightenment will occur with the spreading of this primordial joy on Earth. This joy will also raise the vibrations of other soul feelings, such as love, compassion, freedom, peace, and others. As you find primordial joy in these soul feelings, they join into oneness and become indescribable soul feelings of even higher vibrations.

29

From Suffering to Joy

Buddha is reported to have said, "I have taught one thing and one thing only: dukkha, and the cessation of dukkha." Dukkha is explained in Buddhism to be an all-encompassing term for suffering. How does this teaching of dukkha and its cessation relate to your teaching of primordial joy?

Everything in nature is created in joy and speaks to us in joy if we would simply receive it in joy. This primordial joy is filled with a silent and eternal laughter. This is the true teaching of all enlightened teachers and ascended beings. A tree has a knowingness about the moment of its uprooting, but since it can also sense the primordial joy that lies beyond its death, it does not "suffer" even as it is pulled from the Earth. Though it experiences physical pain in its uprooting, it blesses all with a parting smile of joy!

Unlike trees, humans cannot seem to see the immense beauty of death, which makes it difficult for them to let go when crossing over. Though the enlightened ones speak of celebrating the lives of those who have left them behind, humans are conditioned to mourn and cry over an extended period instead of releasing their tears and returning to joy. Because they do not return to joy, the departed ones are unable to share with them the silent explosion of joy that they experience on the other side. *Know that joy for another can be felt only from a place of joy within oneself.*

If everything is created in joy and speaks to us in joy, then why did Buddha emphasize the truth of dukkha so much?

He emphasized the truth of dukkha because the mind is constantly trying to *escape* from dukkha. This constant effort to escape from the present moment traps one in the duality of cravings and aversions. This creates even more suffering and hides our joyous nature from ourselves. By emphasizing the truth of suffering, Buddha encouraged his listeners to be *fully present to the suffering*, and not bypass it. Such presence ends the subtlest egoic resistance, which dissolves the suffering.

Know that the primordial joy that we speak of precedes all suffering and continues after the cessation of all suffering. While Buddha taught that dukkha has a beginning and an end, *the primordial joy has no beginning and no end.* This joy is empty of everything, by which we mean empty of all causes and conditions connected to mind and matter.

So, emptying ourselves is a way to find this primordial joy?

Yes, and awakening the primordial joy is the way to find emptiness. It goes both ways! As we empty ourselves of everything, we become the unseen heart of the universe. This is why it is said that emptiness is fullness, which is our truest state of being. I shall share with you this high teaching: the truth of dukkha is best seen from the truth of emptiness, for it is not only about acknowledging our suffering, but also about *how the suffering is seen*, either from the conditioning of the mind or from that place beyond the mind. Suffering continues when seen through the conditioning of the mind, but ceases to be when seen through the emptiness that lies beyond the mind. The purpose of breathing, meditation, and expressing gratitude for everything is to find the joyous emptiness that can subsume the mind.

Aha! In the second Noble Truth of the four Noble Truths, Buddha said that the cause of dukkha, or suffering, is *craving, or thirst.* Some have interpreted this to mean that we must give up desire because desire leads to craving or thirst. But isn't the desire to give up desire also a desire?

From trees and stars, to angels and Bodhisattvas, everything in this universe is growing. Even we divine beings are growing through our *desire* to heal worlds within worlds. Desire gives you the basic impetus to grow. So, it is not the desire, but the *attachment to our thoughts about the desire*, which creates cravings or thirst, which is suffering.

What do you mean by our "attachment to our thoughts about the desire"? Isn't desire a thought?

Desire is a thought as well as a feeling, and it creates craving only if it gets crowded by more thoughts associated with it. To free the desire from millions of such thoughts over one's lifetime requires space or emptiness, which is realized in meditation.

Aha! So there is nothing wrong with desire in and of itself?

There is not! The suffering begins when thoughts based on one's past experience with the desire get attached to the desire, which creates craving. This is when the mind infects the soul. To free yourself from a mind full of such thoughts you can first let yourself completely feel the joy of the desire. And then in the next moment you may surrender yourself completely to emptiness. Trust that by freeing yourself completely from the thoughts attached to your desire you increase the likelihood of the desire manifesting in your life. The desire may not manifest exactly in the way you imagined it, but it will manifest in its highest potential if you do this.

This sounds like the *law of attraction.*

Many truths are interwoven, but sometimes their relationships are not seen so clearly. The deeper truth of the law of attraction is not about manifesting your desires—though they manifest with greater likelihood through this law—but to *realize your emptiness* in which all you have ever desired already exists. As you feel the joy of your desire and then totally surrender by freeing yourself from all thoughts attached to the desire, you are bound to taste the primordial joy of emptiness. As this sacred joy takes over your life, desires do not constantly occupy your mind. The primordial joy is so fulfilling that thoughts about your desires occur less and less and your desires become more holistic—about healing worlds within worlds. You are also less affected by whether or not your desires are fulfilled because your cup is already full with this joy of emptiness, which is the ultimate fullness.

Aha! I used to think that the law of attraction was about manifesting our desires and that Buddhism is about getting rid of our desires. It seems neither of these is true!

Exactly! So let me say this again: feeling the joy of your desire and then surrendering to the emptiness increases the likelihood of the desire manifesting. The purpose of the law of attraction is not to manifest the desires that you have, *but to feel the joy of the emptiness* that already contains everything you could ever desire. True freedom from a desire is not attained by negating it, but rather by feeling the joy of desire without the expectation about whether the desire will manifest or not. You attain freedom from your desire because your joy continues whether or not your desire manifests in your life. The more you surrender to the emptiness, the more your desires transform and become wholesome, serving the good of all. On the other hand, if you desire from a place of suffering then your desires turn into cravings and create the divisions of the ego.

This is a great insight, and I think it will help many who think that Buddhism is about getting rid of our desires! It is not the desire but the never-ending thoughts about the desire which create suffering. Most people hold onto such thoughts about their desires because they feel that holding on will be the only way that they will manifest them in their lives.

Most of these thoughts come from a place of lack and not joy. Know that when you are in joy, you do not have as many thoughts. As you feel the joy of your desire and then surrender to emptiness, a new dimension of joy opens up in your heart which is beyond your desires. From this place of emptiness, you do not stop desiring, but you are no longer attached to the outcome of your desire. This is the ultimate *secret* of the law of attraction which frees you from your desires and attracts even more joy in your life.

Earlier you said that suffering ceases when seen from the place of emptiness. And now you are saying that emptiness also frees us from desire, i.e., we do not stop desiring, but our joy is no longer conditional on the *fulfillment* of our desires.

Yes. Emptiness is also the foundation of modern therapies like psychotherapy, hypnotherapy, emotional release work, etc. The job of the therapist is simply to create a safe environment in which the patient can revisit painful memories from this place of emptiness that has no fears, insecurities and judgments. All healing happens from this place of emptiness.

30

Awakening the Primordial Joy

Is there a way to stay centered in this emptiness when we are faced with big losses? For example, if we lost all of our worldly possessions in an earthquake or a fire, how can we not feel overtaken by the sadness and chaos of such an event?

Many humans are going through such experiences at this time because they are attempting to clear their First Chakra. These experiences are like explosions of energy created by those who cannot manifest what they want in their lives. Know that the Earth herself does not suffer through such experiences. From the perspective of Mother Earth, these experiences of loss and destruction are like giving birth to new energies that heal and bring generations together. If you stay in a state of surrender, you too can experience these transitions like the Mother Earth without so much suffering. The main lessons are those of patience, understanding, and to help manifest the realization that people have nothing to run from. Think about when 9/11 happened. While it was devastating, people also surprised themselves with the spontaneous outpouring of care and help. Many were touched deeply by the selfless giving of so many strangers. The miraculous outpouring of love helped many families heal who were affected by a great loss on that day.

The purpose of reaching out to those who have suffered a great loss is to allow them to release their sorrow and make them transition into joy, which is their true nature. However, not all wish to surrender their sorrow. Many decide from their ego to stay in sorrow. By doing this, they slowly close the doors to those around them. Know that even taking very small joyful steps, like taking a walk in nature, cooking a nice meal, listening to a soft melody, and having more laughter, allows the transformation of sorrow into joy, which then flows to others as love.

Why can't humans experience this kind of joy all the time?

Because humans have forgotten their own nature. Many believe that only *outer* abundance gives them happiness; yet, some who experience great devastations come to realize that joy is always living inside of them. They rekindle this inner joy by feeling it in small things; for example, they feel it in the everydayness of their lives instead of waiting for something big to change. Doing this attracts even more joy. Eventually, this joy deepens and blossoms into their hearts as the primordial joy and love spreads as the perfume of this primordial joy. This was my path in my different incarnations on Earth as Sita, Radha, Rukmini, Draupadi, and Yasodhara. I chose this joy to rise above the challenging circumstances of my different lives. As I filled my cup with this joy that was always within me, I was able to love and heal many around me.

Why do we hold on to our sorrow so much?

The ego holds onto many emotions, including sorrow. There are certain times in human life when it is easier to surrender the ego; for example, around puberty when there is an opening in the Third Chakra. Higher choices made at this time prevent the ego from getting unbalanced in one's life.

There are also deep connections between emotional energies, biological rhythms, and planetary cycles that can be used for one's healing. For example, much sorrow can be released during cyclical transitions like solstices and equinoxes.

It is also easier for women to release their sorrow around menstruation, which is connected to the moon cycles. In ancient times, people were more surrendered to nature and felt these profound connections. They cleansed themselves physically and emotionally during these times to get rid of the past and then celebrated to open up to joy. All of this increased their intuitive gifts, which allowed them to connect with us. They honored us with different ceremonies on specific days when all would be more in harmony.

Can we talk about how you released your sorrow in some of your incarnations? For example, when you came as Sita you faced much hardship when your husband, Rama, was exiled; you chose to go with him to the forest and were kidnapped there by Ravana, who sequestered you for 14 years. How were you able to create joy in such difficult circumstances?

While this was a difficult incarnation with many moments of sorrow, I was able to transition to joy with the connection I had with my own Goddesses and guides at that time. As I connected with these beings, it allowed me to have balance in the First and Second chakras and to manifest joy through the Third Chakra. As I completely opened my lower three chakras I found my joy of emptiness and made a connection with my matron and crone aspects. Being alone freed me from the responsibility of serving others and gave me an opportunity to serve the land. My choice to live in the forest over the palace was similar to some who choose to pass to the other side, knowing that they can heal more people from there. It was a choice I had known for many months before I came upon it.

How did you serve the land and heal others?

Think of the enlightened ones like Buddha and many others who would walk on Earth in the times after me. They could sit in those places that were healed and receive my joy by simply sitting there. My path was to heal and bless these lands so that when others would come to rest and even die there at certain times they would be able to move into higher places without sorrow getting in the way.

Aha! Your energy was with the land for many centuries!

It is still there! Laughter! When you sit in any place and others come to sit in that place later they feel the imprint of your energy at a deep level even if they are not aware of it. If you leave joy and love in that place, the Earth shares that with others. If you leave sorrow and suffering, others may feel these energies for some time before the Earth dissolves these with her own joy. Know that Earth expands your higher energies and recycles your lower energies into higher energies.

Oh, really!?

Yes. Mother Gaia shall speak on this in a future book on healing.

I wanted to also briefly touch upon your incarnation as Yasodhara. I imagine that you must have initially felt a great loss when Buddha left the palace so suddenly to find his own enlightenment. How did you deal with his absence in the following days, weeks, and months after he left?

> I briefly lost trust of what I knew was true from my heart. After a period of a few weeks, I transformed that by realizing that I could refill my cup by fully surrendering to the present moment. I realized that having gratitude would allow me to recreate joy in the present moment. So, I removed my attention from what I was lacking and began feeling much gratitude for all that I still had in my life, including my son. I also stayed connected with my husband through my meditations. This allowed me to heal my heart and recreate joy, similar to how celebrating with gratitude allows one to heal from the loss of a loved one.

Aha!

> Think of Buddha's flower again. As he sat and just expressed gratitude to that flower, his joy flowed out and that one seeker surrendered to that energy and smiled from his heart.[24] My path was similar to this seeker's path. After a period of solitude and quiet, I knew in my heart that I could be enjoying each moment, just as the sun comes up each day in great joy. That awareness lifted the burden of my sorrow. I did not go seeking after this joy, but simply surrendered to it. It revealed itself in the smallest of things: in being with nature,

in moments of laughter, in simply breathing in and out.

It took me about a month and a half before I turned my life around in this way, so it was not instantaneous. The main thing is that I let go of my beliefs about what had happened and chose to renew myself through daily meditations. That in and of itself started the healing process for me. It is good for us to know that not everything is turned around in a day. But as we continue to fill our cup with gratitude each day, we respond to the world in joy.

How can one be in gratitude when one is in pain or is being abused?

Staying in fear and self-pity does not put an end to the pain or the abuse. Focusing on the positive, even for a moment—and this may be difficult— would allow one to have more inner resources to deal with the situation. Feeling gratitude for even little things would give some joy, which would allow one to think creatively about one's life situation. Though not all go as deep into gratitude as others, seeing all things in gratitude assists many in over-coming their darkest hours. So, it is again gratitude that heals people by helping them maintain fluidity in their lives. It takes much courage to feel grati-tude and there is also a timing issue in this, espe-cially for children who are too young to cultivate it. Therefore, if people can connect these children with great love there can be a deeper transformation, and these young ones will not be stuck in their pain and will learn to have gratitude and joy again. Many healers can assist in this. Animals in nature, especially mammals, go through much pain and yet they receive all things in joy.

I would like to share an insightful moment I had today. I was getting some work done on my teeth at my dentist's office. There were these lovely trees facing me and there was also some soft music playing in the background. Somehow, I got into a meditative state and felt this deep joy bubbling up from inside me *while they worked on my teeth.*

Tapping into inner joy makes everything easier. The deepest experience of this joy is the emptying of oneself. As you became one with the trees, you went into the void and tasted the timeless primordial joy. As you trusted the trees, they blessed you with their energy, and you felt very relaxed. You felt like you do when I am with you, and there was a fullness to the feeling. This inner joy makes the body heal very rapidly because the mind does not struggle with painful judgments, including that of going to a dentist. Laughter!

31

The Heart is Always Open

We have talked so much about joy. Can we talk about love today?

Yes, we can. While all religions have preached love, one does not truly know unconditional love before glimpsing the *emptiness* of the higher self and the *joy* of simply being in a body and a soul. The music of love becomes melodious after one harmonizes the notes of emptiness and joy within oneself.

Aha! This is so true! Without knowing emptiness and joy within ourselves, our love can become burdensome and/or co-dependent towards others.

Exactly! The essence of the heart center is love since all elements *unite* in this chakra. It is a place of great expansion. It is a place where goddesses of love, such as myself, come to you in a greater fullness. It is a place where, if the woman opens herself in the moment of love, she receives more energy for herself and her partner. If the man is completely connected to the woman in the conjugal embrace, he would feel this energy also. This is why sometimes women cry— it is the heart connection to the goddess energy. Not only does one feel love from this place, but also courage. So the heart-based self-awareness is made up of both love and courage. The green color of this chakra is also the essence of the Earth. As you walk upon the grass, or you look at the trees, or look at all things in nature that are green, you can reconnect with your heart to experience your oneness with all.

Is the love of the heart unconditional?

Love *is* unconditional but it is also what people turn away from most. There has been a great forgetting of what love really is. Love is not desiring and wanting to satisfy one's physical and emotional needs. Love is embracing everything and everyone without any attachment to the self or ego.

Oh, so is that how the heart's love is different from physical and emotional needs?

Heart is love. Heart is courage. Heart is giving. Heart simply is. Think of when you start on your spiritual path and the main thing all teachers ask you to do is to "open" your heart. It is not that we do not want the other chakras to open; it is that your connection with your heart needs more attention.

All Goddesses work with the Heart Chakra even though they may work with one or more other chakras. For example, it is important for Saraswati to work here in the Heart Chakra because she is the divine mother.

Why don't humans pay attention to the heart?

Many humans simply forget about their heart, even though they would deny that. They do not nurture the heart, and thus lose access to it over time. They do not nurture it because they get stuck in the mind around the lower three chakras. It is with the unlocking of these chakras that one realizes that *the heart is always open* since it never shuts down. But humans remain occupied around the lower three chakras, wanting things, wanting love through sexual relations, wanting power, wanting fame, etc. If the lower chakras stay open, a great oneness manifests in the heart. The journey of your life becomes deep and profound by experiencing this oneness in your heart.

Did you say that the Heart Chakra never shuts down?

The mind does not exist around the Heart and higher chakras *so these chakras are always open*. It is the closing of the lower three chakras that cause the dis-ease, or unease of the heart. The heart and higher chakras are part of your higher self, and there is never any Karma in your higher self. So, when healers say, "your Heart or your Third Eye is closed and should be opened," these are things that Goddesses will correct. What occurs is that the higher chakras become *inaccessible* because the lower three chakras are closed. One gets so mired in the mind around the lower chakras that one gets cut off from the higher chakras.

So, know that the *heart is always open*, but since it is always open, it is not protected so easily. It may receive negative energies like fear, hate, and anxiety from the lower chakras. As you heal the lower chakras, the negative energies dissipate, and the heart is experienced in its true fullness, which is love. So, let me repeat that the Heart itself does not need healing since you are bound by your Karma only in the lower three chakras and only these three chakras need to be cleared. The heart can be nurtured like a seed so that it may grow into a tree. This will assist many. There will be those who will listen to this wisdom and receive, and those who will not, and that is okay. But this teaching is the *jewel in the lotus.*

Aha! Sometimes you say that the lower chakras should be *cleared,* and at other times you say these chakras should be *opened.* What is the difference?

As you clear the mind around the lower chakras they open and connect with the higher chakras. The great lesson that we all have kept from ourselves is that there is no closing of the heart. In all my incarnations with Vishnu on Earth, I experienced my heart as open and overflowing with love because it was always accessible from my lower chakras.

32

From Love to Devotion

I want to share a little incident that happened to me last night. As I was beginning to load groceries into my car, my precious little ring that represents my bond with you fell out of my shirt pocket. It was a cold, windy night with snow on the ground, and the ring got lost. At first I searched and could not find it, and then I took a few breaths and went into a deep surrender. As I totally relaxed, there it was right next to me.

The surrender allowed you to become more present to the snow and to the vibration of the ring. If you were too much in your mind, you may have buried the ring under the snow by mistake. Think of your sacred ring as a symbol of our oneness and our connectedness, and your mind as the vast expanse of snow. Similar to your searching for the ring, if you search too much for your spiritual connection with me, you would bury it in the snow of your mind. So again, you discovered that surrender is the key. True surrender is a grand opening to the joy of *what is.*

Aha! With regard to our relationship, my upbringing led to my somewhat traditional beliefs about you and for much of my life I thought of you mostly from the lens of these beliefs that I grew up with. Then, one afternoon many years ago, as I was meditating on you I was able to finally let go of these limiting beliefs and I discovered that you loved me more deeply than I had ever imagined. This allowed me to surrender more fully to your love.

What you are speaking of is that earlier you viewed me through the ego attached to your beliefs. This is not anything that is wrong or bad. There was just a fear attached to viewing me in any other way than the way that you were taught by the culture in which you were raised. You saw me in the most loving way possible with the limited resources you had. As you let go of these beliefs, you also surrendered your ego attached to these beliefs. This increased your devotion towards me and created a grand opening that allowed me to truly bless your life. As you continue to give away the beliefs that have been structured within you through DNA, past patterns, and old Karma, you will experience our oneness even more deeply.

Yes, I do feel very blessed! The beliefs we carry are so subtle, sometimes almost invisible. Is there a way for us to

maintain our connection with that place of joy and innocence from our childhood years?

Don't you remember your own connection?

Yes, I do. My curiosity about meditation and spirituality was a result of many sacred experiences throughout
my early childhood when I felt an expanded oneness with
nature. For example, one day I was walking in autumn and
there were leaves on the ground; I felt myself expand suddenly—then, as now, there are simply no words to describe
that blissful experience. There were no thoughts, only the
nameless bliss I had of seeing myself as the leaves.

This nameless bliss is simply a remembering of
what you knew from your childhood and the time
before you came here on Earth.
You are blessed with a loving mother who
cared for you dearly and who raised you in a way
that allowed you to maintain your openness to
your higher self.

I feel this is the great gift both my mother and you have
given me. With both of your guidance I have surrendered
more and more.

By surrendering to me you have surrendered
to yourself. Our connection is star-born, of infinity.
We are one! Just as Christ said of God, "I am in He,
and He is in me," our higher selves are joined in
absolute oneness. My ring that you wear is not the

only symbol of our love. Let the ring be a reminder of the lessons that you continue to learn by asking these questions: What shall I do in regard to my relationship with Lakshmi? How shall I keep it close to my heart? These questions are not judgments, but reminders that all relationships must be continuously nurtured. The ring is just one pleasant reminder of our relationship.

I feel an incredible lightness when I give away everything that is *mine* to *you*.

So keep surrendering all to me with devotion: every possession you own, every piece of clothing on your body, every fear, every thought, every emotion, every belief, and the most invisible tail of your ego. Through that ultimate surrender, *you shall gain all of me*; you will have my heart and you will have my wisdom. You will have my enlightenment, and you shall realize that we were always one.

The small streams of enlightenment that humanity has witnessed in the past few millenniums will spread like giant rivers as humans surrender to divine beings in this way. Even the physical world will be seen as alive and conscious once this happens.

So even matter is alive and conscious?

Have you ever wondered why the electrons spin, why the moon circles the Earth, and why the sun shines in your universe?

Why?

Because all of them *surrender* to love each moment through the joy of their own free will. While humans have discovered many scientific laws about the universe, they have not asked *why these laws hold*. These laws hold because everything surrenders to everything else in great harmony, without any hindrance from the mind.

Are you saying that an electron would not spin if it did not surrender to love by the joy of its own free will?

It would not! But it has no desire to not surrender in love and devotion, for *love makes the world go round* not just for people, but also for electrons and planets. It is the never-ending celebration of the *living universe* that you have forgotten as you became lost in the prison of your mind.

This resonates with my heart and does not seem to be inconsistent with science. It seems like the continuous occupation with the mind prevents one from feeling the *living universe.*

What do you feel when you think of the center of the Sun?

Hmm...like burning hot, very hot, unimaginably hot...

...And that is your mind's projection of what it thinks and feels is "hot." Let me share with you the *secret of the sun*. The sun lives in a deep ecstasy! If the sun was in pain, then joy and laughter would not be created on Earth. You do not feel the sun's ecstasy because you make up the universe in the image of your mind. You believe that the physical universe is dead, but let me tell you that it is magnificently alive. To experience the universe as it is, you have to simply unknow what you know. That is enlightenment—to empty the mind from your lower three chakras by surrendering all beliefs you hold about everything. The realization happens when the lower three chakras open and align, dissolving the mind with a blissful explosion of primordial joy. All mental suffering comes to an end with this major enlightenment.

Does the ego *completely* dissolve as one is enlightened?

It is a silent explosion that happens with the opening and aligning of the lower three chakras. Building any expectation about a major enlightenment will not get one closer to experiencing this state. To see oneself as enlightened already is the way to surrender towards this state, which happens on its own accord when the body is ready. Ego, emotions, and thoughts all continue to arise even after the great explosion, but now they arise briefly on the surface, and do not exist continuously at the center of one's being. One remains in the bliss of the no-mind for long periods of time and uses the mind only when it is needed. Then as more chakras open, even the residual ego on the surface is dissolved fully as one experiences higher and higher enlightenments that join one with everything—from the magnificently alive Earth to the great compassionate suns to the magical black holes that birth entire universes. Surrendering to this primordial joy frees one from the mind and opens up the door to infinite emptiness both within and without. Everything in the universe exists in this state of primordial joy, except sentient beings who live in the prison of the mind.

Namaste!

Namaste Lakshmi ji!

PART VII

THE PATH OF JOY

DEVI MANTRA

Ya Devi Sarva Bhutesu
Shakti Rupena Samsthita
Namastasyai Namastasyai
Namastasyai Namo Namaha

या देवी सर्व भुतेशु
शक्ति रुपेन सस्मिथा
नम: तस्ये नम: तस्ये
नम: तस्ये नमो नम:

33

The Rise of The Empowered Feminine

Namaste Lakshmi ji!

Namaste!

I am filled with much gratitude for these teachings that have transformed my life. I have discovered a new dimension of inner joy that is unconditionally present beneath the veils of my thinking mind. Often this joy expresses itself with much love and devotion to others.

> When one is flowing with so much joy, one naturally falls in love with life. The immensity of that love is devotion. It is the path of the empowered feminine, the path of affirmation.

How is the path of the empowered feminine different from the path of the empowered masculine?

The empowered masculine creates the path of individuation. The empowered feminine creates the path of union. Spiritual evolution goes in cycles. The world becomes patriarchal and divided when the empowered masculine takes the lead, and it becomes matriarchal and unified when the empowered feminine returns. Divine beings from many pantheons guided humanity on the path led by the empowered masculine for the past 6,500 years to create the *contrast*. I have invited Goddesses from different pantheons to lead the next turning of the wheel of dharma. Together, we shall usher in the *path of joy* led by the empowered feminine so that humanity can rise above the contrast. Now, as we transition into this new Yuga, there shall be a grand merging, not only between Hinduism and Buddhism, but also with the Western pantheons connected with Goddesses such as Mary, Brigid, Gaia, Isis, and others, who will come together to create the most exalted feminine path of spiritual awakening.

So, will Goddesses, and not Gods, lead the way?

Soon Buddhas and Gods will join too, for the divine feminine and the divine masculine energies exist in all beings. Also, as we have said before, the ultimate *nature* of all divine beings is androgynous, even though they may choose to express themselves as either male or female. It is the human mind which is not so open at this time.

As humans open themselves to receiving feminine teachings from either the male or the female divine beings, you will see male Buddhas and Gods step forward, as well. For example, my beloved Vishnu will reveal himself in divine timing.

Aha! So, it is about the *feminine teachings* spreading on Earth, and not so much about the male *versus* the female divine beings.

Yes. Since humanity has become excessively masculine, many humans cannot even recognize the feminine teachings when they show up through the male divine beings. For example, Jesus had so many feminine teachings that he learned from his own mother Mary. However, much separation was created in his name over the past 2,000 years.

It is the desire of the ascended Goddesses from different pantheons to unite humans together in the embrace of the divine feminine at this time. The Goddesses are already seen as unifying in many religions. For example, think of Mother Mary, Saraswati, and Tara.

Mother Mary is seen with much reverence by both the Christians and the Muslims.

Saraswati is seen with the eyes of great devotion both by the Hindus and the Buddhists.

Tara is not only the mother of Buddhas, but she is also a great mother Goddess in Hinduism.

This does not mean that there shall be "one" religion, but that humans will look beyond the boundaries of religions and surrender to the divine feminine aspects in all religions.[25] As you witness this grand shift in the consciousness of humanity, you will see the social, cultural, and economic paradigms shift from a patriarchal system to what historians refer to as a "matriarchal" system.

Why should we have either a matriarchal or a patriarchal system? Why not an egalitarian system in which men and women are truly equal?

The pre-patriarchal systems are labeled as matriarchal by the historians because they evaluate these using the lens of the existing patriarchal system, so relative to the existing system, the ancient systems seem "matriarchal." However, the ancient systems were not known as "matriarchal" by the humans who lived in those times. The political concepts of "matriarchal" versus "patriarchal" had no meaning to the people during these times.

True equality is rooted in the joy of one's being, which does not require equality in every position or every role. A blade of grass and a tree are equal in their freedom to exist uniquely, and they live in harmony with each other and with the whole universe. While the ancient socioeconomic and cultural norms empowered the mother much more than the current norms, the father was also honored for his supportive and protective role. Both had their natural place, and they functioned in harmony with one another.

There was a great period in the ancient past when spiritual awakening was at its peak in many lands on Earth. This was a breathtakingly balanced time when men and women were truly equal. They felt the liberating soul feelings of joy, love, compassion, forgiveness, and others, and not the limiting thoughts and emotions that would create divisions between the sexes. There were many angels on the Earth at this time. Many ascended beings also incarnated at this time and they were sought after to give guidance. So think of these beings as the most holy, and the angels being the messengers for them.

There was a different energy on the Earth at this time. Many lands had an etheric energy, and scholars have yet to realize the deeper spiritual meaning of the writings on the wall. It was a time when children were given a different education. They were taught to understand the stars and the skies and all the things of the Earth first. They were not saddled with a lot of burdens upon their shoulders at young ages. Men were not required to work so hard that they were not able to give attention to their families. Women were not mistreated in any form and their opinions were valued. There was no such thing as a depression. I do not mean "depression" as a historical period. Laughter! I mean there was no depression in the mind and the body. Medicinal herbs were used, but more for just maintaining one's body or for preventative care of the body. If one chose to be a protector over a particular society, a man was not preferred over a woman simply because he was a man. There were women who chose to be warriors as well.

So, there were wars during that time?

Yes, more for protection from those whose energy would become out of balance.

So, what you are saying is that even during this time there were those who were out of balance? But, was this not a time when there was much spiritual awakening in the world?

Yes, there were many teachings at this time, but not everyone was in harmony with these teachings. The teachings were given by the wise ones, or the elders. It was similar to how some of the native cultures of the Earth are at the present time. Also, women were great spiritual teachers in these times and their bodies were in tune with nature.

How were women's bodies in tune with nature?

There were times when women went away for vision quests, or other times when they sequestered themselves away from men. They would often do this during their *moon times*.

Moon times?

Their 29-day moon periods, or menstrual cycles.

Why would they do this?

It would give them an opportunity to maintain their inner strength and be with Mother Earth so that they could have balance in their systems and also harmonize their menstrual cycles with the moon cycles. Some women would go away together, and they were not required to have any work responsibilities during this time. These women would feel a strong emotional bond with one another. They would walk the Earth and lay upon it, conversing in silence with one another and with Mother Earth. As they did this, it balanced the Earth. There were those that took themselves to high places like the mountains. They would commune with those on other planets, and in other solar systems. These were actual conversations from other stars of the *Milky Way*. These gifts were given more to women than men at that time.

Were women more intuitive than men at that time?

Yes. This is because they would be naturally quiet at the end of their moon periods, and they could also leave their bodies more easily at this time. Men overall were still protectors. So, as women would go to these high places, men would stay near the sea or flat lands.

There were also places where some women would go and be completely sequestered from men for a lifetime. Many of these holy places were completely hidden from the explorers who came centuries later. These were not places like the Mayan temples that were found later, but rather they are places that still no one has found. There was a very consistent communion between these women and the heavenly angels.

It would be common for these gifted women to venture into those worlds that exist within worlds. The lack of such communication with these inner worlds is also what is out of balance at this time. The doors to these worlds open in meditative states that lie beyond the mind. Going *within the mind* is still going without, as the mind is just a reflection of what is on the outside. You had to literally be out of your "mind" to explore these worlds within worlds.

So, there are worlds within worlds that are outside of our minds?

Yes, the highest of these are the worlds of primordial joy, or, the spiritual *pure lands*.

Was there any use for advanced technology in such a spiritual world?

Yes, but not in the sense you would think advanced. For example, there was not a need for certain modes of transportation, as in many instances one could teleport oneself, dissolving in one place and recreating oneself in another place in an instant. One could also go into those inner worlds. There are still those who do this.

Do you mean out of body travel?

Except not only can one go outside, but one can also go *inside*. Go within. Hence, the expression, *"go within."*

So, you would explore these worlds?

Yes. Within.

Could you even go outside yourself by teleporting yourself to faraway worlds?

Yes, you could go outside but typically in those times you would go within. Deeply within!

Aha! Worlds within and worlds without! Can you tell us more about the people of those times? For example, what did they wear?

Clothes were mostly loose fitting. There were some that were similar to the saris but much shorter in length. Women's hair would grow quite thick and long, and that would also provide good covering. The warrior women would wear more fitted clothing.

I have noticed that the Goddesses do not wear much clothing when they are depicted on the walls of many Hindu and Buddhist temples.

That is how it was.

So, these depictions were not just a spiritual art form? They represented how real women lived?

Yes. There was no reason to cover the breasts at all times, for the human body was not seen as something unnatural. The clothing was used mainly to protect the body from weather conditions.

Children learned to balance their natures early on from teachings of every kind. They blossomed into adulthood with much maturity and wisdom.

There was not shame as there is shame now. There was not sorrow as there is sorrow now. This is also humanity's future—to live without shame and sorrow in one's heart.

Did the matriarchal societies of the past have no shame at all about the human body?

Women had much reverence for their body, which they considered the temple of the spirit. The sensual carvings in the ancient temples display incredible beauty and passion. Look at how human cultures evolved even in the past five hundred years. The renaissance paintings that reveal the human body versus the cultural taboos that veil the human body created very different social norms in nations that exist very close to each other. When passion is repressed, the fire energy becomes perverted and leads to a more hardened masculine energy.

One of my hidden aspects is *passion*. As this aspect is revealed and accepted, there will be more balance and harmony between the feminine and the masculine.

I have observed two extremes regarding passion: there are those who believe in repression due to religious and cultural reasons, and there are those who believe in unabashed indulgence. Either way the behavior seems somewhat unbalanced. What is the correct conduct, or what should be the guiding rules about this?

Different cultures and societies have different ideas about the rightness and wrongness of behavior. All should examine their conditioning, question their beliefs, and come to a place of knowing from the inside. Neither excessive rules nor indulgences free you from the inside. Following rules allows you to receive the approval of others, but they do not get you to the center of your being and your own knowing.

The great beloved son of Mary came to Earth to show you the futility of "rules." He was misunderstood, and more rules were created in his name when all he desired was for humans to taste their own knowing and their true relationship with their own selves.

Have you seen children sharing their joy unconditionally? This will be one of the great teachings of
this book. A joyful being does not look for approval,
nor does he or she desire to please. Pleasing another for approval creates fissure cracks in relationships
because such relationships are of the mind and not
of the heart; they spring from lack and not from joy.
As humanity shifted from being matriarchal to patriarchal, it created rules and labeled one's joys as
"good" or "bad." The guilt and shame arising from
disobeying such rules divided the self. Seeking the
approval of others and pleasing others became the
primary needs of the ego, and the soul feelings of
joy and love became secondary. This is the cause
of the divisions between sexes, between religions,
and between nations; these divisions manifest from
the many divisions within oneself.

How do we deal with this? Divisions between sexes, cultures, and nations are deep. Do we meditate and observe
our ego and our beliefs?

This is the grand question. We continue to let
go of the many beliefs and illusions that we have
created around ourselves. This is where our guides
come in. Those that are our ancestors can help us.
This is what causes us to have enough pain to have
a desire to be taught differently through enlightened teachers. This is why we go through personal
shamanic experiences, and this is why many desire
to go on spiritual journeys to transform their mind,

body, and spirit. This is the great suffering, the dark night of the soul that initiates the process of awakening.

We will encourage and assist humans to let go of the deep grief that comes through childhood so that this energy will be able to recreate itself and manifest differently upon the Earth. There are angels that shall assist in this process and Goddesses are also moving forward and helping many. Through these teachings many shall find peace and harmony, and ultimately the joy of connecting with their higher self. There shall be room made for everyone who chooses to sit in the boat or on the grand ship. This is a great task before us, for as I have stated before, many suffer deeply at this time. Your choice to help ease the suffering of many by bringing them to us is a blessing to yourself and will open many doorways for you.

Do we have to live alone or in monasteries to get on the boat or the grand ship?

The purpose of remaining alone in a lifetime is to open the heart. And, it is not that the heart is not open, because the Heart Chakra is always open. The heart just becomes unavailable due to the preoccupation of the mind and ego with fears and beliefs. In the past, there were places such as monasteries and temples where those of like nature would be sequestered to experience aloneness. These places were created to maintain balance on Earth. These were not places for physical pleasures such as intimacy between the sexes, but places where a meditative joy of emptiness, a quiet calm and serene oneness could be experienced.

Think of going on a hike. If you go by yourself, you may experience oneness with nature and feel your senses more acutely alive. On the other hand, if you go with a companion—say a charming one—the mind may assume center stage while the heart recedes to the background.

When one incarnates, one has the choice to experience the pleasures and pains of relationships, or grow deeper to find the oneness within. Often, the heart opens through aloneness and meditation after one has experienced disillusionment with relationships, but this is not a judgment. Think of Vishnu and myself: you may wonder what our relationship is. I have had my times of aloneness in my incarnations. I have passed through my physicality, from the density of my mind into the emptiness of the no-mind. Since my heart is already at the center, now I choose ecstasy. I have wrapped myself around my beloved. In our conjugal embrace, there is greatness of joy and bliss. He is the expression of myself and that is our oneness.

Can you tell us more about you? Though all see you as a spiritual Goddess, some pray to you to get more material wealth.

Wealth is a word that has been changed and narrowed over generations of time. However, to answer your question so that humans can understand, I have five aspects of wealth.

First, I transform grief or sorrow into joy, so I am a Goddess of spiritual wealth in that aspect.

Second, I am a Goddess of birth. I am, therefore, the celebration of posterity.

Third, I am a Goddess of Earthly abundance, but that which is also joined with posterity.

Fourth, I am a *just* Goddess. I am one who will bring harmony to the left and right hemispheres of the brain.

Finally, I am a Goddess of passion, of which you and I have spoken many times. And this is what has been hidden. In the ancient times, there were statues that showed me unclothed, and this was not what generations of the past wanted me to represent, so they changed my clothing, and they changed my headdresses and proclaimed me differently.

I am thankful and receive all those who come to me. However, when they do not receive the wealth in the way that they expect, they feel sorrow and then reject me. Know that I desire to help all who come to me.

I want to express the ways in which I feel a deep sense of love and abundance when I contemplate your nature, but praying to you simply to accumulate more material wealth never made sense to me.

When we know what is right inside, we resonate joy through that truth as you have done by contemplating me in so many different ways. That contemplation alone showed you great wealth. For this is the magic of the universe. It is in contemplation of simple things. For in that contemplation, one yet arrives to the joy of no contemplation, a pure joy of being-ness. There is only that moment in its fullness, so there is no lack inside. In other words, there is not a desiring for more in that moment, and there is not a feeling of "I missed out in that moment." You have experienced me in many different ways during times that you have sat in meditation and have released your attachments.

The relationship between us is one that is of the heart. This is true of all who come to me, for my heart is like the sun that warms everyone. There have been times when you have questioned me with your mind, but when you surrendered yourself to a quiet, meditative place, you felt myself in your heart. As you have felt the peace and the oneness, even your senses have heightened. This is the purpose of sitting in those places that are holy. It is to feel the fullness of our being in which all is one. Our relationship is much like the tree that has strengthened over time, and there is much peace that you derive from sitting with me.

Thank you. I have gone through periods of relationship and periods of aloneness and I feel I have grown much from my meditations on you. Is it very normal for all human beings to switch back and forth between being alone and being in a relationship?

No, there are those who find so much peace in their aloneness that they maintain that. They experience love through ultimate solitude and peace, and through finding the union within, for both the feminine and masculine exist within the self. But I understand what you are asking. If you think of the sunrise, the bright sun, and the sunset, all times are beautiful.

The sunrise is like awakening to the sensual love, which is simple and innocent and can be experienced with nature, Earth, and our own bodies. It is felt by being fully present to the senses without any physical or emotional effort.

The bright sun is like the sexual love and also the deep emotional love for our partners and our loved ones.

Finally, the sunset is like returning home to the blissful union with our higher selves. It does not have to be one or the other.

At this time, there is so much light upon this Earth that even individuals who have not harmonized themselves with, say, the bright sun, can relax themselves into the calm of the evening sun. All can complement one another.

Aha! So, could everyone potentially return to their higher selves at this time?

Within the next few years, you will see a great change in the way women present themselves in the world. By this, I mean women from all around the world, not just from one place. Though men may help, look to women, for women will be the ones that change the energy. More and more, they will embrace their spiritual nature instead of questioning it. While some men may question them, there will be lots of women groups through which women will find one another, such as family members finding each other in joy. So, even though these women may not be related to one another through kinship, they will feel spiritually drawn to one another.

There will also be a shift in what many women feel is the proper body form, especially in the western culture.

What kind of shift?

The maiden form will be replaced by the matron form. The matron form has a fuller body, like our dear Saraswati.

So, the slim models will no longer be the only ones representing beauty?

Right! The lower aspect of the maiden form has been ruling for some time. A maiden's sensuality is not a commodity to be purchased, but that is how she is depicted in many commercials that connect her sensuality with material objects. This cheapens sensual love, and it influences many things women do, and men have also followed by upholding this standard. To balance this, the crone will come into position of power. So it may seem the pendulum is swinging from one end to the other. As older women take their place on Earth, you will see commercialism go more into a matronly position, which will create the balance of the masculine and feminine. As a result, there will be more integrity and wisdom in younger people. This does not mean that younger women will behave like older women; rather, they will simply make better decisions for themselves. The young women will learn to trust their intuition and will have more patience. Teenagers who desire to be with each other at a young age will allow themselves to wait so that they grow into more fullness before rushing into relationships. There will be less fascination with material objects and a deeper interest in things of a spiritual or mystical nature. The young ones may be less interested in organized religions and more open to meditation and discovering those universes within. Remember in the beginning we spoke about the art of motherhood? There will be a genuine rise of interest in this lost art in the westernized cultures.

What would inspire all of this?

Love will inspire all of this—the truest love rooted in joy and emptiness—a love that a maiden can learn from a crone, for the crone has much wisdom and compassion. More will come into balance as this happens. This does not take the matron out of the picture, for the love that the crone will teach will allow the maiden to grow into her fullness as a matron.

Will we transition to a post-patriarchal society in the near future?

The natural order of the universe is what historians refer to as "matriarchal." However, remember that the people who lived in the "matriarchal" societies of the past did not see these societies as matriarchal. The masculine and the feminine gets wounded by their separation as either "male" or "female" in a patriarchal system, causing a division between the sexes. The masculine and the feminine join together into wholeness in a matriarchal system, creating an empowered union between the sexes. Thus, patriarchy creates the division of the wounded feminine and the wounded masculine, and matriarchy creates the union of the empowered feminine and the empowered masculine.

This is not a judgment since union cannot arise without division, and divinity cannot arise without experientially knowing the wound of separation. The rhythm of union and division creates the symphony in which order and chaos follow one another in the universe. The matriarchal system was followed by the patriarchal system, which will again be followed by the matriarchal system.

Humanity has become exploitative and divisive in the current patriarchal system. Inequalities have risen and sorrow has overtaken the human heart. The patriarchal system is built to dominate: rich over poor, male over female, and human over animal. All of this will end with the transition into the matriarchal system in which the divine feminine energies will empower the feminine in both men and women, joining them in great love. The transition will happen quickly as the matron assumes her place guided by the crone.

Will we see this happen in our lifetimes?

You will be messengers like many before you and many after you. Yes, the transition will happen in your lifetime. There are many men and women who are in balance with their femininity, and they will continue to assist in this transition. The evolving cultural and social values will once again empower the matron.

Didn't humanity progress much through science and technology mostly under the patriarchal system? Will we regress back to the days of "pre-civilization" as we transition to the matriarchal system in the near future?

Mother Earth was matriarchal until about 6,500 years ago. Even today you can find indigenous people who respect and honor the sacred feminine through their rituals and prayers. Their lives provide hints of a time when all elements were united, when the physical was not separate from the spiritual, when sensuality was the way to realize the sacred.

As the elements separated, there was the creation of both knowledge and ignorance. The separation of body, mind, and spirit created an illusion by which the body suffered because the mind dominated, and thus the spirit was forgotten. The domination of the mind over the body and the spirit represents the unbalance of the patriarchal system. This illusion became our new worldview as the mind trapped and enslaved many with stress and overwork. Even with the wonders of science and technology, many live in near starving conditions, while some consume resources as if there is no tomorrow.

The transition to the matriarchal system does not mean that we will go back to the days of "pre-civilization." The transition will allow humanity to embrace a new world that will unite the mind, body, and spirit once again. The mind would be used for what it does best, guided by the heart and spirit. While you need the mind for continuing with the scientific progress, you do not need it to watch the beauty of a sunset or to enjoy the sensual dance of the peacock. You need the loving heart and the nurturing spirit of a mother to bring back joy on Earth.

But would you not agree that the "thinking mind" has uplifted the human condition overall?

Yes, but it is very unbalanced. While some are uplifted, many remain marginalized. More than one eighth of the world goes to bed hungry at night, while rich nations stockpile weapons that threaten the survival of humanity. Science will deliver its true promise when humans replace their ambition with passion, their greed with generosity, and their ego with their higher self. Much more could have been created through science that has not been created yet, and much has been created that needn't have been created. The transformation needs to occur in the lower three chakras so that the mind can unite with the heart again.

Why did the mind separate from the heart?

The soul must know the darkness before knowing light. Wisdom comes only after losing innocence. All was in balance in the beginning, and the Earth was feminine. Then the divine plan unfolded as teachers of the spirit separated themselves from the mind and hid their teachings in sacred places such as in Egypt, India, and other lands. Even the angels who were here put cultures in various places upon Earth to be hidden from the mind, so that there would be femininity on Earth. As the hidden treasures of the heart were discovered, they spread quickly on Earth but remained hidden from the mind as it continued on its own separate journey. With the sacrifice of the one whom they called Yahweh or Jesus Christ, there was recognition of the separation of the heart and mind. This was His path, and as He and others who were enlightened reorganized themselves, they became one with the Earth and Heavens so that there would always be the feminine heart connection. Without this heart connection, humans would have little hope that all of the four elements would ever come together in the heart. Jesus took all of those aspects and sacrificed His body to rectify some of those teachings that were taken and translated incorrectly from the time of the Egyptians.

Oh! So, Jesus came to rectify the lost teachings from the time of Egyptians?

More than people understand. Though many teachings of this ascended one were either buried or burnt, the feminine spirit of his message survived in what was left behind and what has been discovered again in the recent times.

Was Egypt balanced and feminine in the beginning?

Yes. It was a mystical place full of divinity *before* the time of pharaohs. The pyramids reminded the pharaohs of the feeling of eternity that once existed in these sacred lands. The knowledge from this ancient place was misinterpreted and lost by the patriarchal societies of the Greeks and Romans who followed.

While the Greek philosophers were educated and informed, they did not utilize all of the energies of the chakra system including the seven major energy centers that unite your body with your soul. The Greeks became obsessed with the *mind*, and over a few generations they lost their *heart* connection with the Goddesses they once knew. The Romans represented an even more aggressive nature of the male energy.

So, between the Greek philosophers and Roman conquerors, the connection with the divine feminine was lost. As a result, the energies of present day patriarchal structures seem to have no life. But, remember that everything has life. Even material things! This is why it is important to leave offerings in temples and those places where devotionals are made. It helps the building to renew itself and remain alive with the energies of love and devotion.

You said that the Greeks lost their heart connection with the Goddesses they once knew. When you speak of the *mind* and the *heart*, what exactly do you mean?

As we have already taught in this book, the mind exists around the lower three chakras. One may get a glimpse of the heart in a moment of true forgiveness, or in an offering of unconditional love, but usually what one imagines being the love of the heart is the emotional love arising from the Second Chakra. Only when the lower three chakras open and align does one fully empty the mind and thus enters *that* which is beyond the realm of thought, emotion, and ego. The heart truly opens only after one experiences this infinite emptiness.

As more humans are enlightened into this emptiness, there shall be a great turning point that shall first unite the women on Earth, and then unite both men and women. It will be a new creation. It is an explosion similar to the moment in that ecstasy, that conjugal bliss, in which there is "no-mind." That moment of bliss is neither male nor female.

So, it seems that we may be in the midst of a great momentous time in spiritual evolution. Is this true?

Yes. The separation between the sexes has produced the contrast that will allow the emptiness of one's higher self to expand into an even greater infinity, as it is the nature of emptiness to expand eternally. The next expansion will begin with a new thought in women about embracing their femininity, the fire and water within, and from that the New Earth will be created. All creation begins with fire and water. As thought interacts with fire and water, earth is manifested.

Think of me and my beloved: we did not divide ourselves for eons. There was not a need. As the first thought interfered with our fire and water, there was a creation. Remember the drip?

Oh yes, there is a story of your ecstatic union...

Our attention was taken away for a moment by a single thought. That drop became a universe. A manifestation.

...A whole universe?

Yes.

What do you mean when you say your "fire and water"?

Our union.

So, you were integrated? And then for a moment, there was one thought...

...that separated everything in a single moment.

I see. We know from the scriptures that you and Lord Vishnu have incarnated many times with the deepest devotion to one another. Can you share a story of love between you and Lord Vishnu that we do not know from the scriptures?

Let us take a breath please!

Silence for 10 seconds.

We incarnated in a lifetime in which my beloved did not know how to approach me. After years of travel guided by his intuition, he arrived at the temple where I lived with many other priestesses. This place had a very high etheric energy, and it was protected by warrior women. The walls of the temple opened to the outside world with a single gate. He begged to be let inside, for he felt strongly that I was inside these temple walls. However, his requests were seen as inappropriate by the guardians of this place. I was deeply devoted to my own tasks and so was unaware of his presence outside the gate.

By coming time and time and again with offerings at the gate, he eventually succeeded in getting the attention of the High Priestess of the temple. He revealed his *intuitive* knowing to her: that his beloved, a highly devoted one, was living in this place. The High Priestess let him in and assigned him a set of tasks to be performed daily for two years. Doing these mundane tasks would allow him to let go of his ego attached to having a "wife"— someone whom he could take home to serve him with everyday meals and household work. As he shed his ego, he would be able to see his future wife not as a prized pick, but as *the prize*—someone who could help him grow in spirit and raise his children with a great spiritual awareness. The most important work of a woman in those days was not so much cooking and household tasks, *but to help raise the children with their spiritual gifts.* These were the original teachings until the rise of patriarchy burdened women with many more mundane, domestic tasks than were necessary.

The years passed by quickly as Vishnu surrendered diligently to the many tasks given to him. It had now been six years since he had first arrived at the gate of our temple. Though I became older, his intention remained clear: to claim me in the highest of ways, for he knew that a child was to come from our union. One day as I was sitting alone he sent a messenger through the power of his mind. This messenger eventually manifested as our child. That child showed me the depth of his love and the gate between us was finally opened. Our love was bonded, and there were contracts made by the priestesses for us to be incarnated again and to have children. After a few years of raising our child, I was asked to completely surrender to my devotional practices for a period of one to three years. During this period, he took full responsibility for raising our child. As this child came of age, he was brought back to the temple and taught there. Vishnu was completely devoted to me in that life. He surrendered his ego without any fear, and he did not carry any animosity toward me because of the mundane tasks given to him as I engaged in my spiritual practices.

Was this a "matriarchal" period in human history?

It was the beginning of a matriarchal era in which there was a great harmony between men and women. Humanity has been long-separated, and it is now time for men and women to recreate this harmony. Many are assisting in this task. Beings of pure light from other realms are pouring consciousness on planet Earth at this time. Helping with this transformation is also one of the tasks of Archangel Michael. Divine beings are communicating more easily with humans at this time.

There has also been a shift in the collective consciousness of humanity, which has been accelerated by tragic and destructive events, such as 9/11. There was a vibration upon the Earth that the human race could feel before that momentous event.

So, 9/11 was meant to be?

Yes, it was meant to be. It led more people to turn inward.

Are you saying that a lot of the destructive events are in some ways occurring for humanity to turn inward?

Humanity has been spared even more destructive events that could have occurred, but did not occur because there has been a threshold of spiritual awakening already.

So, the more we awaken...

...the less need there is for destructive events to awaken you. As the transformation speeds up with more people meditating and coming into their own knowing, there is less need for humanity to go through one crisis after another.

There is much help available at this time from divine beings.

Why now?

Everything is unfolding in divine timing. The light of ascended Goddesses shall awaken humans into Satya Yuga after the long dark night of Kali Yuga. Many women and children are suffering with the burden of patriarchal structures at this time. As these structures are overturned, there shall be a spiritual transition to rediscover the harmony that has been lost for thousands of years between the feminine and the masculine. It shall begin with books, art, and songs inspired by the ascended Goddesses from various pantheons. Initially, more women will be attracted to this path that shall eventually weave the whole Earth into joy and oneness.

The sacred union of the sexes guided by the divine feminine will literally recreate Heaven on Earth. As I mentioned earlier, I shall bring together the Goddesses from different pantheons to create a new path of joy from which a great healing love shall flow and unite all. We shall help humans everywhere on Earth in these final stages of their grand spiritual adventure. Billions of souls chose to partake in the creation of contrast in the present soul cycle, which has already expanded emptiness into deeper and vaster realms. It is like a difficult birthing process with contractions of contrast followed by the bursting forth of the joys of sustained, enlightened activity. These vibrations of enlightenment shall spread in this universe and other universes ending the suffering of countless numbers of sentient beings.

I feel so full of gratitude. Do you have a final message for the readers of this book?

The primordial joy that we speak of is pure, unconditional, and beyond all thoughts and emotions, so it cannot be captured fully by any words, even the words "primordial joy." It is possible that your path has brought you to this unconditional, uncaused joy that we speak of, through *love*. In fact, many spiritual paths emphasize *love* as the primary soul feeling of transformation. Other paths emphasize other soul feelings such as *compassion, faith, devotion,* or *peace.* As any of these soul feelings becomes an infinite ocean that takes over your life, other soul feelings join and make the ocean even grander. There is great synergy between soul feelings as they lead, follow, join one another, and ultimately pour together into infinite emptiness.

Realizing the oneness of love, compassion, gratitude, faith, devotion, peace, forgiveness, freedom, and other soul feelings through primordial joy is essential to walking the path of the divine feminine. It is the quickest way to realize emptiness and higher enlightenments in this time of accelerated spiritual development for humanity. Different eras have different soul feelings that become the great oceans of transformation in those eras. Seeing *joy in emptiness* and *emptiness in joy*, seeing *joy in soul feelings* and *soul feelings in joy*, and seeing *soul feelings in emptiness* and *emptiness in soul feelings* is the way to join the oceans of all soul feelings into the infinite emptiness at this time. This is the grand union, the *yoga of soul feelings*, whose time has finally arrived as we transition into the next stage of the evolution of consciousness.

Can you tell us how the teachings in this book relate to the teachings of the religions of the world?

Our divine feminine path of joy nourishes and expands both the lower and higher chakras so that the sacred is not divided from the sensual, and the spiritual is not divided from the physical. These teachings are not new, but have been hidden away. Goddesses are moving forward once again to inspire and awaken humans with these timeless teachings. Many Goddesses from different pantheons shall speak in the books to follow this one. Together, we shall usher in the great transition from Kali Yuga to the Satya Yuga.

We find it amusing that humans have created so much strife in the name of religion. Like the many polluted rivers of the Earth, religions have become polluted by the divisive beliefs of the mind. Religions may still nourish some through those selective writings that have remained hidden and untouched by the mind. However, to nourish all, scriptures have to be purified and renewed so that love can flow with joy and wipe away the tears of humanity.

Our incarnations in different pantheons of Hinduism, Buddhism, Christianity, and other religions have opened new pathways for humans to blossom into enlightenment. This book renews this wisdom for the modern times. The wisdom of this book shall allow the mind to surrender to body sensations and soul feelings with joy, so that one may be enlightened into emptiness with ease. This primordial joy not only expands the human heart with love, but it also allows great Bodhisattvas to ascend from spiritual *pure lands* to the expanding realms of emptiness or Buddhahood.

We give our blessings to all!

Namaste!

Namaste Lakshmi ji!

Thank you! Thank you! Thank you!

Appendix to Chapter 4
Infinities Growing Within Infinities

*(Extended conversation with Mahadevi Saraswati
continued from Chapter 4)*

Hmm...I still do not understand how entire universes arise and dissolve in the expanse of soul feelings.[26]

> The infinity opens at the center of one's being. Since this center is beyond time and space, it is actually beyond the duality of within and without. From the place of the infinite center, both mind and matter are seen as finite, existing as waves on the surface of a bottomless ocean.

Hmm... So what you are saying is that the center is infinite and the surface is finite?

> Yes. One realizes that the *singularity* at the center of one's being is *infinite*.

This is contrary to our everyday intuition according to which the center is a point inside and infinity surrounds the point from the outside.

The *mind* tries to grasp infinity from the surface looking at the expanse of the infinity of universes beyond our universe. The *soul* does not seek outside, but simply surrenders to the infinity within. Just like bigness, even smallness never ends, so the emptiness at the very center has infinities growing within infinities, ad infinitum.

What? This is a bit mind-boggling.

The infinite emptiness at the very center of your being is *out of your mind*.

I could never fathom infinity even though I majored in mathematics.

Infinity cannot be understood by the mind because the mind *is* finite. Not only infinity, but also emptiness cannot be understood by the finite mind, because emptiness *is* infinite.

Emptiness is infinite is like saying zero is infinite? Hmm...

In the spiritual realm, less *is* more and so zero *is* infinite. The way to reach infinity is to empty oneself of everything. Many enlightened ones have taught this truth. Emptiness contains everything, including the largest expanding infinities. The expansion of everything never ends!

If the expansion of everything never ends, then how can everything be "everything"?

> It cannot be! "Everything" is not static. It is continuously expanding into larger infinities, so a final point for "everything" is never reached.

On the topic of infinities, I am reminded of the renowned Indian mathematician, Srinivasa Ramanujan who is considered one of the all-time great mathematicians, such as Euler, Gauss, Jacobi, Pythagoras, and others. He proposed close to 3,900 results consisting of highly sophisticated equations and identities,[27] all of which came to him in his visions. Ramanujan claimed that he received the equations and identities directly from Goddesss Namagiri who is considered a form of the ascended Goddess Lakshmi. He would tell his friends that Goddess Namagiri would visit him in his dreams with visions of equations, whisper equations into his ear, and write equations on his tongue.

So, my question is, did Goddess Lakshmi give these mathematical equations and identities to Ramanujan?

> Yes! Writing down mathematical results that dear Lakshmi gave him brought him immense joy. Lakshmi communicated using all his senses, such that not only he could see these results in his visions, but he could also hear them and taste them. He wrote down these equations and identities with great devotion to her. His main frustration was that those around him did not believe that he received

these results from a *Goddess*. Conditioned by their formal education and scientific worldview, his peers found it difficult to understand that his truest devotion was towards Lakshmi, and not to mathematics.

What is the metaphysical significance of mathematical equations and identities?[28]

Mathematical *equations* reveal the magnificent harmony present in a specific universe like yours.

Mathematical *identities* reveal the absolute harmony that joins all universes into oneness.

There are universes that do not follow the equations followed by your universe.

Oh, really?

Yes. The physical reality is made up of infinite diversity. The infinite singularity of emptiness contains infinite information about everything. From this place of ultimate nothingness all fields of knowledge in all universes—whether it is mathematics, or language, or logic, or philosophy—are fully accessible. Ascended Goddesses like Lakshmi and myself can communicate with sentient beings in other universes in languages made up of completely different words and sounds.

Do you actually communicate using words and sounds?

We transmit energies, which sentient beings interpret as words or sounds in their own languages. If one's mind is empty, one receives our information without any filter. If one's mind is filled with thoughts and emotions, the information we send gets clouded.

Even Ramanujan was not perfect, and on rare occasions he did make mistakes about what he received from Lakshmi. However, this did not bother him. He grew up with great humility and devotion. He was born in a family that came from a line of devotees. His mother was Lakshmi's great devotee, as was her mother. His grandmother could even channel Lakshmi's words.

As Ramanujan's soul passed over to the other side and was immersed in love and light, his fascination with mathematics dissolved immediately. He saw an infinite number of equations and identities of the type that he received from Lakshmi and had no interest in pursuing these further.

Are science and spirituality connected in some way?

Science and spirituality are deeply integrated and complimentary. Science gives you the roots to survive; spirituality gives you the wings to fly. Science is like the solid trunk that supports you; spirituality is like the beautiful flower that blossoms within you. Science creates the conditions for spirituality to spread on an entire living planet like Earth. As humanity shifts its obsession with survival and dedicates itself to expanding consciousness, many humans will be enlightened.

Aha! This resonates deeply with me. However, I am still not clear about the purpose of sending thousands of equations and identities to Ramanujan. Could you explain why Goddess Lakshmi did this?

She did this to create a curiosity among those around him about larger spiritual truths that transcend the mind. This happened as he received these beautiful equations and identities from her *without any proofs*. Because Ramanujan did not worry about the proofs, he felt the joy of his divine connection with her. His collaborator also experienced the joy of discovering these results of great beauty, but he got caught up in the mind around his Third Chakra, worrying about the approval from peers who demanded proofs. This closed the door to having more mystical experiences of joy through these mathematical results. Ramanujan simply wanted to share the joy of his devotion to Lakshmi through these mathematical results. Ramanujan knew in his heart that that which can be proven is finite and a vanishingly small part of consciousness. He sensed that the infinite emptiness, or one's higher self, lies beyond the confines of a finite mind. He would express this by saying that "God" is realized when zero and infinity become one. He felt that God could never be *proven* using the mind.

Why can't God be proven? What if God were to appear in front of us?

Gods and Goddesses have appeared in front of each one of you many times. But you need to be awakened to see these infinite divine beings, just like you need to have eyes to see light. Even thousands of proofs about the existence of light will not convince a blind man about the reality of light. Ramanujan glimpsed absolute divinity in the form of Lakshmi as he emptied his mind through his devotion to her, and expressed this devotion through the numerous equations and identities that she gave to him.

Thank you!

Namaste Saraswati ji!

GUIDED MEDITATIONS

1.Blessing Oneself
2. Blessing all Sentient Beings
3. Blessing the Earth and the Universes Within

1

Blessing Oneself

Sit comfortably with your eyes closed and become aware of your breath. Now take a deep breath in...and breathe it out slowly. Continue to breathe slowly and deeply. Become aware of time.

Become aware of the time before you incarnated in this lifetime on Earth. See yourself as a soul, a being of divine light born from your own higher self, full of joy, love, freedom, compassion, gratitude, forgiveness, peace, and other soul feelings. See your parents, your siblings and relatives, your friends and everyone else you know in this life, also as souls born from their higher selves. Consider that your soul, like all souls, chose to know darkness by going through a cycle of physical incarnations so that your higher self may expand into an even greater emptiness. Know that the highest divine beings, like Buddhas and ascended Gods and

Goddesses, have also experienced contrast by incarnating in the physical realms. Take another deep breath in...and breathe it out slowly.

Now, become aware of the time of your early childhood in your body. Remember the long and joyous days of presence followed by sweet nights of rest. Recall those moments of completeness when you felt a deep connection with the mountains; when you became totally silent watching the colors of a sunset; when you were immersed in the beautiful night of star lights; and when an unspoken joy filled your senses and your soul for no reason.

Now, recall the time during your childhood and puberty when you became identified with your mind. Remember your emotions, both positive and negative. The emotions of love and affection shared with family members, as well as the emotions of sadness, anger, and loneliness when you were disappointed or when you felt alone. Remember the emotions of fear and anxiety when you felt threatened in some way, either physically or psychologically. Remember the emotions of shame and embarrassment when you felt inadequate and exposed. Remember the birth of your ego, and how your suffering increased over the years as you became more strongly identified with your ego.

Now, become aware of the inner child who still lives in you from your childhood. The child who was not loved enough or was abused. The child who is sad or angry about what occurred in your childhood. The child who is fearful and anxious because of the threatening experiences of your childhood. The child who is carrying the feelings of shame and embarrassment from your childhood.

Visualize a soft white light entering from your higher self from the top of your head. The light reaches all of your seven chakras one by one. As you breathe in, visualize the light shining brightly through all seven chakras. As you breathe out, visualize the light spreading into your body with joy, compassion, gratitude, love, forgiveness, freedom, peace, and other soul feelings. See the light joining your body and soul into an expanded oneness that transcends the mind. Continue breathing in and out with this visualization.

Hold your inner child to your heart. Nurture him or her with the magnificent light of your higher self, shining out through your body and your soul with each cycle of your breath. Let the suffering of your inner child dissolve fully as you synchronize your breath with the child's breath. Let the child feel safe being held in your arms. Nourish the child with compassion and forgiveness emanating from your heart. Let the child feel the joy and laughter arising through your belly. Let the child feel your devotion through your higher heart. See yourself merge into oneness with your inner child. May you be safe. May you be healthy. May you be happy.

With blessings to you,

Mahadevi Saraswati

2

Blessing all Sentient Beings

Sit comfortably with your eyes closed and become aware of your breath. Take a deep Ujjayi²⁹ breath in. Feel the energy of your breath in your Solar Plexus Chakra. As you breathe out, keep the attention on the area around your Third Eye and feel the air moving out through your nostrils. Take another Ujjayi breath in... and breathe it out slowly. Continue to breathe in and out in this relaxed manner.

Now, return to normal breathing. Visualize a beam of a beautiful golden light from high above entering your body through your Seventh Chakra and going into your Heart Chakra. Imagine receiving the blessings of many ascended Goddesses as this divine light flows from your heart into your lower three chakras.

See the different emotions in your lower chakras with the help of this light. As this light reveals your anger towards another, see even more light shine upon their suffering, and your an-

ger transform into compassion. As this light reveals your hate towards another, see even more light shine upon their pain, and your hate transform into forgiveness. As this light reveals your apathy for another, see even more light shine upon the interconnectedness of all souls, and your apathy transform into love. As this light reveals your attachments for people and things, see even more light shine on the impermanence of everything, and your attachments dissolve into freedom. Let this light reveal all emotions hidden within you and transform these into soul feelings. From this expanded awareness see that all sentient beings are suffering and all desire an end to their suffering, just like you do.

Now, visualize your torso as a hollow bamboo filled with this golden light. Imagine the light traveling down even more connecting your Root Chakra to the Earth below. See the light going deeper and deeper until it reaches the very center of the Earth. Become aware that you are connected though this light with both Heavens and Earth. Rest in this place for some time.

Now, visualize this light pouring out from your heart, gently moving and spiraling into your room creating a soft golden aura around you. From your room the light goes into the whole house and then spreads in your entire neighborhood. See the birds, trees, and all of nature bathe in this golden light. See even the buildings and other structures delight in the joy of being touched by this divine light. See this light spread into the town or the city you are living in, and from there expanding even farther and enveloping the whole Earth in joy and love. From this place of oneness with everything, send the light of joy, compassion, peace, and freedom to all sentient beings in the universe..

With blessings to all sentient beings,

Mahadevi Lakshmi

3

Blessing the Earth and the Universes Within

Sit comfortably with your eyes closed and become aware of your breath. Now take a deep Ujjayi[30] breath in. Feel the energy of the breath relaxing your Solar Plexus. Breathe out through your nostrils, and as you do this become aware of your Third Eye. Take another Ujjayi breath in...and breathe it out slowly. Breathe in and out in this manner a few more times.

Now, return to normal breathing. Using both your Solar Plexus and your Third Eye, see yourself in a divine circle holding hands with myself and other ascended Goddesses. As we smile with love to one another visualize the whole world between us. Imagine a soft white light expanding out from your heart and joining with the light emanating from our hearts. See this light shine upon the world as we walk a full circle around the Earth in a clockwise direction. You may feel a gentle rhythm of peace walking with us at the speed of your heartbeat.

See our light pushing through every part of Earth, including all continents, oceans, trees, grass blades, and living beings. As we walk slowly and sure-footedly with a feeling of a joyous dance in our hearts, the light blesses the Earth and returns back into the vast empty space. It is as if the Earth had innumerable pores through which the light pours out, reaching beyond our circle to even other planets and stars. A great harmony is formed from which great blessings are given. As taught by many enlightened teachers, what is given is received back many fold!

Take another breath in. See the light heal every cell and every organ of your body as you breathe out slowly. Now, invite the light into your mind as you continue to circle the Earth with the ascended Goddesses. Let the pure radiance of this light allow any lack, fear, hate, sadness, anger, guilt, shame, jealousy, envy, and other emotions to melt and transform into soul feelings, such as joy, love, compassion, forgiveness, gratitude, freedom, peace, and others. As your emotions transform into soul feelings, see your ego dissolve.

Find any dark places within you as you continue to circle. Let these go and see the darkness absorb them. With light expanding with more light and darkness absorbing darkness, the whole universe expands with more space. This balance of opposites transforms everything to a higher vibration using the universal law of attraction. As you continue to circle, place your requests of experi-

encing more light in your belly around your Third Chakra, and see those requests manifest in the world at the center.

Take another deep breath in...and breathe it out. Feel the infinite vastness inside of you that contains the whole universe. Nurture that universe for it is a part of your divine mother. She has carried you, so you carry her now. Nurture the light within you and allow it to manifest from the emptiness of no-thought. Again, this is a representation of darkness holding light, which creates the balance of opposites. Visualize yourself opening your mouth and let the light within you reach outward and fill the great abyss of darkness. Consider that it may look like the Milky Way with some stars emanating from you shining more brightly than others. Now expel the Earth into the center and see the light that remains inside. Open your arms towards the sky with your chin up and smile. Relax into the vast emptiness.

This visualization is our gift to you this day. The more you practice this and get used to it, the more aware you shall become of those universes within your infinite higher self.

With blessings to the Earth and the universes within,

Mahadevi Lakshmi

Acknowledgments

First and foremost, I would like to express my profound gratitude to Ma Lakshmi, Ma Saraswati, Ma Parvati, Ma Kuan Yin, Mother Mary, Archangel Michael, Lord Vishnu, Lord Shiva, and Lord Ganesha for your many blessings in my life. I reach for you with joy and I melt into your emptiness with love. I bow to you with humility and rise to you through forgiveness. I celebrate all of you and all divine beings of this universe. Next, I would like to thank my dearest soul-friend, Jade Devi Kamala for walking with me on this magnificent journey with the ascended Goddesses from different spiritual pantheons. It is our hope to weave together and unify the divine feminine teachings of the ascended Goddesses from many spiritual pantheons of the world. Finally, I would like to thank my dearest mother, my late father, my spiritual teachers Jiddu Krishnamurti and Sri Sri Ravi Shankar, my loving brothers and their families, and many friends and supporters, especially Gabrielli, Jessica, Nancy, Andjela, Apurva, Eva, Melissa, Rebecca, Amy, Michele, Deepa, Devina, Shakkuntala, Erica, Brooke, Gisele, Madhu, Mira, Michael, Saloni, Shalini and Vijay for their love and care, and for assisting me in many small and big ways during the writing and publication of this book.

With much gratitude,

Ananda Karunesh

About the Author

Ananda Karunesh

Ananda Karunesh (a.k.a. Sanjay Nawalkha, Ph.D.) experienced a Zen awakening at the age of 19, which opened the door to an expanded spiritual awareness. He has engaged in meditative and spiritual practices for the past 35 years. He is the founder of *Path of Joy*, a humanitarian organization dedicated to spreading the teachings of Mahadevi Lakshmi, Mahadevi Saraswati, Mahadevi Parvati, and other ascended Goddesses from different spiritual pantheons of the world. He worked as the Chairman of the Finance Department at the Isenberg School of Management, University of Massachusetts, Amherst, from January 2011 until August 2018.

Jade Devi Kamala
(*contributor*)

Jade Devi Kamala (a.k.a. Jade Moser) is a Spiritual healer, spiritual mentor and teacher, and shamaness. She resides in the United States, where she leads retreats and classes, and also does individual healing sessions.

More information related to this book and the Ascended Goddesses Series can be obtained on the following website: www.pathofjoy.life

To learn more about the events and activities related to this book and connect with the author, please visit:

Facebook:
https://www.facebook.com/pathofjoy.life/ (Page)
https://www.facebook.com/ananda.karunesh.2 (Profile)

Instagram: Ananda.Karunesh

Endnotes

1 For the sake of brevity, we simply say Goddess when we refer to any ascended Goddess or Mahadevi in this book.

2 My curiosity about the metaphysics of infinities led
   to many additional questions and answers which are
   given in the Appendix to this chapter towards the end
   of this book. These questions and answers in the Appendix also explore the mystery of how the famed Indian mathematician Srinivasa Ramanujan received
   close to 3,900 mathematical equations and identities
   through divine inspiration *without any proofs*. The content of this Appendix was in "Chapter 5" of the first
   edition of this book.   Also, Chapter 6 of the first edition has become Chapter 5 in the revised edition of this
   book, and Chapter 7 of the first edition has been
   broken into two chapters— Chapter 6 and Chapter 7—
   in the revised edition of this book. Chapters 1 through 4,
   and chapters 8 though 33 in the revised edition are iden-
   tical to the corresponding chapters in the first edition of
   this book. However, not a single word has changed from
   any of the original 33 chapters in the first edition of this
   book. They are simply presented in a different format
   as 33 chapters plus an appendix in the revised edition of
   this book.

3 According to a Christian legend, God created Adam as
   the first human being in his own divine image and then
   created Eve from Adam's rib. God's original plan for
   Adam and Eve and their human progeny was thwarted by

Satan, who, in the form of a serpent, tempted Eve to eat the forbidden fruit from the tree of knowledge. When Eve persuaded Adam to eat the fruit, God expelled both of them from the Garden of Eden. Because of this original sin, God punished all humans with death, and women with painful childbirth. He also gave man the power to rule over woman because Eve persuaded Adam to commit the first sin.

4   Different legends about Adam and Eve appeared in the scriptures of Judaism, Christianity, and Islam as these religions replaced the ancient Goddess religions. Legends in Judaism and Islam are kinder to Eve. In Judaic legends, there are two accounts, one suggesting that Adam and Eve were created together, and the other suggesting that Eve was created after Adam. In Islamic legends, the Garden of Eden was a heavenly realm, and Adam and Eve were sent to Earth because they both ate the forbidden fruit. They were sent to two different mountain peaks, Adam to al-Safa and Eve to al-Marwah. Adam repented by weeping for 40 days, after which God sent the Black Stone and taught him the Hajj. The concept of "original sin" does not exist in Islam because God forgave both Adam and Eve and reunited them near Mecca.

5   Saint Gregory I's sermons backed by papal authority proved more influential than the Bible, especially since he was also a prolific writer and a commanding dialogist. He confused her identity with Saint Mary of Egypt, another repentant prostitute in the evolving religious literature. Medieval artists and patriarchal theologians

further popularized Mary Magdalene's image as a repentant sinner. In contrast, the fourth century theologian Augustine honored Mary Magdalene with the honorific "apostle of the apostles." She was also declared a saint by some denominations of Christian churches. Yet, many Christians saw Mary Magdalene as a sinner for the past 1400 years, notwithstanding the fact that she was present both at his crucifixion and his burial, and was the first person to see him after his resurrection. Her portrayal as a repentant sinner and prostitute continued by many writers and artists until the end of 20th century *despite the official rejection of this characterization by Pope Paul VI in 1969.*

6   For much of the prehistoric time, humanity believed in a *Goddess* as the supreme deity of our universe. The invention of a male God occurred in Abrahamic religions (i.e., Judaism, Christianity, and Islam) about 4,000 years ago in the Canaan region as patriarchy replaced matriarchy and God replaced the Goddess as the creator of the universe. The historical evidence—including archaeological and scriptural—suggests that male monotheism spread rapidly as competing Goddess religions were suppressed in the Middle East and the Western world. The strict monotheism of Abrahamic religions is not shared by all religions. For example, the Goddess religions that flourished before the arrival of Abrahamic religions had many female deities such as Isis, Hathor, Gaia, Athena, Aphrodite, and Brigid, to name a few. Non-Abrahamic religions such as Hinduism and Buddhism allow female deities. For example, the followers of Hinduism are divided into different sects: some be-

lieve in *Adi Shakti* as the great Goddess who created the entire universe and is the Mother of all other divine beings, while others believe in different Gods and Goddesses such as Brahma and Saraswati, Vishnu and Lakshmi, Shiva and Parvati, and others. Similarly, while the Theravada followers of Buddhism practice a non-theistic view of liberation from Samsara (i.e., the world of suffering) to attain enlightenment, the Vajrayana followers of Buddhism meditate on different forms of Tara, Prajnaparamita, and other female deities. Tara and Prajnaparamita are seen as the mothers of all Buddhas of the past, present and future. However, even Vajrayana Buddhism is not *theistic* because all deities, male or female, are considered creations of the minds of the Vajrayana practitioners.

7 Siddhis is a Sanskrit word for psychic powers.

8 Krishna became friends with his cousins, the *Pandavas*, who belonged to the Kuru clan that ruled the kingdom of Hastinapur.

9 Based on the Hindu legend, Radha is an incarnation of Goddess Lakshmi, and Krishna is the eighth incarnation of Lord Vishnu. Krishna was born as the eighth son of Devaki and her husband Vasudeva. Devaki's brother Kansa became King of Mathura by overthrowing and imprisoning his own father. Afraid of a prophecy of his death by Devaki's eighth son, King Kansa imprisoned both Devaki and Vasudeva. Krishna was born in the prison cell but was secretly moved to the home of his foster parents, who lived in Vrindavan. Even as a young boy

Krishna revealed his supernatural powers by dancing on the hoods of a serpent, and in another instance, vanquishing the ego of Indra, the heavenly King of Devas. Krishna grew up as a divinely playful child and spent his youth in the company of Radha and other gopis (milkmaids) who loved him dearly. As Krishna would play his flute, the gopis would leave whatever they were doing and join him in singing and dancing.

10 The *Bhakti* path spread in different parts of India during the medieval period as sages shared the mystic visions they had about the devotional love between Radha and Krishna. Interestingly, during the same period, the Buddhist devotional path of *Vajrayana* also spread with practices of Mantras, Tantras, and Mandalas.

11 The five *Pandava* brothers were the sons of Kunti and Madri, the two wives of Pandu. The throne of Hastinapur switched between Pandu and his blind half-brother, Dhritarashtra, until Pandu died due to a curse. Dhritarashtra was the father of the hundred *Kauravas*. The Kurukshetra war was caused by a dynastic struggle between Pandavas and Kauravas to inherit the kingdom of Hastinapur.

12 When the time came for the next generation to inherit the kingdom, the eldest Pandava brother, Yudhisthira, and the eldest Kaurava brother, Duryodana, both claimed the throne. Though the family elders brokered a peace agreement by dividing up the kingdom, events unfolded that made Duryodana feel jealous of

the Pandavas. By challenging and tricking Yudhisthira into a dice game, Duryodana enslaved the Pandavas, and had Draupadi—the beautiful Panchala princess who married the five Pandavas—humiliated by his brother, Dushasana, who attempted to strip her naked in the royal court of Kauravas. Draupadi was a great devotee of Krishna, and as she prayed to him, Krishna added ample lengths to her Sari, making it impossible for Dushasana to disrobe her. Learning of this miracle, Dhritarashtra became afraid for his own sons. He freed Draupadi, and returned all that had been taken away from the Pandavas back to them. However, with more trickery, Duryodana had the Pandava brothers exiled for thirteen years, and then refused to give them the share of their kingdom after the completion of their exile. This led to the great Kurukshetra war between the Pandavas and the Kauravas.

13 All of the Pandava brothers were conceived as sons of Gods with the help of a divine mantra that Kunti received as a boon when she was a young princess. Eager to test the power of the mantra, Kunti called upon God Surya, and Karna was born to her as her first son. Due to the fear of becoming an unwed mother, Kunti abandoned Karna by putting him in a basket and setting him afloat in a river. Karna did not find out until much later in his life that the Pandavas were his younger brothers, and he grew up thinking that he was the son of the charioteer who adopted him.

14 A royal ceremony in ancient India in which a princess would select her husband from many contenders.

15 Growing up as the son of a charioteer, Karna had to fight
for his rights. Drona, the royal guru of the Pandavas and
the Kauravas, refused to accept Karna as his student, and
Draupadi—the young and beautiful princess of Panchala—refused to allow Karna to participate in her Swayamvara. Karna was wounded deeply by the rejection of
Draupadi.

16 Karna got the attention of Duryodana when he
arrived uninvited to an archery competition organized by Drona, and beat Arjuna, the best ar-
cher among all Pandava and Kaurava cousins.
Recognizing his skill and courage, Duryodana be-
friended Karna and made him the king of Anga. Karna
became a loyal friend of Duryodana, and was seen as a
noble and generous King by the people of Anga. Even
Krishna admired Karna, and considered him more
skilled, more courageous, more generous, and more
virtuous, than all of the Pandavas.

17 Karna was cursed by many in *Mahabharata*.
According to one curse by his own teacher *Parashura-
ma*, Karna would be unable to use his most powerful divine weapon, Brahmastra, when he needed it most. On
his soul path, Karna would face formidable opponents
with similar weapons. Also, there was another curse
that stated that Karna's enemy would kill him when
his chariot was stuck in the ground. Many months after this conversation, we asked Goddess Lakshmi how
these curses would manifest on Karna's soul path. She
replied as follows:

If Krishna could save Arjuna from the mighty Karna, why would he not save Karna from his opponents, if needed? The curse did not say that Karna would die with his inability to use the Brahmastra, when he would need it the most. The curse would manifest in his inability to save the ones dearest to him like his children. Each and every curse would manifest, as they were spoken with a strong intention from the higher chakras. Since Karna was the most cursed person, do you not think that at least one curse would have said that his own blood brother, Arjuna, would kill him? Why was such a curse never uttered by anyone? It was not for the simple reason that his blood brother, Arjuna, was not supposed to kill Karna on his soul path. Karna's curse was to be killed by his enemy, and Duryodana would become his staunchest enemy on his soul path. Duryodana would die in the war in the same way, but with feelings of bitterness and betrayal by Karna, whom he would not forgive even as he was dying. This would create Karma for Karna. After the Pandavas won the war, Karna would be anointed as the King. He would rule with much generosity and kindness for the remainder of his life. Karna and Krishna would have a deep soul connection and both would work to usher in the change of Yugas. They would be killed in the same manner and around the same time. A hunter would accidentally shoot Karna as he would be digging his chariot out of a ditch. The hunter would have been his enemy, Duryodana, in his previous life. This would be similar to how Krishna died, as Krishna and Karna shared similar soul paths. Krishna was a King who served as a Charioteer, and Karna became a King after being raised by a Charioteer. Both were abandoned by their mothers after birth, and both were supposed to die accidentally by hunters to fulfill their Karma.

18 The actual events related to Karna unfolded as follows: Karna stayed loyal to Duryodana, despite learning from Krishna before the war that he was the "abandoned" first son of Kunti and a blood brother of the Pandavas. The war lasted 18 days during which Karna defeated all of the Pandava brothers except Arjuna, in duels, but chose to spare their lives because of a promise he made to their mother, Kunti. Without the help of Krishna, Karna would have defeated Arjuna as well, but he died at the hands of Arjuna in a vulnerable moment when he was digging his chariot out of the mud.

19 Angulimala was a murderer who had killed 999 people and was on the lookout to kill his last victim in order to fulfill a vow he had taken to make a garland of a thousand fingers.

20 See endnote 7.

21 See endnote 19.

22 The original Sanskrit names of *The Diamond Sutra*, *The Lotus Sutra*, and *The Heart Sutra* are *Vajracchedikā Prajñāpāramitā Sūtra, Saddharma Puṇḍarīka Sūtra, and*

Prajñāpāramitāhṛdaya, respectively.

23 Unlike traditional astrology that is based upon the time and place of one's birth, Naadi astrology is based upon the matching of one's thumb print with a particular Naadi scroll that contains predictions about that person's life. It is believed that these Naadi scrolls were written by great sages thousands of years ago, initially in Sanskrit, and then translated in Tamil and other south Indian languages.

24 Goddess Lakshmi is referring to Mahakasyapa in the Flower Sermon story of Buddha.

25 The divine feminine is honored in the mystical paths associated with most major religions. For example, the *Kabbalah* in Judaism, *Gnosticism* in Christianity, *Sufism* in Islam, the *Bhakti Path* and *Shaktism* in Hinduism, the *Vajrayana path* in Buddhism, the *Great Mother* in Taoism, and the ancient *Goddess paths* in most Pagan religions.

26 See endnote 2.

27 An *equation* represents a *specific* relationship of equality, such as $E = MC^2$ or $X + 1 = 6$, that holds for *specific* variables and/or with *specific* values of the variables. An *identity* represents a *general* relationship of equality that always holds by the laws of mathematics, such as $(X + 1)^2 = X^2 + 2x + 1$. Many of the equations and identities that Ramanujan received deal with infinite sums, infinite products, and infinite continued fractions. Ramanujan's British collaborator, Godfrey Hardy, who

was also a great mathematician himself, considered Ramanujan to be in a very select group of mathematicians in history such as Euler, Gauss, Jacobi, Pythagoras, and others.

28 See the previous endnote.

29 Ujjayi breath is an ancient yogic breathing technique that produces a sense of deep relaxation in the body somewhat similar to what one experiences when asleep. The inhalation is deep with an oceanic sound made through a slight constriction of the throat, while the diaphragm is used to bring the breath all the way to the lower three chakras, followed by the Heart Chakra and the chest area. The exhalation is slow and deep, also with an oceanic sound made through a slight constriction of the throat. Both the inhalation and exhalation are done with the mouth closed, through the nose. One can learn Ujjayi breath from a qualified yoga practitioner.

30 See the previous endnote.

Made in the USA
San Bernardino, CA
13 August 2020